Reflections
of Western Historians

Reflections

(Papers of the 7th annual conference of the)
Western History Association,
on the history of Western America,
San Francisco, California:
October 12–14, 1967

Western Historical Studies 1967

f Western Historians

JOHN ALEXANDER CARROLL
editor

with the assistance of
JAMES R. KLUGER

 THE UNIVERSITY OF ARIZONA PRESS

THE UNIVERSITY OF ARIZONA PRESS

Copyright © 1969
The Arizona Board of Regents
Library of Congress Catalog
Card No. 68-9335
Manufactured in the U.S.A.

CONTENTS

A PREFACE

FOR PROFESSOR WEBB

"THIS IS MORE THAN JUST A JOB OF WORK, JACK," said the serious-minded man as he cleared a spot among the galleys on his desk, "and we shouldn't hang a 'Men at Work' detour sign on it. You historians are supposed to reflect on the past as well as record it, aren't you? Well, that's really what we have here — an assortment of reflections on the Western past, in the shape of articles, from fifteen writers who know what they are talking about." Smiling, he paused then to let me simply "reflect." "Why scare off the lay readers, and maybe the academics too, by nailing some fuzzy old pedantry like 'Papers' or 'Proceedings' on this interesting book? Let's call it *Reflections of Western Historians* and make the label suggest what the package contains."

The man making the hard sell was Marshall Townsend, the perspica-cious director of the University of Arizona Press. On the receiving end was the editor of this volume, a booted and spurred professor of history who was more conservative in his taste for some things — book titles, for instance — than might at first be imagined. He had decided that the title should be something quite formal, like "Western Historical Studies, 1967," and he had come in to talk rather than to listen. But the words of the publisher were persuasive. The high-hatted editor scratched a match on his heel, lit another cigar, and sat back to hear the full argument for the name which this book has been given.

At the seventh annual conference of the Western History Association, held at the Palace Hotel in San Francisco in mid-October, 1967, I was assigned by the Council of that organization to select the outstanding papers of its three-day meeting, prepare them for publication, and arrange with a university press to bring them out between hard covers. What the Council wanted, and what many members of the Western History Association had long requested, was a formal publication of the fine papers of the annual conference. For this important project I chose the press of my own institution, the University of Arizona, for special reasons. One was that I looked forward to working closely with Press Director Townsend and his gifted chief of design and production, Doug Peck, whose output I had admired for almost a decade. This volume, then, is collaborative in more ways than its multiple authorship, and by tracing the title to its actual source I am trying to make adequate acknowledgment by parable. Some years ago, in one of his great essays, the late Walter Prescott Webb urged historians and other writers — but particularly his fellow historians — to begin their books with "An Honest Preface." Believing with Webb that the hallmark of historianship is total adherence to the truth, even in one's preface, I am going to tell it true. The title of this volume is Mr. Townsend's, not mine. But, like Oscar Wilde upon hearing a certain beautiful line in a poem of W. B. Yeats, I damn well wish that I had said it first.

Having opened with one little confession, I am going to follow Webb's advice again and make a second. Another reason why the University of Arizona Press was contracted to produce this volume is that publication under its imprint fulfills in a sense, an old dream of mine. From the moment of arrival at the University of Arizona exactly ten years previously, I started to dream of editing something of this sort. Like the hotshot reporter in New York who thought that Broadway ought to be his exclusive beat, I have nurtured the notion of "covering" the West as an historical editor. It was an egocentric desire, of course, and perhaps akin to the urge which energized another oddly dressed editor, Charles F. Lummis, out in Los Angeles three quarters of a century ago. Mimicking the eccentric founder of the monthly which came to be called *Out West,* a rival publisher once ascribed these words to Lummis:

> I am the mountains and the sea,
>
> And all the desert plain between;
>
> You've seen the Western sky? That's me,
>
> I made it with my magazine.

However pertinent this analogy to old aspirations of mine, the point is simply that some people sit for years in editorial chairs, just as in the United States Congress, not because they are getting rich there but because they like to feel powerful. Elsewhere in print I have said, and I think correctly, that the chair of the scholarly editor is sometimes a showcase for his psyche. Let me now add the observation that most of the professional scholars who start editing quarterlies and annuals do so because there is a tedious task at hand, a veritable "job of work" which no available colleague is anxious to undertake. Most scholars are quite naturally more interested in their own research and writing than in handling the learned copy of others. A few, however, may become editors because they have fondly conjured up a challenge which they mistakenly imagine no one else has recognized before. So it was with me in 1958. Armed with a prize for historical writing and full of the professional juices that agitate the glands of younger academics, I wanted a crack at something that no one else had yet tried. Within the quarterly numbers of a learned journal of history I hoped to bring together the best of the West, the cream of the shorter writings (i.e., articles, annotated documents, and book reviews) of the hundreds of specialists in that broad field embracing the "frontier" hypothesis of Turner, the "borderlands" concept of Bolton, and the "desert" theory of Webb. In a word, I wanted the editorial range of the North American West to be mine.

With the generous support of the regents and administrative officers of the University of Arizona, a journal of such pretensions was born in the spring of 1959. *Arizona and the West* was not everything that I hoped to make it, but in the five years that I edited it I had a perfectly grand time on the job. The hours at the editorial desk were often overlong and my teaching responsibilities by choice quite heavy, but no professor of history ever enjoyed earning his keep more than I did in those days. In the pages of the journal I had the pleasure of publishing the mature work of the most distinguished of senior Western historians, and the equal pleasure of putting into print the early efforts of some younger scholars who subsequently have become leading figures in the field. Thus I had the best of both worlds, so to speak, as well as the stimulation of contact with many non-academic but deeply knowledgeable students of Western history in every corner of the continent.

Out of this admixture came the ideas that led to the Santa Fe conference of 1961 and the launching of the Western History Association. Herein lies a tale best left to be told someday by the indefatigable young scholar who was then serving voluntarily as my book-review editor, John Porter Bloom, the secretary-treasurer of the new organization and its helmsman in that office for seven years. Suffice it to note here that "JPB," and such believers as Ray A. Billington and Robert M. Utley, were contributing regularly to the University of Arizona journal at the same time that they were laying the keel of the Western History Association. Ray Billington, as the old organizers will well remember, served magnificently as its founding president; Bob Utley, now the chief historian of the National Park Service, presided over the term during which these pages were readied for press. To Billington,

Bloom, and Utley, whose tripartite endeavors in the cause of coalescence in Western historical studies I have a special reason to know intimately and to appreciate profoundly, this last editorial effort of mine is hereby dedicated. Without what they did in 1961 and thereafter, there would be no Western History Association and I would not have had the privilege of editing these *Reflections of Western Historians*.

Continuing to speak only the truth, I am frankly very happy with this book. Like I sought to make the quarterly issues of *Arizona and the West* (and much as they have become under the skillful management of my successor, Harwood P. Hinton), the present volume is greatly diversified in both geography and chronology. Its contents range from Canada to Mexico, from the sixteenth century to past the middle of the twentieth. With the exception of the opening paper, which was delivered on the first day of the San Francisco conference, the flow of these *Reflections* is essentially chronological. Each of the fifteen articles selected for inclusion stands proudly on its own as an original contribution to the fuller understanding of the West, and each provides the reader with something to think about. Each, therefore, is indeed a "reflection," just as Mr. Townsend saw so clearly. A word on each of the papers, in the order of their appearance in the volume, may help to guide the reader on what I am very sure will prove to be a pleasant and intellectually profitable journey into the Western past.

The opening paper, Richard A. Van Orman's "San Francisco: Hotel City of the West," emphasizes that the public houses of the Bay City were of great economic and social importance to its general growth, and that in few other metropolitan communities of nineteenth-century America did hotels rise and fall so rapidly.

In "Guzmán's 'Mayor España': A Study in Conquistador Ambition," Donald E. Chipman examines the ambitious project of a sixteenth-century Spanish adventurer who attempted to reserve all of northern Mexico for himself, and whose colossal ego led him to propose that his conquests deserved recognition as a "Greater Spain."

Iris H. Wilson's "Spanish Scientists in the Pacific Northwest, 1790–1792" treats a significant facet of the participation of Spain in New World exploration that has been largely overlooked because the rich documentary sources, replete with illustrations, have remained untranslated and unpublished until now.

"Juan Bodega y Quadra and the Spanish Retreat from Nootka, 1790–1794," by Michael E. Thurman, presents a detailed analysis of the activities of the most important Spanish naval officer on the West Coast at the time of the brink-of-war diplomatic controversy between Spain and Great Britain over territorial jurisdictions in the Pacific Northwest.

In "California's Economic Imperialism: An Historical Iceberg," W. H. Hutchinson suggests that the financial and commercial tycoons of nineteenth-century California extended their interests — and consequently their economic grasp — considerably farther than historians hitherto have guessed.

Thomas R. Cox, in "The Passage to India Revisited: Asian Trade and the Development of the Far West, 1850–1900," treats the Pacific trade in the less glamorous and neglected years following the decline of the clipper ships, stressing the point that the economic emergence of the coastal and interior states of the Far West was not dependent on domestic factors alone.

Richard Maxwell Brown's "Pivot of American Vigilantism: The San Francisco Vigilance Committee of 1856" implies that William T. Coleman's famed vigilantes deserve more from historians than a colorful chapter in the annals of old San Francisco, and that their activities actually signaled the transition from an older concern with rural crime on the frontier to an increasing preoccupation with the growing pains of urban America.

In "The Prospectors: Some Considerations on Their Craft," Otis Young ventures beyond the familiar but superficial descriptions of mining life and translates into comprehensible terms the special language of the gold fields, showing the relation of what the gold-seeker did to how he behaved.

"The Umbrella and the Mosaic: The French-English Presence and the Settlement of the Canadian Prairie West," by Lewis G. Thomas, presents the premise that the quiet conquest of the Canadian prairies has been the result of a fortuitous combination of factors: the "umbrella" of French-English biculturalism protecting the "mosaic" of a highly polyglot pattern of settlement.

In "The Significance of the Small Town in American History," John D. Hicks recalls how the old town-and-country society that was dominant in the United States before World War I provided a viable way of life that the urbanized America of recent times has not yet attained.

In "George W. Littlefield: From Cattle to Colonization, 1871–1920," David B. Gracy II observes that the stereotype of bitter friction between Western stockmen and "sod-busters" did not even begin to prevail at Littlefield, Texas, and that such conflict occurred on the Panhandle-Plains so infrequently as to be of no real historical significance.

James B. Allen, in "The Company-Owned Mining Town in the West: Exploitation or Benevolent Paternalism," examines this thorny question from all sides, and concludes that the much-maligned company town was a curious experiment in what might be valled "benevolent exploitation."

Joe B. Frantz, in "Kennedy and Johnson: A Political Look at the Recent West," offers a close analysis of the voting records of Senators John F. Kennedy of Massachusetts and Lyndon B. Johnson of Texas on issues of importance to the Western states during the 1950's, and shows their views to have been in general harmony.

In "The Modern Texas Rangers: A Law Enforcement Dilemma in the Rio Grande Valley," Ben H. Procter describes the labor unrest that agitated South Texas from the summer of 1966 to June, 1967, culminating in an ugly clash between the strikers and Captain A. Y. Allee's Texas Rangers. (Professor Procter's suggestion that the modern Rangers "maintain, indeed project, a proper public image" has already been taken under advisement by the Texas Department of Public Safety. For this reason, and because his response to Professor Procter's paper has impressed me as a singular example of what "comments" at historical conferences ought to be but seldom are, Philip D. Jordan's chiseled and perceptive commentary is included here just as he gave it at San Francisco. P.S. to future program chairmen and enterprising editors: Why not apply a little benevolent blackmail by reminding the commentators at historical conferences that their utterings should be like those of Professor Jordan, both fit and fit to print?)

The concluding paper, "The West and New Nations in Other Continents" by Earl Pomeroy, calls attention to the possibilities of deriving new perspectives on Western history from studies of the comparative development of new nations. The author has described his paper as "an attempt to borrow from the ideas of social scientists in a field that seems particularly active today." It provides a most appropriate finale to a book of *Reflections* such as this.

Beyond the fifteen papers, the volume contains an appendix which should be interesting to most readers and of great practical value to those members of the Western History Association who spend much of their time with students. One of the most exciting sessions at San Francisco, "The Training of Western Historians," was given the subtitle of "A Seminar" by its chairman, Walter Rundell, Jr., and it proved to be that and more. Short papers from a panel of four experienced and erudite teachers of Western history — Vernon Carstensen, C. Gregory Crampton, Wilbur R. Jacobs, and Howard R. Lamar — were followed by a flood of comment from the floor. This outpouring of viewpoints on how Western history should be approached in the classroom, and outside it, produced much electricity in the audience, and few were ready to quit when Professor Rundell finally had to turn off his taping machine and adjourn the session. Among those who rose to speak their minds on the one hand were such senior historians as Ray A. Billington, John W. Caughey, Oscar O. Winther, W. Turrentine Jackson, and the chief papal delegate of the Western History Association, Father John Francis Bannon, and on the other hand, such interesting "interlopers" as the renowned ethnologist John C. Ewers (who called himself an "eavesdropper" but was indeed a welcome one), a young archaeologist (a very pretty one, and likewise welcome), and an alert undergraduate major in history. Professor Rundell has prepared the proceedings of his "seminar" for publication here, and in extending my editorial thanks I should like to commend him on a first-rate piece of work. Those who read his pages will agree that *Reflections of Western Historians* has been greatly enhanced by their inclusion.

Webb's plea is still ringing in my head, telling me to stop while my statements are still pure. I am not going to disappoint that dear old Texan, but a few things do remain to be said. The very valuable contributions of Marshall Townsend and Doug Peck have already been noted, but to that acknowledgment must now be added my appreciation of the cooperation in the editorial offices of the University of Arizona Press by Mrs. Karen Thure, and of the labors of Miss Judy Corbett, an English major from Kentucky who pitched in to help me with the galleys while I was teaching the summer session at the University of San Francisco. Finally, there are two more names that must be mentioned, and they happen to be the most important of all to me. When a preface contains some such statement as "this book could not have been done without . . .," there is reason to question whether the writer has taken Webb seriously. I have tried to do so, however, and therefore I am hoping that what is about to be said here regarding two individuals will be taken quite seriously by all who know them. There are two people, one a senior and the other a junior Western historian, without whose spiritual and material aid (*i.e.*, endorsement, encouragement, pushing, pulling, prodding, backing and filling, etc.) this volume surely would never have been edited by me.

The senior person is Russell C. Ewing, distinguished scholar of the borderlands and head of the Department of History at the University of Arizona through the decade that I was around that pleasant place. I would never have been there at all if this magnanimous man had not welcomed me warmly in 1958, surrendering his favorite course so as to make room for me in the faculty of his department. Once on the campus, I would neither have become an editor, nor remained one for long, without his unfailing and unstinting support, enlightened counsel, and habit of gentle handling of halter-shy or headsore colts in his corrals. To Russ Ewing I am more grateful than he knows, or than I can say here, for ten years of kindnesses and all the friendship aggregate in them. To state it simply, he gave me the chance of a lifetime for professional fulfillment.

The junior person is James R. Kluger, whose name appears on the title page of this book. Where I could not have gotten into editorial work without Ewing, I could not have gotten out of it without Kluger; where the one provided me with the opportunity to make an editorial reputation, the other helped me to salvage it. As my regularly assigned research assistant for the 1968–69 academic year at the University of Arizona, this bright young Iowan put in triple the hours that his contract·specified in order to get these pages to press. He typed countless paragraphs of text, verified many hundreds of footnotes, read galleys against copy and then repro proofs against galleys, prepared the index alone, and mopped up after me as I made ready to leave for Texas to try my hand at motion picture scripts. (Somewhere along the trail I got to thinking that the life of a scenarist might be yet more fun than that of an historical editor!) More even than this, Jim Kluger furnished me with some of the sharpest editorial suggestions I have ever received from an assistant. He has an eye for the work, a sense of rhythm and pace which is finally far more important than an impeccable command of the commas. Over the years I have known a few young scholars, but not more than just a few, who were happily endowed with the editor's knack. Jim Kluger is the most recent of these, and one of the very best. When he is holding his doctorate, he may prefer the professorial leisure of the classroom to the editorial ardors of iron pants and blue pencil. I rather hope not, because historical editors are in short supply in the Western field. If he is given an opportunity to combine the two careers, as I was, he will be a lucky man. I will then expect him to buy me a Texas T-bone steak, rare, out of gratitude for having been worked so hard on these *Reflections of Western Historians*.

And now, Professor Webb, what do you think of that "dark-eyed dude" who urged you to come to the Denver conference in 1962 so that we could hang on you the first honorary membership in the Western History Association? At least that dude has tried to write an honest preface in your memory.

JOHN ALEXANDER CARROLL

Reflections
of Western Historians

SAN FRANCISCO:

HOTEL CITY OF THE WEST

by

RICHARD A. VAN ORMAN

A member of the faculty of Purdue University teaching at the Calumet campus, the author took his undergraduate and master's work at Michigan State University, then earned the Ph.D. at Indiana University. His dissertation, *A Room for the Night: Hotels of the Old West,* was published by the Indiana University Press in 1966.

DURING ITS EARLY YEARS, San Francisco looked like anything but the great hotel city of the West. Its first hotels were more bar than bed, offering little peace and less quiet. San Francisco was no different from hundreds of other western communities where landlords threw up hotels with little concern for their guests, as long as the money poured in from liquor, gambling, and prostitution.

So it began in San Francisco in 1840 when Jean Jacques Vioget, a French sailor who had fought with Napoleon, opened the town's first public house. If anyone did spend the night at this combination bar and billiard parlor, it was more than likely that he had been drinking and passed out. By the mid-1840's the one-story, frame Vioget House had been leased to a genial young Englishman, Robert T. Ridley. More taken with rum than running

[3]

the hotel, Ridley soon hired as his assistant a fellow Briton, John Henry Brown, who had been steward at Sutter's Fort.

A few months after Brown started to work, he had a most unnerving experience. Each night Lieutenant Henry B. Watson, of the small United States marine detachment, would rap on Brown's window and whisper, "The Spanish are in the brush." This phrase was the signal to Brown to fill the lieutenant's jug with brandy. One night Brown had been drinking heavily and fell sound asleep. Watson appeared at the window and knocked — no response. He rapped again — nothing. Watson, immoderate in the best of times, was already drunk. Having no intention of foregoing his nightly jug, he fired his pistol and bellowed at the top of his voice, "The Spanish are in the brush!" Brown sprang out of bed in an instant, while the townsfolk rushed into the streets firing at shrubs and shadows.

The town was growing at a steady pace in 1846 when Brown bought a saloon directly across Kearny Street from Vioget's and turned it into Brown's Hotel. This adobe house, the first in California to be called "hotel," became the center of activities in the town. Meetings, elections, dances, funerals, and other legal and illegal functions took place at Brown's.

There now arrived upon the San Francisco scene a likeable Bostonian named Robert A. Parker, who had been a sailor and merchant. He soon uttered those all too familiar words, "What this town needs is a good hotel!" Parker, a persuasive man, easily convinced Brown, and a site was selected on Kearny across from Portsmouth Square. That was the easy part, for building anything in San Francisco was not a simple task. Lumber sold at one dollar per foot and carpenters were difficult to find. But the friendly New Englander and the able Englishman persevered, and by May of 1848 the hotel was nearing completion. Just then news of the gold discoveries on the American River reached the town, and the workers took off for the mines.

Construction costs skyrocketed; carpenters, when available, charged sixteen dollars a day, and weekly expenses topped $3,000. Brown and Parker decided that their best course of action would be to renovate Brown's Hotel and divert the profits into finishing the new house. Brown's was reopened auspiciously on the Fourth of July, 1848. A United States ship in the bay joined in the patriotic fervor by firing a number of salutes — the last one almost leveling the hotel. Fortunately no one was hurt, and a few of the better fortified guests thought it was merely a terrific firecracker.

Due to the sudden burst in population, Brown and Parker were soon making $3,000 a day in the bar, and the miners who stayed at Brown's paid the owners $200 a day plus a percentage of the profits for the use of a room for gambling. This space was filled with ten tables for monte, faro, and roulette. Betting was brisk, and the construction costs of the new hotel were quickly met.

Late in 1848 the handsomely furnished Parker House was opened with a gala ball and supper. Although a few rooms were rented out for sleeping, it was primarily a gambling house. The entire second floor was taken over by gamblers, who leased it for $10,000 a month; another $7,000 came from renting other rooms to gentlemen and their lady-friends. Altogether, the Parker House received $175,000 yearly for the use of its facilities.

The noises at the Parker House were the sounds of San Francisco. At the roulette tables the gamblers call, "Make your game," "All set!" "Roll," "Red wins." In one end of the long smoke-filled room a three-piece Mexican band of bugle, harp, and viol tears into a *paso doble*, only to be drowned out by the commotion around the monte table. A gunshot quiets the room, and the miner who has attempted to take back his gold is carried bleeding through the swinging doors. That was all — back to the gambling.

Because of the Parker's swift success, and with thousands of gold seekers entering the city, other public houses opened in 1849 and the early 1850's. Most were gambling resorts or bordellos; those few that were respectable houses rented rooms for thirty dollars a week. Two of the better ones were the Graham House on Kearny and the Pacific (a prefabricated structure whose frame had been ready-cut in Baltimore and then shipped around the Horn), and the three-story St. Francis on Clay and Dupont, the city's best hotel for nearly two years. What was commonly true of nineteenth-century western hotels was especially true of San Francisco houses: a new hotel opened, it became successful — a year or two passed, another house opened, and the first one became outdated in the popular mind.

Others that flourished in the early 1850's were the town's first brick hotel, the Union; the fashionable International; the expensive Oriental; and the strange-looking Niantic, built around the hull of a ship, at the corner of Clay and Sansome. With the great expenses and the numerous delays in construction work, plus the fact that sailors were daily deserting to the mines, ships might be converted into stores, saloons, jails, or even hotels.

Since some of the first hotelmen like Vioget and Parker had been sailors, ship design greatly influenced early San Francisco hotel architecture. Rooms with row upon row of wooden or canvas bunks, three and four tiers high, were common. Because the beds reached to the ceiling, a guest in the top bunk often bumped his head, while those on the lower berths could get kicked in the head, spat upon, or worse.

During its first boom, San Francisco's hotel construction was unending, not only because of the increasing population but also because the town was ravaged by six major fires in a period of nineteen months. Frame and canvas hotels were built, burned down, and rebuilt with monotonous frequency. Many were destroyed at least once, and the Parker House burned down and was rebuilt three times.

No great loss was suffered when most of them were destroyed. They were sorry hotels to begin with. Rooms were little better than torture chambers, with partitions so thin that one could hear what went on both inside and outside the house. To fall asleep was often impossible, what with the constant hotel noises of billiard balls and roulette wheels, sneezing, snoring, and the usual heated conversations revolving around the question of whether the window should be opened or closed.

Always a problem were the creepy, crawly things that attacked sleeping guests. It was a fact of hotel life that the more clothes one wore, the better off one was. Bugs were so numerous and large gray rats so aggressive that a few houses posted signs that read: "Keep your shoes on and cover your head with the blanket." But it was the stench that was most unforgettable. A noxious mingling of tobacco smoke, fumes from the stove, the pungent scent of bedbug powder, and the human odors prompted more than one guest to stick a clothespin on his nose.

In these human stables, guests were given directions to the distant outhouse (the better ones being papered with *Harper's* and *Scientific American*), along with a piece of dirty soap and a towel as black as the landlord's heart. Sheets were a rarity; pillows were stuffed with straw and crockery; and blankets, smelling of horse, rented for one dollar a night.

On occasion a guest shared not only a room for the night but a bed as well. A drunken sailor, a dirty miner, or some nondescript character might crawl in next to you and end all hope of sleep with his jerking and snoring. This situation is reminiscent of the story about a traveler in Illinois who was promised the room recently vacated by Senator Stephen A. Douglas. When the guest entered the apartment, he found seven men sleeping in four beds. Rushing back to the landlord, he exclaimed that it was indeed an honor to sleep in a room so recently occupied by the great Douglas — "But I will not sleep with the whole damn Democratic Party!" It may well be that one of the reasons drinking became the town's major recreation was that it was easier to suffer such indignities when drunk.

Among the dozens of San Francisco hotels, some catered especially to the foreigners. The Prescott and the Hansa were known as *gemütlich* German houses, and more than one was considered a French hotel. There was a Chinese hotel named the Globe; another, a large cellar, was facetiously called the Palace. But the most unusual, and indeed in some ways one of the best, was the What Cheer House. Opened in 1852 at 527 Sacramento Street, it catered to mechanics and miners. Upon signing the guest register, the men were often requested to take a bath and go to a special delousing room. Although the hotel was not fancy, it was clean and the owner, R. B. Woodward, intended to keep it that way.

At the What Cheer beds were fifty cents a night, and a substantial meal cost fifteen cents. At that price it is easy to see why more than 4,000 meals were served each day, and that the daily consumption of food included 100 dozen eggs, 100 pounds of butter, 500 pounds of potatoes, 400 quarts of milk, and 150 pies. Aside from the amount of food devoured there, this house was exceptional in other ways. There was no bar, and considering its clientele, one might question Woodward's sanity. But like some other hotels of the time, the What Cheer was a temperance house. Its most uncommon feature was the rule that no women were allowed in the house, not even maids. A bachelor's paradise! And this strongly suggests one of the reasons why it was so popular.

The rooms were furnished with mahogany bedstands, curled hair mattresses, pin cushions and needles, and combs and brushes. (Some hotels of the time even offered a communal toothbrush.) Since there was an excellent laundry connected with the What Cheer, the miners no longer had to ship their shirts to China.

Two extraordinary rooms in the hotel were the museum and the library. The museum, one of the best in the West, contained twenty-five species of preserved animals, 600 assorted stuffed birds, and some 1,200 variegated eggs from ostrich to humming-bird. The What Cheer's outstanding attraction was its library. Begun in 1856 after Woodward had traveled to New York to consult with Harper Brothers, in a short time it was filled with more than 4,000 volumes. The only requirement that a book had to meet was that it encourage morality. Besides works on gardening, bee-keeping, grape-growing, and stock-raising, there were 300 volumes of history and biography and 400 volumes devoted to fiction. Dickens, Scott, Cooper, and Irving were especially popular with the miners. The library also had a varied collection of periodicals and an excellent selection of newspapers, including *The Times* of London. Woodward's yearly bill for papers and periodicals was

$1,200, but it was well worth the money, for this was the most popular room in the house.

In the late 1850's a decline in the California mines and an exodus of the miners to new areas ended the first boom period of hotel construction in San Francisco. Many hotels changed owners, managers, and names; a few burned down; others were razed to make space for a city hall, a new bank, or a theater. Some were removed to the Barbary Coast to become well-paying parlor houses. But by the early 1860's, with the Nevada mines pouring new wealth into the city, the second boom began — and San Francisco was on her way to becoming the hotel city of the West.

One of the factors that helped San Francisco to win this enviable reputation was the unlimited optimism that this influx of bullion created in the minds of her citizens. But there were other aspects of life in San Francisco that played their part. As a town made up largely of miners, sailors, and men on the make, it was primarily a town of young bachelors who had neither the time nor the inclination to build a house and then worry about its upkeep. For such a youthful and unsettled population, hotel life was the only life.

During the last decades of the nineteenth century, over fifty per cent of San Francisco hotel guests were permanents, including young married couples as well as bachelors. It may seem strange that a young couple with a child or two would decide to live in a hotel, but there were numerous reasons why they did. Many considered it less expensive than buying a home or paying fifty to one hundred dollars a month rent. Many who did have the money for a house felt it was easier and much more convenient to live in a hotel, especially if several of their friends also resided there. One of the social problems in upper-class America at that time was the difficulty in obtaining servants. One San Francisco woman in a month's time had a turnover of eighteen maids. In a hotel the servant problem was solved, what with chambermaids, bartenders, bellboys, and doormen at the guest's beck and call.

Concern was expressed, especially by British travelers, over the harmful effects of hotel life on the American home and family. Children, they cautioned, would become spoiled and ill-mannered from lack of supervision, while mothers frittered away their time gossiping with the ladies; and even morality might suffer a decline, for a place with 300 beds could not be pure! Increasingly fearful of such hotbeds of sin, the San Francisco press finally brought the evils of hotel living to the attention of the public.

An editorial in the *Evening Bulletin* began by conceding that there were obvious advantages to residing in a hotel where one was "upholstered, fed, wined, newspapered, amused and attended"; further, one could maintain a style of living that in private most could not afford. But there was another side of the coin. "What a waste," the irate editor wrote, "does hotel life make of all the finer social instincts and all the sweeter joys of social intercourse! How it saps the virtues that originate in the private household! How it dissipates health! How it blights womanly modesty and divests childhood of its simplicity!" It might be all right for the unmarried or for childless couples to live in these palaces of pleasure, for such people pass through them "comparatively unharmed." But for those with children, the flash and glitter and extravagance of hotel living would bring forth "spicy scandals." In conclusion, the editor warned that "every American who is anxious for the growth of a strong, manly, healthy, National character, must deprecate the growing tendency to prefer hotel to domestic life. The typical woman who is to be the future Mother of America cannot be formed in six story palaces; she must develop in the private dwelling."

Between 1862 and 1864, as it happened, four new threats to American motherhood appeared in San Francisco. (If the divorce rate increased because of them, there is no record of it.) Run on the "American Plan," these new hotels charged two to three dollars in gold per day for a room and three meals, and even then they were being compared with the better hostelries of New York, Chicago, and St. Louis. The first of these was the plain but popular Russ House, owned by the experienced hotelman Adolph Russ and located on Montgomery Street between Bush and Pine. As

Kearny had been the important hotel street of the 1840's and 1850's, Montgomery, one block east, was becoming the new center of hotel life. The $350,000 Russ, whose first year's income was $400,000, opened its 275 rooms in 1862 and for a short time was the largest hotel on the Pacific Coast. Because many of its guests were farmers and small-town businessmen, there was little excitement at the Russ other than an occasional robbery or the visits of the amorous actress Adah Isaacs Menken, of *Mazeppa* fame, with one of her many lovers. Before writing off the old Russ as being too staid, it might be noted that there were a few rooms on the second floor set aside for certain diversions. San Franciscans were virtuous, according to their lights, but at times their lights were a little dim.

The Lick House also opened in 1862 on Montgomery Street, between Post and Sutter. This 250-room structure was built by the eccentric millionaire James Lick. Besides being the first palatial hotel in San Francisco, it was also the first one in California to have a bridal suite. The Lick was a family hotel, and the Lick set included some of San Francisco's most prominent people. Elegantly attired men and women could be seen there, especially on Sunday evenings, eating in the grand dining room. In roisterous earlier days the walls of the bars and dining rooms of San Francisco hotels were covered with paintings of buxom nudes attacking satyrs, but now in the decorous year of 1862 the Lick dining room was hung with paintings of tranquil California scenes.

The Occidental, the third new hotel on Montgomery Street, was opened on New Year's Day, 1863, with appointments luxurious enough to cause Mark Twain to describe it as "heaven on the half-shell." This handsome four-story house had 400 rooms and — wonder of wonders — a bath on every floor. In addition to the usual reading room, the Occidental had a telegraph office, mineral museum, and billiard room with thirteen tables, plus the first elevator on the Coast, which was in service from 6 A.M. to 12 P.M. daily. As famous as the hotel itself was the Occidental's luxurious white marble bar where presided that master mixologist, Professor Jerry Thomas. The author of a popular book on how to mix drinks, Thomas, behind the bar, was resplendent with diamonds as he prepared two of his own creations — the fiery Blue Blazer, made with Scotch and boiling water, and the ever-popular Tom and Jerry.

Lewis Leland was the Occidental's first manager, and his younger brother Jerome the steward. In America of the nineteenth century, the name Leland personified all that was grand in hotel-manship. The dozen Lelands in the business from coast to coast comprised what was certainly the great hotel family of the United States.

On August 31, 1864, the $500,000 Cosmopolitan Hotel opened at Bush and Sansome. If New York could have her Metro-politan Hotel, then San Francisco, always competing with eastern cities, must have her Cosmopolitan. This five-story house was built with silver from the Comstock Lode, and naturally its set included the wealthy Nevadans.

Most hotels had either grand opening balls or, like the Cos-mopolitan, an inspection by the public. What was expected to be a leisurely tour of the new hotel by a few sightseers turned into a mob scene. More than 20,000 people stormed the house as if it were the Bastille. Toughs from the Barbary Coast out for a little fun, got it that night. Women fainted, children screamed, and men were slugged. A policeman, trying to maintain order, was picked up and carried through the lobby. The pickpockets had a profitable eve-ning, and some of the girls from the Coast were seen propositioning men in the crowd.

What a shambles it was after the house was cleared! Anything and everything that could be stolen was gone — sheets, pillow-cases, silver, glasses, and even a bed. The final humiliation came when the staff discovered that many of the guests had been locked in their rooms by the rowdies.

Stealing in hotels grew worse and more widespread as time passed. In fact, next to fire it was the plague of hotelmen. Silver-ware disappeared from tables along with salt and pepper shakers, ashtrays, and on occasion the table itself. Owners could not even trust their employees. Two bellboys stole $12,000 from the Russ House safe, and later the What Cheer was robbed of $25,000. The professional hotel thief not only stole from the hotels, he also relieved the guests of their money, jewelry, clothes, and anything portable. As night watchmen were usually ineffective and locks easy to jimmy, the hotel bandit continued on his felonious way. Often taking a room at the house to remove suspicion, the thief, if apprehended, could play drunk and claim that he had gotten into the wrong room by mistake.

Another problem that San Francisco hotelmen could do even less about was the incidence of suicide in their hotels. For the despondent guest there was not only the dramatic value of being found dead in the morning by the chambermaid, but it was also one way —albeit drastic — to beat the bill. Twenty-four suicides occurred in San Francisco in 1865, many of them in hotels. A man at the Lick House cut his throat; a guest at the Occidental swallowed strychnine; at the William Tell a roomer shot himself. The frequency of such deaths climbed steadily in the last decades of the nineteenth century until San Francisco newspapers editorialized on the "suicide mania" sweeping the city.

One of the most famous hotels in the West was the Cliff House, located six miles west of downtown San Francisco. A "must" on all tourists' agenda was breakfast at the Cliff House. The drive there along Bush Street to Point Lobos Road, and then through Golden Gate Park, was one of the city's most scenic routes. First built by the enterprising Mormon apostate Samuel Brannan in 1858 with lumber from a ship that had run aground, the Cliff House — perched on rocks overlooking the Pacific Ocean — offered a superb view from its wide veranda. The most popular sight was the Seal Rocks where, during certain weeks of the year, hundreds of barking sea lions frolicked. Two of the animals were especially famous — "General Grant," called that because he was very quiet and slept a great deal, and "Ben Butler," so named because he was big, cross-eyed, and ugly.

For years the Cliff House was run by "Pop" Foster. When business fell off in the 1870's, Pop hired a few of the girls from the Barbary Coast and things picked up again. Adolph Sutro, of Nevada tunnel fame, later bought the none-too-respectable house and rebuilt it into a fine seven-story hotel, only to have it destroyed by fire.

In the 1870's San Francisco truly became the hotel city of the West, a title she won away from St. Louis. The hotels that gave her that distinction were the Grand, the Baldwin, and the Palace.

The Grand Hotel opened in the spring of 1870 on the corner of Market and New Montgomery streets. Covering two and one-half acres of ground, it consisted of two separate buildings joined by a bridge. This luxurious 400-room structure cost one million dollars, with most of the money coming from the Nevada mines. Built in the Second Empire style, the Grand was the best hotel west of Chicago. Hosts Johnson and Ridgeway were from the firm of Johnson & Company, which had previously managed the Lick House. The owners were the Montgomery Street developer, Asbury Harpending, and the head of the Bank of California, William C. Ralston.

The Baldwin, opened in April of 1877 at Market and Powell, was a monument to the name and fame of its owner, Elias J. "Lucky" Baldwin. A six-story, 400-room structure with mansard roof and Ionic columns and towers, it cost $3,500,000 to build and contained $300,000 worth of furnishings. More than any other edifice on the Pacific Coast, the Baldwin embodied the imposing and ornate Second Empire style. Inside the house were hung paintings depicting incidents in the owner's unusual life. Baldwin purchased carpets at twenty-five dollars a yard in Philadelphia, and on the recommendation of Mark Twain, paid Tiffany's of New York $25,000 for a clock which Twain claimed "not only tells the hours and minutes and seconds but the turn of the tides, the phases of the moon, the price of eggs, and who's got your umbrella."

Among the hotel's well-known features were a billiard parlor and reading room just for women, and a conservatory where studious guests could contemplate the mysteries of botany. Baldwin's Academy of Music, the hotel theater, featured on its bill such names as Edwin Booth, Maurice Barrymore, Otis Skinner, and Julia Marlowe. American Plan rates were four dollars a day for a room with bath and three meals. Not much profit was made, for the food costs came to three dollars and fifty cents per guest. For twenty-one years the Baldwin was one of the great hotels of the West. On November 23, 1898, it burned to the ground.

When the Palace Hotel opened on Saturday, October 2, 1875, it was not only the largest and most talked-about hotel in the United States, but also the very best. If any hotel ever represented a town and a time, it was this symbol of San Francisco's coming of age. The Palace was the last major undertaking of that banker extraordinaire, William C. Ralston. His good friend Asbury Harpending reminisced that it was built simply to satisfy Ralston's ambition to have in San Francisco the biggest and best hotel in the world. For almost two decades the Palace reigned supreme over American hotels — until the Waldorf of New York was opened in 1893 — and for more than thirty years the Palace was the finest hotel in the West.

Construction began early in 1873 on a tract of two and one-half acres bounded by Market, New Montgomery, Jessie, and Annie streets. Ralston had estimated that the hotel would cost $1,750,000, but that amount alone went for the "earthquake proof" foundation of twelve-foot thickness. The last major San Francisco quake had occurred in October, 1868; and the fear of earthquakes gave San Francisco the most solid hotels on the continent. The great size of the Palace, however, taxed even California's resources. Part of Ralston's plan was to prove California's self-sufficiency to the rest of the country. He purchased a ranch to supply the oak flooring, a foundry to forge nails, a lock and key shop, and a factory to turn California timber into Palace furniture. But difficulties in getting bricks, as well as strikes by the three hundred bricklayers, delayed construction.

Up the hotel went and up, too, climbed the cost. By the time the seventh and last story was completed, seven million dollars had been spent. In part because of this financial drain, the Bank of California closed its doors on August 26, 1875. The next day Ralston resigned as president of the bank, deeded his many holdings to his business associate William Sharon, and left the bank building. As was his habit, he went to the Neptune Bath House at North Beach, changed into his swimming trunks, and dived into the Pacific. Some fifteen minutes later his body was pulled from the water. Five weeks after Ralston's death, the Palace opened its doors with a concert by Chris Andre's band and a tearful speech by Sharon. Appropriately, on that same day, the Bank of California reopened.

The immensity of the Palace was truly staggering. The hotel was a city within a city. Besides thirteen dining rooms, one of which was just for children, there were numerous businesses within the house: clothing stores, Doxey's famous book store, a luggage shop, a travel agency, and a barber shop. Each new guest was given a prospectus which told of the size and facilities of the Palace. The hotel had been built with thirty-one million bricks, ten million feet of lumber, and 3,300 tons of iron. Within its structure, curling like great snakes, were twenty miles of gas pipe and twenty-eight miles of water pipe. The house had 755 rooms, 437 bathtubs, 492 water closets, five hydraulic elevators (one of which was large enough to carry forty passengers), and no less than 900 cuspidors.

Guests made various comments on its size. A Chicago newspaperman described the Palace as a house made up of houses, "a kind of architectural Surinam toad that swallows . . . little toads to keep them out of danger." Rudyard Kipling, who stopped there in 1889, called the Palace "a seven-storied warren of humanity." Another guest of the 1880's thought that its hundreds of bay windows gave it the air of "a mammoth bird-cage." A popular hotel magazine advised its readers that guests at the Palace need not go outside for exercise. "Once around the corridors," the writer noted, "is equal to a mile, and half an hour on the top floor equivalent to a couple of weeks at a mountain or seaside resort."

Besides its great size, the most talked-about feature was the Grand Court, reminiscent of the Grand Hotel in Paris, into which coaches turned from New Montgomery Street to deposit arriving guests. From the Court rose six tiers of balconies, and above it all was a magnificent arched roof of glass. Separated from the main entrance area was the Palm Court, laid with alternate blocks of black and white marble. Palm, banana, lemon, and lime trees grew there, along with hundreds of flowers and tropical plants. Cages filled with chirping birds added to the garden effect.

Just as the Palace was the great meeting place of San Francisco, so the Palace Bar was the great mecca of the hotel. The specialty of the room was oysters on the half shell. Here, as Evelyn Wells has noted in her book, *Champagne Days of San Francisco,* between the hours of four and six in the afternoon "centered the West." Beautiful by day, the Palace at night took on a magical luster. Then the fashionably dressed ladies and their escorts would promenade along the plush halls and through the courts below. The strains of Strauss waltzes, the glow from the gigantic chandeliers, and the rainbow of colors all added up to an unforgettable evening for many a resident of San Francisco or visitor to the city.

Since Ralston also had owned the Grand Hotel, a bridge, called the Bridge of Sighs, was built across New Montgomery Street to connect the two hotels. Where distinguished travelers had once resided at the Grand, they now stayed at the Palace. Leland Stanford was the first of a long line of world-famous guests. Others included Generals William Tecumseh Sherman and Phil Sheridan, Presidents Benjamin Harrison and William McKinley, the preacher Henry Ward Beecher, the prizefighter James J. Jeffries, and the first royal visitor, Dom Pedro II, Emperor of Brazil, who told San Francisco's mayor that nothing caused him to be so ashamed of his country as the Palace.

The greatest reception ever given at the hotel was the one that welcomed former President Grant back from his world tour in 1879. On this occasion the balconies were brilliantly lit and bedecked with the Stars and Stripes and pictures of the General. As his carriage entered the Grand Court, confetti was dropped from above, flags were waved, and 500 vocalists under the direction of Madame Fabbri sang a specially-written ode to Grant. The good General suffered through the lengthy ordeal, made more trying because of the loss of his false teeth.

Some of the Palace employees were almost as distinguished as the guests. Warren Leland, of the great hotel family, was manager and lessee for the first three years. Among his many innovations, Leland introduced Negro hotel employees to San Francisco. Of the Palace's staff of 300, there were 150 Negro waiters and forty Negro maids. The hotel's best known Negro employee was old "Muffin Tom," celebrated for his delicious corn bread and waffles. Another famous Palace employee was the chef, Jules Harder, who had left Delmonico's in New York to start the new hotel off gastronomically.

Because of its size, the Palace had few money-making years. With the opening of the St. Francis by the Crocker family in 1904 and the construction of Tessie Fair Oelrichs' beautiful $5,000,000 Fairmont on Nob Hill, it was apparent that Ralston's great house was becoming outmoded. There was talk of completely remodeling it and even of tearing it down.

But the problems of the Palace were solved on Wednesday, April 18, 1906, the morning the earth opened up and closed again along the ancient line of the San Andreas fault. No structural damage was done to the Palace since the brick walls, two feet thick, were supported by 300 tons of iron strips. Following the quake, however, scores of fires broke out all over the city. Although the city's water mains were cracked, there was little panic at the Palace, for the guests were reassured that the 630,000 gallons of water stored in the basement and the 130,000 gallons on the roof could handle the emergency. Yet by two in the afternoon the water supply had been pumped dry and the Palace began to burn — the upper floors first and then the entire house. By five o'clock the Palace was destroyed; only its massive walls stood, almost defiantly. (Later it would cost almost $100,000 to tear those walls down.)

Out of the tangle of rubble grew a new San Francisco. It would never catch the charm and flavor of that older city, but its hotels — the rebuilt Palace, the St. Francis, and the Fairmont, and later the Mark Hopkins and the Sir Francis Drake — would make San Francisco once again the hotel city of the West.

The Colonial West

GUZMÁN'S "MAYOR ESPAÑA": A STUDY IN CONQUISTADOR AMBITION

by

DONALD E. CHIPMAN

A professor of history at North Texas State University and a native of Kansas, the author did research in Spain while working toward his doctorate at the University of New Mexico. His study of Guzmán's governorship in Pánuco was published by the Arthur H. Clark Company in 1967 as a volume in its series on "Spain in the West."

"God, gold, and glory" have traditionally been ascribed as the personal motives and psychological goals of the Spanish conquistadores. Religious motivation in the conquest has received much attention, as well as the conquistador's appetite for gold and silver. But ambition was a powerful factor, too, perhaps paramount in importance. While the ambition of the conquistadores was directed partly to the accumulation of wealth, it was also aimed at recognition, prestige, and at least a measure of political power. Hernán Cortés received impressive titles and grants in 1529, but he was denied the one distinction which meant the most to him — reappointment as governor of New Spain. His frustration drove him to the costly and unsuccessful enterprises of the 1530's.

Cortés was not alone in this; there was hardly a single conquistador who, in the twilight days of his life, could express any measure of contentment over his accomplishments and rewards. No doubt this sense of failure was prompted by a dilemma that faced the conquistador. If he became too successful or ambitious, he constituted a real or imagined threat to royal absolutism and to the predominance of the crown over its possessions in the New World; if he failed, he faced anonymity or worse. Spanish bureaucrats or corporate bodies such as the audiencias inevitably replaced the conquistadores whether they were good, bad, or indifferent.

Nuño de Guzmán repeatedly failed, except for a few brief moments, to taste the sweet wine of success. Of a moderately wealthy family with important connections at court, he was appointed governor of Pánuco, a province to the north of Veracruz, in November of 1525. An appointee with Luis Ponce de León (the judge of residencia for Cortés), Guzmán contracted malaria after his arrival at Española and was bedfast for seven months. In the meantime, Luis Ponce continued on to Mexico City where he soon died.

Several months later, in May of 1527, Guzmán took up his duties as resident governor of Pánuco. Pánuco was a bitter disappointment to his ambitions. Its only readily exploitable wealth, the unfortunate Huastec Indians, Guzmán shipped by the thousands as slaves to the West Indies. Moreover he faced an imagined threat of encroachment by Pánfilo de Narváez to the north, and a very real threat from the friends of Cortés in Mexico City who recognized Guzmán as a person hostile to their interests.[1]

After a year and a half as resident governor of Pánuco, Guzmán received one of his few triumphs in New Spain — the presidency of the First Audiencia, with orders to conduct the long-delayed residencia of Cortés and his lieutenants. But his twelve-month stay in Mexico City was anything but pleasant. He faced the determined opposition of the partisans of Cortés, and he

---

[1] For a detailed treatment of Guzmán's governorship in Pánuco, see Donald E. Chipman, *Nuño de Guzmán and the Province of Pánuco in New Spain, 1518–1533* (Glendale, Calif., 1967).

acquired a potent enemy in Bishop Juan de Zumárraga who had arrived with the judges of the First Audiencia.

The rule, or misrule, of the First Audiencia was one of the most dismal periods in the history of sixteenth-century New Spain. Guzmán accelerated the slave trade and conducted the residencia of Cortés; the surviving judges of the Audiencia, Matienzo and Delgadillo, adopted moral standards that left much to be desired; encomiendas were revoked and reassigned; and quarrels between the Franciscans and the civil government were unseemly at best. Underlying the tone of government was the knowledge that the First Audiencia was a temporary agency, and that a new Audiencia and Viceroy would soon arrive to replace it. Also, contacts at court advised Guzmán that the climate of opinion there was favorable to Cortés.[2]

By the summer of 1529 Guzmán had begun to lay plans for a new conquest to the west and northwest of Mexico City. While he was careful to build up the undertaking as one which would benefit the crown, there is no doubt that the conquest was, in large measure, designed to serve Guzmán's personal ambitions. Within a short distance of Mexico City was the "Tierra de Guerra," from which the "Teules-Chichimecas" raided the settled portions of New Spain. Thus the proposed conquest would simultaneously secure and increase the lands and revenues of the crown as well as bring the cross to pagan Indians. A persistent rumor that a land of Amazons awaited the army lent an air of excitement and expectation to the preparations.

But unquestionably Guzmán found the prospect of his removal as president and the inevitable residencia exceedingly unpleasant. Further, if the residencia went against him, it could bring a premature end to certain goals as yet unrealized. He hoped to discover rich cities that would exceed the splendor of Tenoch-

---

[2] A study of the First Audiencia of New Spain is in progress by the author. The residencia of this agency is preserved in the Archivo General de Indias, Sevilla (cited hereafter as AGI), Justicia 226–229. (Microfilm or Xerox copies of this and other documentation cited below are in the possession of the author.)

titlán and thus eclipse the fame of Cortés. To insure that all wealth in the unconquered portions of New Spain lay within his jurisdiction, Guzmán planned a coordinated expansion to combine the new areas of conquest with the province of Pánuco. Accordingly, he appointed a *teniente de capitán general* for Pánuco in mid-December of 1529. The appointee, Juan de Cervantes, received detailed instructions to carry out a military campaign in the region of los Valles de Oxitipa. Ostensibly this campaign was to pacify troublesome Indians in the area of modern Valles, but in reality Cervantes was to link up with the main army of Guzmán in Jalisco.[3]

The main army was assembled with much care. It was probably the best equipped force for a conquest in New Spain to this time, and in the ranks were seasoned troops experienced in Indian warfare. Shortly before Christmas of 1529 Guzmán marched out of Mexico City. Accompanying him was the Cazonci, the most prominent of the surviving Indian nobility of New Spain.[4]

As civil and religious head of the Tarascans, the Cazonci had had a precarious existence since the mid-1520's. At times he was free, but always he faced the possibility of arrest and extortion because Spanish control over Michoacán, both civil and religious, was considerable by the late 1520's. Some four months before Guzmán left Mexico City, he had ordered that the Cazonci be brought there and detained. In the march through Michoacán, he

---

[3] Hubert H. Bancroft, *History of Mexico* (6 vols.; San Francisco, 1883–1888), II, 283–289; Vicente Riva Palacio (ed.), *México a través de los siglos* (5 vols.; México, [1958]), II, 203; Manuel Carrera Stampa, *Nuño de Guzmán* (México, 1955), 13; *Memoria de los servicios que había hecho Nuño de Guzmán desde que fue nombrado gobernador de Pánuco en 1525,* Estudio y notas por Manuel Carrera Stampa (México, 1955), 63–64 (hereafter cited as *Memoria de Guzmán*); Título y instrucciones a Juan de Cervantes, factor, como teniente de capitán general en la provincia de Pánuco por Nuño de Guzmán (México: 13 de diciembre de 1529), AGI, Patronato 76-2-1.

[4] Estimates of the number of Spaniards and Indian allies in the army vary widely from 300 to 800 in the case of the former, and from 2,000 to 20,000 in the latter. A study of documents contemporary to the conquest (see note 8 below) would suggest 300 to 400 Spaniards and 5,000 to 8,000 Indian allies; Bancroft, II, 294n. For the estimate of 20,000 Indian allies, see Antonio Tello, *Libro segundo de la crónica miscelánea, en que se trata de la conquista espiritual y temporal de la Santa Provincia de Xalisco en el nuevo reino de la Galicia y Nueva Vizcaya y descubrimiento del Nuevo México* (Guadalajara, 1891).

intended to use the Cazonci as his hostage and the key to untapped treasure.[5]

In early February of 1530 the army crossed the Lerma River north of Puruándiro and entered Tierra de Guerra for the first time. There the Cazonci was brought to trial and executed. The charges against him are not germane to this paper except to note that included in them was the accusation that the Tarascan chief had planned to ambush Guzmán's army in the environs of Lake Chapala.[6]

While camped on the Lerma River, Guzmán put into action another phase of his master plan of expansion. Antonio de Godoy, a former muleteer and civil official in Michoacán, was given a small force and dispatched in the general direction of Pánuco with orders to pacify all intervening pueblos.[7] Presumably, Godoy was to join forces with Juan de Cervantes in the Valles area while, in the meantime, Guzmán was to continue the conquest toward the South Sea and eventually control everything from the Pacific Ocean to the Gulf of Mexico. This plan failed for several reasons. First of all, Guzmán consistently underestimated the size of New Spain; he thought his possessions in Pánuco to be no great distance from the South Sea. Secondly, Cervantes and Godoy were not able to contact each other. And finally, Guzmán ran into a number of difficulties, slowing down what he hoped would be a swift and profitable conquest.

---

[5] The best treatment of the conquest of Michoacán is Fintan Warren, "The Conquest of Michoacán, 1521–1530" (Master's thesis, University of New Mexico, 1960; manuscript in preparation for publication). The same author has resolved the status of the Cazonci at this time in his *Vasco de Quiroga and his Pueblo-Hospitals of Santa Fe* (Washington, D.C., 1963), 78.

[6] Preliminary investigation of charges against the Cazonci was first made in Tzintzuntzan; the trial continued on the Lerma River. For a scholarly discussion of these events, see Warren, "The Conquest of Michoacán, 1521–1530," 130–163; for the trial record itself, see France V. Scholes and Eleanor B. Adams (eds.), *Proceso contra Tzintzicha Tangaxoan, el Caltzontzin, formado por Nuño de Guzmán, año de 1530* (México, 1952).

[7] Godoy was somewhat familiar with the terrain, and in late 1528 he had carried news to Pánuco of Guzmán's appointment as president of the First Audiencia. For Godoy's selection to lead the expedition, see [El fiscal] con Antonio de Godoy sobre el derecho del pueblo de Cinagua que le había sido encomendado (1542), AGI, Justicia 197–4.

On the northeastern shores of Lake Chapala, the army ran
into stiff opposition. This added support to Guzmán's contention
that the Cazonci had indeed organized Indian resistance against
him. From Lake Chapala, campaigns were conducted to Tonalá
and to Nochistlán. At Nochistlán Guzmán divided the main army
between himself and the former *veedor* of New Spain, Pedro
Almíndez de Cherino. Later the two forces rejoined at Tepic, and
from there Guzmán led a small detachment to the Pacific and
founded a port near San Blas.[8]

The conquest now moved north of Tepic late in May of
1530. Arriving at a large river on May 29, Guzmán, with much
pomp and ceremony, named it the Río Grande del Espíritu Santo
(now the Río Grande de Santiago). Then, on the north bank, he
proclaimed grandly that his army would now proceed with the
conquest of "Mayor España,"[9] a declaration reflecting his supreme
ego. But the notion that his conquests deserved a title greater than
Spain itself did not strike a responsive note when it reached
the court.

After crossing the Río Grande de Santiago, Guzmán experienced one failure after another, broken only by his recognition
as governor and captain general of the areas of conquest. Indian
resistance north of the river was fierce. Armed with excellent bows
and arrows and protected by huge shields of alligator and buffalo
skin, these Indians attacked with the boldness and ferocity of

---

[8] The most reliable secondary account of the conquest of New Galicia remains in
Bancroft, II, 341–374. Documentary sources of considerable value are: Residencia
tomada á Nuño de Guzmán al tiempo que fue gobernador de la Nueva Galicia; por
el Licenciado Don Diego de la Torre, juez nombrado para este efecto (1536), Justicia,
337–338 (hereafter cited as Residencia de Nueva Galicia); Carta á su majestad del
presidente de la Audiencia de México, Nuño de Guzmán, en que refiere la jornada
que hizo á Michoacán, a conquistar la provincia de los Teules-Chichimecas, que confina
con Nueva España (Omitlán: 8 de julio de 1530), *Colección de documentos inéditos
relativos al descubrimiento, conquista, y organización de las antiguas posesiones espa-
ñolas en América y Oceanía* (42 vols.; Kraus Reprint Ltd., 1966), XIII, 356–393
(hereafter cited as *DII*); Relación hecha por Pedro de Carranza sobre la jornada que
hizo Nuño de Guzmán, de la entrada y sucesos en la Nueva Galicia (1531), *DII*,
XIV, 347–373; and the four anonymous accounts of the conquest in *Memoria de Guzmán*, 93–176.

[9] Carta á su majested (8 de julio de 1530), *DII*, XIII, 388.

Spanish soldiers hardened by a lifetime of warfare. Temporary camp was made at Omitlán on the Trinidad River. While the area had abundant foodstuffs — fish, corn, and fruit — it was a horrible place to spend July. Guzmán complained of the unbearable heat, of streams filled with alligators, and of all too many poisonous scorpions.[10]

By the end of summer the army had arrived at the Acaponeta River. Here a letter arrived advising Guzmán of the return to New Spain of his arch-enemy Cortés. Then disaster struck again. On September 20, 1530, a sudden rising of flood waters hit the army in the dead of night. Most of the supplies and food were washed away or ruined. Massive sickness among the Indian allies followed the flood. Both Spaniards and Indians clamored to quit the expedition; but a few hangings, on orders of Guzmán, restored enthusiasm. Guzmán also dangled before the disgruntled troops the prospects of soon reaching the land of the Amazons.

Stories of the Amazons, who supposedly lived at Cihuatlán, were more than a mere palliative for the troops. On two occasions Guzmán reported accounts of them in official documents sent to the crown. Rumor had it that these remarkable women were rich, whiter than other Indians, and consented to cohabitation only on certain occasions. Their offspring, if male, were killed immediately; but the females were protected. When an advance party of the army finally reached the pueblo of Cihuatlán and found it to be an ordinary Indian village, Guzmán began to circulate stories of the fabled Seven Cities.[11]

---

[10]Ibid., 391.

[11]Irving Leonard notes that Guzmán was the immediate heir to the legend of Amazons on the Pacific Coast — a legend given credence by Cristóbal de Olid, Francisco Cortés, and the Conqueror in his Fourth Letter. See his "Conquerors and Amazons in México," Hispanic American Historical Review (November 1944), XXIV, 574–578; Bancroft, II, 364, 392; Carta á su majestad del presidente de la Audiencia de México, Nuño de Guzmán (Omitlán: 8 de julio de 1530), DII, XIII, 392; Carta de Nuño de Guzmán al emperador (Chiametla: 16 de enero de 1531), ibid., 408–409; Relación del descubrimiento y conquista que se hizo por el gobernador Nuño de Guzmán y su ejército en las provincias de la Nueva Galicia. Autorizada por Alonso de Mata, escribano de S. M. (1530), DII, XIV, 436–437.

By the fall of 1531 Guzmán had extended the conquest to
the north of Culiacán. At this time word reached him of his
appointment as governor and captain general of New Galicia. This
momentary triumph, however, was lessened by an apparent
upbraiding from the Empress herself for his presumption in suggesting that the area of conquest carry the title "Mayor España."
Guzmán's explanation for the proposed title is something of a
classic. "Mayor España," he contended, came from his veneration
for Santa María la Mayor, whom he had beseeched to uplift a
country lacking in Faith; it was not meant to suggest that his conquests were greater than Spain. Besides, argued Guzmán, good
parents are never displeased when their children outstrip them;
and he implied that Spain as the Mother Country could afford
to sponsor an enterprise that would eventually surpass her. Left
unsaid was the further implication that he, as a strong and devoted
son of Spain, was just the person to carry out such a project.[12]

At the very time that Guzmán's appointment as governor and
captain general arrived, representatives of Hernán Cortés chal-
lenged him in the Jalisco-Tepic area; and he found the Second
Audiencia increasingly unfriendly to his government. He strengthened his control in the South by marching from Culiacán to Jalisco,
but the continuing presence of potent enemies in Mexico City and
Michoacán caused him to return to the project which had mis-
carried in the first months of 1530.[13]

Guzmán had retained his office as governor of Pánuco, and
now he transformed his goal of creating a Greater Spain into a
Greater New Spain. His lieutenants in Pánuco, perhaps at the

---

[12] Guzmán received appointment as governor and captain general of New Galicia on
February 25, 1531 (the document is apparently no longer extant). See Chipman,
Nuño de Guzmán, pp. 236–237; Carta a la emperatriz, de Nuño de Guzmán, dando
cuenta del estado en que se hallaba la conquista y población de la Nueva Galicia y
quejándose de los daños que le hacían la Audiencia y el Marqués del Valle (Compostela: 12 de junio de 1532), Francisco del Paso y Troncoso (comp.), *Epistolario de
Nueva España* (16 vols.; México, 1939–1942), II, 144–145 (hereafter cited as *ENE*).

[13] Guzmán's return to southern New Galicia and his confrontation with Luis de Castilla is adequately treated in Bancroft, II, 365–372. Partisan accounts are *Memoria de
Guzmán*, 70–71, and Carta a la emperatriz, de la Audiencia de México, dando aviso de
haber enviado a don Luis de Castilla a poblar en Jalisco y que lo había preso Nuño de
Guzmán . . . (México: 19 de abril de 1532), *ENE*, II, 112.

prompting of Guzmán, had already written to the crown suggesting that Pánuco be incorporated with Guzmán's conquests in the
Northwest. The advantages of such a union, they argued, were
evident in the geographic proximity of the two areas. It would elim-
inate the cost of separate governments and officialdom; and, most
important from their point of view, it would provide funds for
Pánuco, which was so poor that royal officials in the province had
never been paid their salaries.

In mid-1532 Guzmán sent orders to Pánuco for another military campaign in the area of Valles. Then, in the first months
of 1533, Guzmán and a small force left Nochistlán for the difficult
march to Pánuco.[14] He founded Santiago de los Valles in the
spring of 1533 and placed it within the province of New Galicia.
With his combined governorships of New Galicia and Pánuco,
Guzmán now controlled northern Mexico from the Pacific to the
Gulf. He was in a position to deny Cortés the right of discovery on the west coast, a privilege which had been extended to the
Conqueror by his grants of 1529. Further, Guzmán could block
rival expeditions to the northern frontier of New Spain where,
little more than a decade later, the rich silver mines of Zacatecas
were discovered.

Guzmán's plans for a Greater New Spain were a reality for
some seven months. But in the fall of 1533 a royal decree stripped
him of his office as governor of Pánuco. It obliged him to depart
from Pánuco and retire to Santiago de los Valles. On February 20,
1534, an unexplained fire destroyed Valles with the exception of
five or six houses. A day later Guzmán wrote the Second Audiencia
in Mexico City requesting that it assume responsibility for the pro-
tection of the villa, but did not suggest that it be removed from

---

14 Chipman, *Nuño de Guzmán,* 242–245; Manuel Carrera Stampa traces the march
from Nochistlán to Pánuco: "pasó al Este por el valle del Tejas, pasó el río San Pedro
rumbo al Norte, hasta encontrar el río Chicalote, encumbrando la Sierra Madre, descen-
diendo al entonces valle de Tangamanga, hoy de San Luis Potosí. Siguió el río Verde
y el Tamuin hasta Pánuco," *Memoria de Guzmán,* 78n. Several witnesses in Residencia de Nueva Galicia maintained that Guzmán departed from Compostela; Carta al
rey de Bernaldino Iñiguez, Juan de Cervantes y Rodrigo de Garay, suplicando que se
incorporase a la provincia de Pánuco lo que Nuño de Guzmán andaba conquistando, y
que se les confirmasen los oficios que tenían (Santisteban del Puerto: 15 de mayo de
1531), *ENE,* II, 86–88.

New Galicia. Indeed, the purpose of his letter appears to have been a kind of desperate attempt to prevent the incorporation of Valles into the province of Pánuco. Perhaps Guzmán had genuine concern for the safety of the settlers of the villa; but if this were the case, then for practical considerations it should have been placed under Pánuco — a decision the Second Audiencia was soon to make. More likely, Guzmán saw his ambitious plan to control northern New Spain collapsing and now found it necessary to return to the Pacific coast to secure his more valuable possessions. If the Audiencia could be persuaded to protect his claim to the Valles area, then he would still have legal authority stretching from Culiacán to Valles with only a few miles between Valles and the mouth of the Pánuco River excluded. But the Audiencia was not disposed to cooperate with him.[15]

Two years later, on March 17, 1536, the crown appointed Diego Pérez de la Torre as judge of residencia for New Galicia and Guzmán's successor in the province. Arriving in Mexico City in early 1537, Pérez de la Torre found Guzmán living in the splendor and good company of Viceroy Antonio de Mendoza, who had persuaded him to come voluntarily to the city. Pérez de la Torre ordered Guzmán confined in the public jail while his residencias for Pánuco and New Galicia were in progress. After a year and a half in jail, Guzmán returned to Spain where he lived another twenty years.[16] He probably died a prisoner of the court in 1558 in a kind of judicial limbo. Apparently there was no final sentence on charges arising against him from three residencias. In any case, the last years of Nuño de Guzmán's life were an ignominious end to the career of a conquistador whose ambitions had included the founding of a Spain greater than Spain itself.

---

[15] Chipman, *Nuño de Guzmán*, 247–249; Vasco de Puga, *Cedulario* (2 vols.; México, 1878–1879), I, 287–289; Carta de Nuño de Guzmán al presidente y oidores de la Audiencia de Nueva España, dándoles parte de varias cosas de su gobernación (Santiago de los Valles: 21 de febrero [de 1534], *DII*, XIII, 418–420.

[16] For a discussion of Guzmán's status after his return to Spain, see Donald E. Chipman, "New Light on the Career of Nuño Beltrán de Guzmán," *The Americas* (April 1963), XIX, 341–348.

SPANISH SCIENTISTS IN THE
PACIFIC NORTHWEST, 1790–1792

by

IRIS HIGBIE WILSON

The author, an associate professor at the University of San Diego, is a
native of California who earned her three degrees at the University of
Southern California. She has done research in Spain under grants from
the Del Amo Foundation and the American Philosophical Society. Author
of several books and numerous articles, she has a translation of Moziño's
Noticias de Nutka under publication by the University of Washington
Press.

SPAIN IS a country of extremes, of absolute alternatives. Spaniards
strive to achieve impossible goals or they remain astonishingly
inert. With the discovery of America their ambitious undertakings
excelled those of other European countries, but subsequent neglect
brought failures of equal magnitude. In the sixteenth century they
thought to conquer the world; in the next they washed their hands
of greatness and sank into helpless indifference. But out of the
apathy of the seventeenth century came a new elite of intellectuals
who sought to revive their country and bring Spain once again into
contact with European thought. The ideas of the eighteenth-century Enlightenment were imported and absorbed. Men of learn-

ing made plans to regain for their country the primacy of the past.[1]

Under the relaxed censorship of the able Bourbon monarch, Carlos III (1759-1788), channels of communication were widened, conveying many new concepts to the Iberian Peninsula. The field of natural science was one that benefitted conspicuously. The flow of thought across the Pyrenees brought French zeal for the promotion of useful knowledge. Centers of learning in London, Stockholm, Frankfort, and Philadelphia carried ideas of the Enlightenment into Spain's church-dominated educational institutions, and these in turn were transmitted to the overseas colonies.[2] The reforming efforts of Carlos III found expression in the support of intellectual pursuits. During the last quarter of the eighteenth century his encouragement of scientific studies promoted no less than half a dozen exploring expeditions designed to survey and examine the natural resources of Spain's colonial empire. Unfortunately, his death in 1788 signalled the end of Spain's final period of greatness.

Factors influencing the flurry of scientific activity in Spain and her colonial possessions were rooted in the whole climate of European thought. The concept of naturalism — the assumption that the whole universe of mind and matter was guided and controlled by natural law — caused men of the Enlightenment to turn with enthusiasm to rediscover their own lands, studying and

---

[1] John W. Crow, *Spain: the Root and the Flower* (New York, 1963), 226–27, observed that the " . . . eighteenth century in general was characterized by a struggle between two opposing tendencies: the Europeanization of Spain, espoused by the intellectuals and by the crown, on the one hand, and, on the other, the attempt to recapture some of the essence of Spain's past glory simply by intensifying the use of measures utilized two centuries previously. This latter attitude was supported by the mass of the Spanish people. . . . With such a populace the best intentions of the most liberal monarchs would in the end come to a mere inching forward. The Spaniards resisted progress all the way." See also Arthur P. Whitaker (ed.), *Latin America and the Enlightenment* (New York, 1958), 5–20.

[2] The travel of officials, merchants, and scientists between Europe and the Americas allowed a constant exchange of information. Despite some effort at censorship, ideas of the Enlightenment reached the Spanish colonies with almost the same speed as they entered other areas. Further, books and periodicals from the United States influenced Spanish colonial and peninsular thought. Benjamin Franklin was the first American to attain membership in the Spanish Academy of History at Madrid. He became a Hispanist and his work was sent to Spanish America.

recording fauna and flora, minerals, and agricultural products, as well as customs and history. Ancient authority was no longer sufficient to establish the truth of long accepted propositions; everything on earth, and even beyond, was submitted to questioning and new investigation. In the natural sciences men broke with Aristotelian tradition and constructed a system based on direct observation and reason. The critical spirit with which Spanish intellectuals approached the entire body of knowledge inherited from previous ages inspired them to project a geographical, historical, and statistical survey of the New World — one which would leave no corner of Spain's possessions uncatalogued.[3]

The essential motive which set into motion this re-examination of the existing order was a search for the physical and moral improvement of man, rather than the age-old pursuit of riches. Knowledge would, of itself, release the natural wealth which lay unexploited. Intellectual interests shifted gradually from supernatural religion to a natural science separated from magic and superstition. The first issue of the *Gaceta de Madrid* in 1787 proclaimed the eighteenth century "the most scientific of all those composing the extensive epoch of seven thousand years."[4] Subjects under discussion ranged from practical inventions and the increase of population to abstract theories of physics and chemistry.

New institutions were founded under the patronage of Carlos III. The Royal Botanical Garden, the Museum of Natural Science, the Astronomical Observatory, and the Royal Academy of Medicine at Madrid each trained scientists for participation in overseas expeditions. Encouraged by the works of Carolus Lin-

---

[3] For general works on the participation of Spain and Spanish America in the Enlightenment, see Marcelino Menéndez y Pelayo, *Historia de los heterodoxos españoles* (2d ed., 7 vols., Madrid, 1911–32) and *La ciencia española* (4th ed., 3 vols., Madrid, 1915–18); Vicente G. Quesada, *La vida intelectual en la América española durante los siglos XVI, XVII y XVIII* (Buenos Aires, 1917); John Tate Lanning, *Academic Culture in the Spanish Colonies* (New York, 1940); John H. R. Polt, *Jovellanos and his English Sources* (Philadelphia, 1964); Richard Herr, *The Eighteenth Century Revolution in Spain* (Princeton, 1958); and Whitaker, *Latin America and the Enlightenment.*

[4] "Idea de la Obra" (July 2, 1787), No. 1.

naeus, Swedish classifier of all existing botanical knowledge,[5] and excited by the amount of new information contained in Buffon's encyclopedic *Natural History of Animals*,[6] Spanish naturalists desired to extend their knowledge to the vast and virtually unexplored territories of North and South America.

The second Count of Revilla Gigedo, Viceroy of New Spain from 1789 to 1794, carried the enlightened tradition of Carlos III into the New World. An able administrator, Revilla Gigedo was vitally concerned with every aspect of his realm. He firmly believed in the value of scientific exploration and investigation, and continually offered his full support to excursions in Mexico, California, and the Pacific Northwest.[7] On his visit to New Spain in 1803, the celebrated German naturalist Alexander von Humboldt noted the extent of this recent patronage:

> Since the final years of the reign of Carlos III and during that of Carlos IV, the study of the natural sciences has made great progress not only in Mexico, but also in all of the Spanish colonies. No European government has sacrificed greater sums than that of the Spanish in order to advance the knowledge of plants. Three botanical expeditions, that of Peru, New Granada and New Spain, . . . have cost the state nearly four hundred thousand pesos.[8]

---

[5] Born Carl von Linné (1707–1778), his major works on scientific nomenclature were *Systema naturae* (1735), *Genera Plantarum* (1737), and *Species Plantarum* (1753). His student, the botanist Peter Loeffling, studied in Spain and conducted scientific investigations in Venezuela.

[6] Georges Louis Leclerc, Count of Buffon (1707–1788), celebrated French zoologist, was director of the Royal Museum, member of the French Academy of Science, and fellow of the Royal Society of London.

[7] Viceroy Revilla Gigedo aided the expeditions of Martín Sessé, José Longinos Martínez, José Moziño, and Antonio Pineda, and encouraged the scientific aspects of naval explorations during the years of his administration. See Cayetano Alcázar Molina, *Los virreinatos en el siglo XVIII* (Barcelona, 1945), 92–97, for a description of Revilla Gigedo's government.

[8] Juan A. Ortega y Medina (ed.), Alexander von Humboldt, *Ensayo Político sobre el Reino de la Nueva España* (México, 1966), 80. Whitaker, in "The Dual Role of Latin America" (*Latin America and the Enlightenment*, 15), commented that when " . . . Humboldt went to Spanish America to begin the long residence that was to furnish the material for his classic accounts of that region, he was only following in the footsteps of many of his fellow countrymen. And it is to be noted that, although Humboldt was the spiritual heir of the philosophers, personal acquaintance with Spanish America emancipated him from their stock ideas about it, and he painted a portrait of it that was perhaps more generous than just. . . ."

Unfortunately these zealous efforts resulted not in fame or lasting contributions, but only in the collection of a mass of unpublished data read by few contemporaries of the scientific world. The dynamic intellectuals under Carlos III who thought their country could be revitalized, and who worked to bring about Spain's resurgence as a great power, were destined to fail. The palace despotism of Godoy, the lethargy and incompetence of Carlos IV,, and finally the blood and confusion of the French invasion brought ruin to their ambitious plans. Spain, once more at the pinnacle of success, reached instead the extreme of absolute failure.

The participation of Spain in the Enlightenment has been little recognized.[9] Evidence of its influence in the Americas has seldom received more than a passing note in historical literature. Moreover, the fact that Spanish scientists were not able to publish the results of their observations precluded recognition even in contemporary journals. This is not to say, however, that their contributions were not significant or not used by investigators who examined the same areas. The activity, the writings, and the enthusiasm of these men are still inspiring today. They are no less inspiring because they failed. Their work was thorough and accurate, their investigations based on the latest scientific methods; but their zeal could not change the circumstances which forced their accomplishments into near obscurity.

Preparations for the visit of Spanish scientists to the Pacific Northwest were begun during the 1780's. The ministers of Carlos III formulated plans for two expeditions which would spend a considerable portion of their time and efforts examining the northwest coast. The first, the Royal Scientific Expedition of New Spain, was created by *real cédula* issued on October 27, 1786, and placed under the direction of Dr. Martín Sessé.[10] The royal order called

---

[9] Spaniards notable for their contributions during the period of the Enlightenment included Padre Benito Jerónimo Feijóo, Pedro Rodríguez Campomanes, José de Cadalso, Gaspar Melchor de Jovellanos, Antonio de Ulloa, Casimiro Gómez Ortega, and the Basque Elhuyar brothers, Fausto and Juan José.

[10] Licensed in medicine at the University of Zaragoza, Sessé served as a physician with the army during the siege of Gibraltar, was transferred to Cuba under the command of the Conde de Gálvez, and was eventually sent to México where he rendered medical service in prisons and houses of correction.

for the "establishment of a botanical garden and a scientific expedition to survey and examine the natural resources of New Spain."[11]
The botanical institute, established in Mexico by the members
of this group, supplied scientists to accompany exploratory efforts
throughout the viceroyalty — and particularly to the expedition of
Juan Francisco de la Bodega y Quadra to "the limits to the north of
California" in 1792.[12]

The second scientific enterprise organized in Spain, the
around-the-world expedition of Alejandro Malaspina (1789-
1794), reached the northwest coast in 1791. Plans for the project,
another manifestation of the enlightened monarchy of Carlos III,
were formulated shortly after the incorporation of Sessé's expedition. Malaspina, a naval officer, had circumnavigated the globe in
1786–88 as captain of the vessel *Astrea*. He and a fellow officer,
José Bustamante y Guerra, submitted a "Plan of a Scientific and
Political Voyage Around the World" to the Spanish Minister of
Marine, Antonio Valdés, on September 10, 1788. The introduction to this plan reflected the expanded vision of these late eighteenth-century naval officers:

> For the past twenty years the two nations of England and France, with
> a noble rivalry, have undertaken voyages in which navigation, geog-
> raphy, and the knowledge of humanity have made very rapid progress.
> This history of human society has laid the foundation for more gen-
> eral investigations; natural history has been enriched with an almost
> infinite number of discoveries; and finally, the preservation of Man in
> different climates, in extensive journeys, and among some almost
> incredible tasks and risks, has been the most interesting acquisition
> which navigation has made. The voyage which is being proposed is
> particularly directed toward the completion of these objects; and the
> aspect which is being called the Scientific Part will certainly be carried

---

[11] Real Cédula del 27 de Octubre de 1786, Flora Española — Año 1786, archives of
the Museo Nacional de Ciencias Naturales (Madrid), hereinafter cited as AMCN.
Describing the sums spent by Sessé's expedition in México, Dr. Samuel Latham
Mitchill of Columbia College, in an address to the New York Historical Society in
1813, said: "I wish it was in my power to state the particulars for the improvement of
American botany made by the Kings of Spain. There is not perhaps a government upon
earth that has expended so much money for the advancement of this branch of natural
history as that of the Castilian monarch."

[12] Sessé to Viceroy Revilla Gigedo, México, May 9, 1793, Archivo General de la
Nación (México, D.F.), Historia 527, hereinafter cited as AGN.

out with much care, continuing with effectiveness the paths of Cook and La Perouse.[13]

These two expeditions brought to the remote areas of the Pacific Northwest the studies of botany, zoology, anthropology, ethnography, astronomy, and cartography. Their efforts were pursued in cooperation and in competition with those of English, French, American and other visitors, but the reports of Spanish investigators, unlike those of their contemporaries, were not published.[14]

A major objective of the Malaspina expedition in the Pacific Northwest was to find the elusive strait of Ferrer Maldonado, or a Northwest Passage, leading to the Atlantic.[15] Discovery of the long-sought water route would return Spain to the forefront in her competition for supremacy in the Americas. A second objective involved the Spanish claim to Nootka Sound, where the seizure of British ships in 1789 had touched off a five-year controversy with England.[16] A third objective, reflecting the overall plan proposed to Valdés, concerned scientific investigation.

In order to carry out projects of natural history, the expedition was staffed with personnel handpicked for their skills in botany, zoology, cartography, astronomy, and artistic reproduction. Felipe Bauzá, Chief of Charts and Maps, had previous experience in gen-

---

[13] Plan de un Viaje Científico y Político a el Rededor del Mundo Remitido a el Exmo. Sr. Bailio Fray Antonio Valdés de Madrid en 10 Sept. de 1788, MS 316, archives of the Museo Naval (Madrid), hereinafter cited as MN.

[14] Captain James Cook's description of Nootka and its inhabitants is found in his principal work, *A Voyage to the Pacific Ocean Undertaken . . . for Making Discoveries in the Northern Hemisphere in the Years 1776, 1777, 1778, 1779 and 1780* (3 vols. and Atlas; London, 1st ed. 1784, 2nd ed. 1785); James K. Munford (ed.), *John Ledyard's Journal of Captain Cook's Last Voyage* (Oregon State University Press, 1963) gives supporting information. See also Frederick W. Howay, "The Early Literature of the Northwest Coast," *Transactions of the Royal Society of Canada*, XVIII (May 1924). Judge Howay edited the letters and journals of many early participants in the Northwestern fur trade, including John Meares, James Colnett, Nathaniel Portlock, George Dixon, and the American captains John Kendrick, Robert Gray, and Joseph Ingraham.

[15] Lt. José Espinosa y Tello extracted the narrative of Ferrer Maldonado from the Archivo General de Indias prior to departure of the expedition. See "Correspondencia relativa al viage del Malaspina," MN, MS 583.

[16] See William R. Manning, *The Nootka Sound Controversy* (Washington, D.C., 1905) for a thorough study of the negotiations between Spain and England.

eral mapping on the Spanish Peninsula; Tadeo Haënke, a Bohem-
ian-born botanist recommended for the expedition by the Sardin-
ian ambassador, took charge of the collections of natural history.[17]
Luis Neé, a Frenchman employed for many years in the Royal
Botanical Garden of Madrid, was to assemble, classify, and describe
plant life.[18] Pedro María González assisted in astronomy and natural science.[19] The two official artists on the expedition were Tomás
de Suría from the Mexican Academy of San Carlos,[20] and José
Cardero, a talented member of Malaspina's crew.[21]

Two corvettes, the *Descubierta* and the *Atrevida,* commanded
by Malaspina and Bustamante y Guerra respectively, were specially
built for the project and outfitted to facilitate the work of scientific
investigation. Departing from Cádiz in 1789, the expedition visited
Spanish possessions in South America and reached Acapulco in
the spring of 1791. To make the best use of the time available,
Malaspina left a number of officers and scientists in Mexico to
make a detailed examination of the coastal and inland regions during the summer and fall.[22] The *Descubierta* and the *Atrevida* then
set sail for the Pacific Northwest in May.

Malaspina's first major stop was at Mulgrave Sound (Yakutat

---

[17] Haënke's observations are scattered in numerous archives of Europe. See Josef
Kuhnel, *Thaddaeus Haënke, Leben und Wirken eines Forschers* (Prague, 1960).

[18] Luis Neé, Dibujos de Plantas, Vols. I, II, and IV, 6ª División, and 2ª División:
Papeles de la Expedición de Malaspina, Legajos Nos. 1, 2; and archives of the Real
Jardín Botánico (Madrid), hereinafter cited as ARJB.

[19] González, the official "cirujano" on the *Atrevida,* wanted to obtain some instruction
in botany "in order to contribute to the progress of this science"; MN, MS 583. While
in Acapulco González described a number of zoological specimens, and later he made
botanical observations in the Pacific Northwest. His reports are in the archives of the
Museum of Natural Science in Madrid.

[20] A native of Madrid, Suría was twenty-nine years old and an engraver for the Casa de
Moneda in México. See José Torre Revello, *Los Artistas Pintores de la Expedición
Malaspina* (Buenos Aires, 1944). His diary and illustrations are in the Malaspina
Papers, Beinecke Collection, Yale University Library.

[21] Donald C. Cutter, *Malaspina in California* (San Francisco, 1960), 12–16, gives
biographical data on Cardero.

[22] Antonio Pineda, Malaspina's chief of natural history, spent from May to December,
1791, in the company of botanist Luis Neé and several artists making an intensive
survey of the natural resources, fauna and flora, and native inhabitants of México.
See Iris H. Wilson, "Pineda's Report on the Beverages of New Spain," *Arizona and
the West,* V (Winter 1963), and "Antonio Pineda y su viaje mundial," *Revista de
Historia Militar* (No. 15, 1964).

Bay) in the vicinity of 59° 30'N. Here his men spent nine days among the Tlingit Indians gathering native weapons, articles of dress, manufactured items, and other artifacts. They attempted to learn the language and compiled a vocabulary consisting primarily of words used in trade. The nearby glacier, later named for Malaspina, was investigated and the height of Mount Elias calculated.[23] Botanist Haënke prepared a summary of available wood in the area,[24] and Pedro González scientifically described a number of animals, birds, and plants.[25] The artists prepared zoological and botanical plates.

The next stop was Nootka Sound on the west coast of Vancouver Island. The expedition arrived on August 12, 1791, and spent two weeks inspecting the Spanish settlement at Friendly Cove, gaining the friendship of the Nootka Indians and seeking whatever information Viceroy Revilla Gigedo might find helpful in negotiating a settlement of the controversy between Spain and England. The artists sketched local inhabitants and their cultural activities while the scientists gathered samples of fauna and flora. Appropriate maps of the coastal regions and charts of the labyrinth of canals inland from Nootka Sound were prepared; astronomical data were assembled at the observatory built by Felipe Bauzá. All projects completed, the group set sail for the port of Monterey, capital of Alta California.[26] They returned to Acapulco in October of 1791 and rejoined the members of the expedition remaining in Mexico.[27]

---

[23] The table of apparent altitudes of Mt. St. Elias is in "Curiosidades Sueltas," MN, MS 169.

[24] "Relación de maderas de Mulgrave, de Nutka, de Monterrey in Pacífico América," MN, MS 126.

[25] "Descripciones del Sr. Gonzales hechas en el viaje a los 60° N," in notes of Antonio Pineda, AMCN.

[26] Malaspina to Josef Espinosa, Nutka, Aug. 17, 1791, in "Apuntes, Noticias correspondencias pertenecientes a la Expedición de Malaspina," MN, MS 427. See also Donald C. Cutter, "Spanish Scientific Explorations Along the Pacific Coast," in *The American West: An Appraisal,* ed. by Robert G. Ferris (Santa Fe, 1963).

[27] See Pedro de Novo y Colson, *La Vuelta al Mundo por las Corbetas Descubierta y Atrevida al Mando del Capitán de Navío D. Alejandro Malaspina desde 1789 a 1794* (Madrid, 1885). The career of Malaspina is summarized in "Antiguedades de los oficiales de guerra de la Armada," MN, MS 1161 bis. His expedition did not actually circumnavigate the globe, but returned from the Philippines, Australia and New Zealand by way of South America.

An extension of the Malaspina effort was the further exploration of the northwest coast by Dionisio Alcalá Galiano and Cayetano Valdés, commanding the schooners *Sutil* and *Mexicana*. Viceroy Revilla Gigedo accepted Malaspina's offer of these two able officers to carry out a detailed reconnaissance of the Strait of Juan de Fuca. In addition to charting the coastlines, Alcalá Galiano and Valdés were instructed to investigate the natural resources, describe the animals, birds, and fish, look for valuable metals or precious stones, and note any objects of scientific curiosity. Several other of Malaspina's men, including José Cardero as official artist and cartographer, also sailed on this voyage.[28]

After a brief stop at Nootka Sound, the *Sutil* and the *Mexicana* proceeded into the Straits of Juan de Fuca and Rosario in June of 1792. Upon leaving present-day Bellingham Bay, the Spaniards encountered the English vessels *Discovery* and *Chatham* under the command of Captain George Vancouver, the commissioner sent to negotiate a settlement of the terms of the Nootka convention. They informed Vancouver that his Spanish counterpart, Juan Francisco de la Bodega y Quadra, commandant of the Naval Department of San Blas, was awaiting arrival of the British at the Nootkan post. Alcalá Galiano and Vancouver compared findings of their respective explorations in the straits, and continued together for a short time. The English ships reached the Pacific through Johnstone's Strait and anchored at Nootka Sound on August 28, 1792. The *Sutil* and *Mexicana* subsequently entered the Pacific and reached Nootka two days later.[29] The results of this expedition, which included a series of illustrations by Cardero,

---

[28] The official journal of the expedition is "Relación del Viaje hecho por las Goletas Sutil y Mexicana en el año de 1792 para reconocer el estrecho de Fuca," MN, MS 468. See also José Espinosa y Tello, *Relación del viaje hecho por las goletas Sutil y Mexicana en el año 1792* (Madrid, 1802), a new edition of which was published by Chimalistac at Madrid in 1958.

[29] See Edmund S. Meany, *Vancouver's Discovery at Puget Sound* (New York, 1907), 236–302; Henry R. Wagner, *Spanish Explorations of the Strait of Juan de Fuca* (Santa Ana, Calif., 1933), 65; and Bern Anderson, *The Life and Voyages of Captain George Vancouver*, (Seattle, 1960), 100–109.

a set of excellent maps, and a resumé of places visited, were then transmitted to the viceroy.

When Lieutenant Alcalá Galiano's official journal was published in 1802, it included the description of Nootka Sound and its inhabitants prepared by José Mariano Moziño, official botanist-naturalist of the last Spanish expedition to the northwest coast — that of Bodega y Quadra in 1792. The commander of the *Sutil* believed it "preferable to study the accounts given by the distinguished Naturalist than one's own impressions." He wrote:

> We are indebted to Mosiño for almost all the knowledge and accounts that we possess in regard to the inhabitants of Nutka. . . . The insight of this worthy subject, his perserverance, the intelligence by which he was able to acquire the Nootkan language, the intimate friendship which he gained with the most distinguished and most knowledgeable persons of the settlement, and his long residence with them are the reasons why our impartiality demands that we give preference to his investigations over our own.[30]

Bodega y Quadra's voyage was Spain's final effort to explore the Pacific Northwest.[31] Headed by New Spain's senior naval officer, its political objective was the reconciliation of differences between Spain and England at Nootka Sound. At the suggestion of Dr. Martin Sessé,[32] two highly trained scientists and a botanical illustrator from the Royal Scientific Expedition of New Spain were appointed by the viceroy to accompany Bodega y Quadra to the northwest. José Moziño, a Mexican-born naturalist, was placed in charge of scientific investigation. He was assisted by José Maldon-

---

[30] "Relación del Viaje hecho por las Goletas Sutil y Mexicana," MN, MS 468.

[31] Bodega y Quadra's official journal bears the title "Viaje a la Costa N. O. de la América Septentrional por Don Juan Francisco de la Bodega y Quadra, del Orden de Santiago, Capitán de Navío de la Real Armada, y Comandante del Departamento de San Blas en las Fragatas a su mando Sta. Gertrudis, Aránzazu, Princesa y Goleta Activo en el año de 1790," MS 145, Archivo del Ministerio de Asuntos Exteriores (Madrid), hereinafter cited as AMAE, and Revilla Gigedo Collection, vol. 30, Bancroft Library, University of California, Berkeley. Its 169 folios give a good description of the visitors and their activities at Nootka from May to September, 1792.

[32] Sessé to Viceroy Revilla Gigedo, México, May 9, 1793, AGN Historia 527.

ado, a botanist and anatomist, and Atanásio Echeverría, the best artist then working with the expedition in Mexico.[33]

Moziño, a kind of universal scholar, was a graduate of the School of Medicine at the University of Mexico and a former professor of ecclesiastical history and theology in Oaxaca. His commission under Bodega y Quadra resulted in the preparation of *Noticias de Nutka,* a thorough and comprehensive survey of Nootka Sound. His study included history, ethnography, botany, and zoology.[34] In addition, Moziño learned the Nootkan language and became the expedition's official interpreter. He prepared a vocabulary of Nootkan words and compiled a catalogue of more than four hundred species of plants, animals, and birds described by himself and José Maldonado.[35] Moziño's work was fully illustrated by Echeverría.[36]

---

[33] Viceroy Revilla Gigedo approved the employment of Moziño, Maldonado, and Echeverría as official members of Bodega y Quadra's expedition. A shortage of funds made it difficult to keep the men on the payroll of the Royal Scientific Expedition of New Spain, especially after the viceroy's petition for additional support was unrealistically denied by Carlos IV (Orden del Rey Carlos IV, 1792, 4ª División, Legajo No. 15, ARJB). Their new appointment to accompany Bodega y Quadra afforded Revilla Gigedo an excellent temporary solution to his dilemma.

[34] Its full title, "Nootka, an Account of its Discovery, Location and Natural Products; about the Customs of its Inhabitants, Government, Rites, Chronology, Language, Music, Poetry, Fishing, Hunting and Fur Trade: with an Account of the Voyages made by Europeans, particularly Spaniards, and of the Agreement made between them and the English," indicates the extensive nature of Moziño's work. A copy was published in several parts in vols. 7 and 8 (1803 and 1804) of the *Gazeta de Guatemala.* Albert M. Carreño edited and published another copy, in the library of the Sociedad Mexicana de Geografía y Estadística, in 1913. Other copies may be found in the Revilla Gigedo Collection of the Bancroft Library; in the Biblioteca del Palacio Nacional (Madrid); in two separate volumes in the archives of the Museo Naval, Ministerio de Marina (Madrid); and in the Agrand Collection of the Bibliotheque Nationale (Paris).

[35] "Breve Diccionario de los términos que se pudieron aprender del idioma de los naturales de Nutka," and "Catálogo de los Animales y Plantas que han reconocido y determinado según el sistema de Linneo los Facultativos de mi Expedición Don José Moziño y Don José Maldonado," MS 145, AMAE.

[36] "Planos geográficos y dibujos para ilustrar el Diario de D. Juan Francisco de la Bodega y Quadra," AMAE, MS 146. Archibald Menzies, naturalist with Vancouver's expedition, commented in his journal that Moziño, Maldonado, and Echeverría "were part of a Society of Naturalists who were employed of late years in examining México and New Spain for the purpose of collecting materials for a Flora Mexicana which they said would soon be published, and with the assistance of so good an Artist it must be a valuable acquisition"; *Menzies' Journal of Vancouver's Voyage April to October, 1792,* ed. by C. F. Newcombe (Victoria, 1923).

In the eighteenth-century sense of natural science, *Noticias de Nutka* was perhaps the most "scientific" study made during the Spanish occupation of that area. Although other expeditions had made surveys, Moziño's investigation was the first done by a person schooled in scientific methods. His visit to the Pacific Northwest was solely for the purpose of botanical and zoological observation. He also described the daily life of the Nootka Indians with unusual insight. Moziño wrote:

> Our residence of more than four months . . . allowed me to learn about the various customs of its natives. I believe that I am the first person for whom it has been possible to gather information about their religion and system of government because of having learned their language sufficiently to converse with them.[37]

If Spain's plans for the publication of *Noticias de Nutka* in a universal history of the Indies had materialized, Moziño's account would have served to acquaint Europeans with the natives of a strategic area of the Pacific Northwest and to provide natural scientists with an abundance of untapped source material.[38] The study consisted of twelve separate articles, the first two of which described the geography and natural resources of Nootka and noted the physical characteristics and material culture of its inhabitants.[39] The following four articles concerned Nootkan religious beliefs, social customs, ceremonies, and occupations. In the seventh and eighth articles Moziño analyzed and recorded the language, poetry, and music of these Indians, and attempted to explain their chron-

---

[37] *Noticias de Nutka.*

[38] Alexander von Humboldt wrote in 1803: "In spite of the exact accounts which we owe to the English and French navigators, it would be very interesting to publish in French the observations which Moziño has made about the customs of the natives of Nootka, because they include a great number of curious facts." Humboldt was especially impressed with "the union of civil and religious power in the person of the prince or *Tais;* the struggle between the powers of good and evil which govern the world . . . the education of the first man . . . the genealogy of the nobility of Nootka . . . the calendar of Nootkans, which begins the year in the summer solstice . . . etc., etc." Humboldt, *Ensayo Político*, 215.

[39] These natives were members of the Moachat Confederacy which occupied the Nootka Sound area. The term "Nootkan" today is a linguistic designation for members of the Wakashan stock extending from Cape Cook to Cape Flattery.

ology and method of counting the days, months, and years.[40] He then traced the history of Nootka Sound from the arrival of Juan Pérez in 1774 through 1792, describing the problems of the Spanish establishment under Esteban Martínez in 1789 and the subsequent progress made by Francisco de Eliza and Pedro de Alberni in 1790. The last two articles concerned the commission of Bodega y Quadra and George Vancouver, to which Moziño added a description of his role as a scientist and interpreter. He concluded his study with various recommendations for the future of Spain in the Pacific Northwest.[41]

Moziño's aide, the naturalist José Maldonado, spent three months in the company of Lieutenant Jacinto Caamaño investigating points northward in the straits of Bucareli and Font. Under orders from Bodega y Quadra, Caamaño set sail from Nootka on June 13, 1792, in the *Aránzazu* to inspect the coastline north of the Queen Charlotte Islands and the southern shores of Alaska. Maldonado gathered specimens of plants and animals and prepared a list of the natural resources of the places visited. This list was submitted to the viceroy upon Maldonado's return to Nootka in September.[42]

The meeting between Bodega y Quadra and Vancouver failed to settle the rights of Spain and England in the Pacific Northwest. Despite a most cordial relationship, the two commissioners could

---

[40] Moziño noted that the Nootka Indians "divide the year into fourteen months, and each month into twenty days. They then add some intercalary days at the end of each month, the number of which varies and is determined by the importance of the object which that month characterizes for them."

[41] Moziño advised withdrawal from Nootka. He warned: "Anyone can perceive that six or eight thousand men would scarcely be enough to guard the area, and that even by taking exclusive possession of the fur trade, it probably would not defray the enormous expense which our defense would demand." On the other hand, Moziño praised California: "There our conquest has taken roots, our Religion has been propagated, and our hopes are greatest for obtaining obvious advantages to benefit all the monarchy."

[42] "Extracto del Diario de las navegaciones, exploraciones y descubrimientos hechos en la América Septentrional por D. Jacinto Caamaño," MS 10, AMAE. The list is preceded by the following note: "El Botánico D. José Maldonado que conduge para inspeccionar las producciones de estos países, y acompaño para el mejor desempeño de su encargo a el reconocimiento del Puerto, encontró las siguientes . . .," MS 10, AMAE.

only agree to refer the matter back to Madrid and London.[43] Bodega y Quadra departed from Nootka on September 22, 1792, and Vancouver set sail three weeks later. Moziño, Maldonado, and Echeverría returned to Mexico early in 1793 to work with the Royal Scientific Expedition in New Spain and Guatemala.[44]

The Malaspina venture, completing its sixty-two-month exploration of the Americas, the Pacific Islands, Australia and New Zealand, reached Cádiz in 1794. Malaspina was praised for his success, but his fame was short-lived. A court intrigue involving the wife of Carlos IV resulted in his exile, and even though Malaspina was eventually allowed to return to Spain he was never able to secure publication of the expedition's material.[45] Not until almost a hundred years later was there an attempt made to publicize the significant contribution of Malaspina's "Viaje Alrededor del Mundo" in the last decade of the eighteenth century.[46]

The Royal Scientific Expedition of New Spain received an extension of its original six-year contract and continued in Mexico until 1803. In that year the director, Dr. Martín Sessé, and José Moziño returned to Madrid. Like Malaspina, though for different reasons, Sessé was also unable to publish the results of his work. Matters other than the patronage of natural history were commanding the attention of Carlos IV. Sessé and Moziño requested assis-

---

[43] According to the terms of the Convention finally agreed upon, both Spanish and British ships could have free entry into any port north of the Spanish settlements and British subjects could not set up any establishments on coasts of the Americas occupied by Spain.

[44] Upon their arrival in México, Moziño and Echeverría were immediately sent southward to investigate the volcano then erupting at San Andrés de Tuxtla. Consequently, Echeverría was unable to finish many of his drawings. He left his sketches with the Academy of San Carlos in México where they could be completed and copied. More than a half dozen artists, including Francisco Lindo, Vicente de la Cerda, Tomás Suría and others, dedicated themselves to this task. These drawings consisted of general scenes as well as botanical and zoological plates.

[45] Humboldt summed up the unhappy ending of Malaspina's expedition with these words: "... this able navigator is more famous for his misfortunes than for his discoveries. The works of Malaspina lay buried in the archives, not because the government feared revelation of secrets that it thought useful not to reveal, but because the name of that intrepid navigator had to remain in eternal oblivion."

[46] Novo y Colson's La Vuelta al Mundo was published in Madrid in 1885.

tance to organize and edit their papers, but saw their work shelved for lack of official interest. Their efforts came to share a fate similar to those of Felipe II's naturalist Francisco Hernández two centuries before.[47] The futility felt by the scientists from New Spain was reflected in a letter written by Moziño in 1808 reporting the death of his friend and parton, Martín Sessé. Moziño rightly feared that "the precious collection which has been the fruit of our long and difficult voyages, which has cost more than two million pesos of the public treasury, and which could be of such honor and utility to the nation" would be lost.[48]

In the fall of 1808 the French forces under Napoleon invaded the Spanish peninsula. Joseph Bonaparte was placed on the throne which had been abdicated by Carlos IV in favor of his son, Fernando VII. Napoleon's brother became interested in the work of the expedition and appointed Moziño director of the Royal Museum of Natural History, a position which proved to be the Mexican scientist's downfall. When the French withdrew from Madrid in 1812, Moziño was looked upon with disfavor by Spanish patriots and was forced to flee with his remaining manuscripts, drawings, and herbaria to Montpellier. As a result, the expedition's work became scattered even farther. Moziño finally received permission to return to Spain in 1817, but there is no evidence of his ever again reaching Madrid.[49]

---

[47] Dr. Francisco Hernández and his son Juan studied the botanical, animal, and mineral kingdoms of New Spain from 1570 to 1576. Upon his return to the Spanish peninsula, Hernández prepared sixteen volumes of his findings for publication; but they were left unprinted in the archives of El Escorial near Madrid, where most of them were destroyed by fire in 1671. Six volumes were later discovered and published in 1790 under the editorship of Casimiro Gómez Ortega, director of the Royal Botanical Garden of Madrid.

[48] Moziño to Pedro Cevallos, Madrid, October 24, 1808, *Flora Española — Año* 1808, AMCN. In 1870 the Sociedad Mexicana de Historia Natural learned that the manuscripts and drawings of the Royal Scientific Expedition existed in the archives of the Real Jardín Botánico in Madrid. Through correspondence covering a period of fifteen years, the Sociedad finally managed to secure a copy of the botanical descriptions and in 1888 published *Flora Mexicana*. A second work, *Plantae Novae Hispaniae*, was published by the Sociedad in 1889 and reprinted for the Chicago Exposition of 1893.

[49] Some of Moziño's botanical plates were deposited in the Conservatoire Botanique in Geneva, but the majority were lost after his death in Barcelona in 1820.

Thus the several tragedies which befell the returning members of the eighteenth-century expeditions allowed a disorganized mass of information to be buried in archives, lost, given away, or sold to foreign collectors. But these unfortunate occurrences were overshadowed by Spain's imminent loss of her colonial empire. The same spirit of inquiry and enlightenment, initially responsible for European scientific interest, subsequently awakened liberal ideas of revolution in Latin America which led to the wars of independence.[50]

If Spain contributed little to science, it was not for lack of ideas and worthwhile experiments but rather because of events which defeated her ambitious undertakings. The final days of the eighteenth century saw many excellent projects dissolve uncompleted into dusty nothingness. Spanish scientists would never again have the opportunity to examine, describe, and catalogue the natural resources of the New World. It seems only fair, however, that due credit be given to those men whose names and contributions have remained virtually unknown until the present day.

---

[50] Whitaker believes the final days of the Spanish empire in America to be exemplified by the case of Alexander von Humboldt. The German naturalist's favorable report showed, according to Whitaker, that "Latin America's active role as participant in the Enlightenment was at last altering its passive role as an exhibit in the case prepared by the Philosophers; but the change had been too long delayed, for by the time Humboldt's new portrait was completed, the waters of the Enlightenment had run out in the marshes of war and revolution." *Latin America and the Enlightenment,* 16.

JUAN BODEGA Y QUADRA
AND THE SPANISH RETREAT
FROM NOOTKA,

1790–1794

by

MICHAEL E. THURMAN

A member of the history faculty at Southern Methodist University, the author taught previously at East Texas State University and the Universiy of New Mexico. He earned the doctorate at the University of Southern California after research in the archives of Madrid, Seville, and Mexico City. His major work, *The Naval Department of San Blas,* was published in 1967 by the Arthur H. Clark Company.

SAN LORENZO DE NOOTKA on the west coast of Vancouver Island was the northernmost bastion of Spain's North American empire. An official garrison post for Spanish naval operations and scientific studies from 1789 to 1795, it was at the same time an important depot for Pacific traders who sailed to such distant places as Manila and Canton. The commercial value of Nootka Sound was not fully realized by the Spaniards who made the original discovery in 1774;[1] rather it was the English maritime explorer James Cook who first publicized the potential of the northwest coast in luxurious furs then in great demand in the ports of the

---

[1] "Primer exploración de Juan Pérez . . ., 1774" (331) and Tomás de la Peña, "Diario en la Fragata Santiago . . ." (331), MSS in Museo Naval, Madrid. This archive is hereafter cited as MN.

Orient. Cook's crew had bartered casually for otter skins while the *Resolution* was anchored in King George's Sound in 1778.[2] Soon the word was out, and English and American merchantmen began plying Alaskan waters and taking aboard cargoes of fine peltry in exchange for the copper, iron, and shells prized by the local Indians. Within a decade the port of Nootka was known to the seafarers of several nations for its timber, water, and friendly native population, and had become a favorite supply point and wintering refuge.

Disputes inevitably arose among the nations. The most notable of these, the diplomatic tangle precipitated by Ensign José Martínez in 1789, has been explored in depth by others[3] and will not be treated here. Instead this study will focus on the military aspects of the Spanish occupation of Nootka, with emphasis on the role of the leading personality involved: Capitán de Navío Juan Francisco de la Bodega y Quadra.[4]

Born of Spanish parents in Lima in 1743, Bodega took midshipman training in the Department of Cádiz (1762–65) and was commissioned in the Royal Navy on October 12, 1767.[5] He arrived at Vera Cruz in September, 1774, in company with six other officers, and reported for duty at San Blas in December of that year. His voyage in the *Sonora,* a frail craft of thirty-six feet, was undertaken with a crew of fifteen and a fellow officer from Spain, Francisco Mourelle.[6]

Spain's first thorough exploration of the Pacific Northwest had begun in 1774 when a Mallorcan captain, Juan Pérez, touched at Nootka and made a brief reconnaissance of the harbor. His expedition was not altogether successful, however, because of lack

---

[2] James Cook, *A Voyage to the Pacific Ocean Undertaken ... for Making Discoveries in the Northern Hemisphere in the Years 1776, 1777,1778, 1779 and 1780* (3 vols. and atlas; 2nd ed., London, 1785), II, 260–272.

[3] The best diplomatic study on this subject is still William R. Manning, *The Nootka Sound Controversy* (Washington, D.C., 1905).

[4] For a detailed study of the naval activities of Spain along the entire Pacific Coast, see Michael E. Thurman, *The Naval Department of San Blas* (Glendale, Calif., 1967).

[5] "Guardias Marinas de Cádiz" (1073), and "Antigüedades de los oficiales de guerra de la armada," Tomo II (1161), MSS in MN.

[6] "Relación de los méritos y servicios del Capitán de Navío Francisco Mourelle" (999), MS in MN.

of supplies and widespread scurvy.[7] Six years earlier, officials of New Spain had put into motion the plan for the settlement of Alta California — a vast project which required the shipment of large quantities of food, tools, and clothing out of the port of San Blas in the province of Nayarit. To accomplish this venture additional men and ships gradually were allocated to the Naval Department of San Blas; and the viceroy, in assuming responsibility for the annual supply voyages to Alta California, became responsible also for the exploration of the northwest coasts.[8]

In 1775 Viceroy Bucareli sent a new frigate, the *Santiago* under Captain Hezeta, and the schooner *Sonora* under Juan de la Bodega y Quadra to explore the northern waters, but neither vessel made port or established formal claim to Nootka. Bodega's schooner sailed farther north than Hezeta's flagship, however, and this lengthy voyage earned the young officer his fame as an intrepid explorer.[9] He made a detailed survey of the coast from 52° to 57° N. latitude, complete with maps and charts of harbors deserving of future occupation, and filled his journal with prolific descriptions of the natives and the flora and fauna.[10]

The difficulty of this operation was quickly apparent to his superiors. Upon his return to San Blas he was praised by Viceroy Bucareli, recommended for the title of Knight of the Order of Santiago — a title which required exceptional valor in a military assignment together with unimpeachable lineage of highest purity[11] — and promoted to the full rank of lieutenant in the Royal Navy.

---

7 "Primer exploración de Juan Pérez . . ., 1774" (331), MS in MN. See Thurman, *The Naval Department of San Blas,* 133–139, for a detailed account.

8*Ibid.,* chs. 11–13.

9 Bodega y Quadra, "Primer viaje hasta la altura de 58 gr . . ." (618), Francisco Mourelle, "Navegación con la Goleta Sonora . . ." (575), and "Segunda exploración en 1775 con la Fragata Santiago y Goleta Sonora" (331), MSS in MN.

10 In the Museo Naval there are at least two more MS journals kept by Bodega (618 and 622). His charts, both originals and copies dating from 1775 to 1792, are in Cartas y Planos, MN.

11 "Ordenes Militares Santiago, Pruebas de el teniente coronel D[o]n Juan Fran[cis]co de la Bodega, Las Llanas, Mollinedo, y Losada teniente de Navío de la R[ea]l Armada, natural de la ciudad de Lima, Reyno de el Perú, pretendiente al Abito de Caballero de la orden de Santiago, año 1776" (1119), MS in Archivo Histórico Nacional, Madrid. This archive is hereafter cited as AHN.

By 1778 Bodega had earned a rest, and he sailed to Lima where he joined his family in festive thanksgiving and warm reunion.[12]

The voyage of the *Sonora* marked the beginning of a decade of American duty for Bodega, most of it with the Naval Department of San Blas. This apprenticeship took him to Las Islas Marías, Callao in Peru, the presidios of Alta California, and finally to Alaska — up the continent, across the Gulf, and down the Kenai Peninsula. His specific assignments included those of shipbuilder, repair supervisor, commanding officer of supply vessels, and "diplomatic agent" to Madrid. In 1785 he was promoted to the rank of captain and transferred to Europe. Sailing by way of Havana, he arrived in Spain and reported for duty at the Department of Cádiz where he had trained as a midshipman twenty years before.[13]

During the next four years Captain Bodega y Quadra was used primarily as a naval adviser. On official visits to Cádiz and Cartagena he was apparently appointed to instruct midshipmen, and in this work he must have utilized the experience obtained through his Pacific Northwest explorations. Rest and relaxation had a place in his schedule also, and he spent some time in Madrid, Aranjuez, and the small towns of the Basque country which had been the homeland of his parents.[14] During Bodega's tour of duty in the Department of Cádiz he came to know two junior officers who later served under him at San Blas — Manuel Quimper and Juan Bautista Matute.[15]

In 1789, during official conferences at Aranjuez, Captain Bodega y Quadra was called upon to testify regarding Pacific Coast

---

[12] Bodega y Quadra, "Segunda salida hasta los 61 gros en la Fragata la Favorita . . ." (618), MS and Diario in Californias, vol. 8, Archivo General de la Nación, México, D.F. This archive is hereafter cited as AGN.

[13] According to Admiral Julio F. Guillén, distinguished scholar and archivist and director of the Museo Naval, such an appointment to the Department of Cádiz was indeed an enviable assignment in those days. I spoke with Admiral Guillén on this and other points while a Del Amo Fellow in Spain in 1961–62, and wish again to acknowledge gratefully his cooperation.

[14] Bodega's regional and family ties are indicated in "Ordenes Militares Santiago, Pruebas de . . . D[o]n Juan Fran[cis]co de la Bodega . . ." (1119), MS in AHN.

[15] Oficiales: Asuntos particulares desde el año 1784 (1163), MS in MN.

defenses and the need for further exploration and development. He had firsthand knowledge of all the new ports north of San Blas,[16] and his comment on them was essentially negative. At any of these locations, Bodega reported, Spain could only fire a few pitiful salvos and then pray that no foreign power might burst in. If the enemy were to attack in force or approach by land from any northern boundary, the presidial garrisons of Alta California were too scanty and untrained to make effective resistance. An even more serious deficiency, and one reiterated by the viceroy himself, was the woeful lack of ships in the Naval Department of San Blas. Without ships, the coasts could not be patrolled and defended.[17]

Some of these problems were resolved in Court meetings or through advice from ranking naval officers, Captain Bodega y Quadra included. It was commonly known that Carlos III had appointed the Count of Revilla Gigedo to the viceregal office in Mexico, and sometime in the spring of 1789 Bodega was approved as commandant of the Naval Department of San Blas.[18] It was apparent that the Court had agreed to augment the naval forces of New Spain with personnel as well as ships. On May 26 Revilla Gigedo's party took passage from Cádiz; it included Bodega and six junior naval officers, together with a group of craftsmen. Their ship, the *San Ramón*, docked at Vera Cruz in mid-August, and after additional conferences Bodega left for San Blas. The new commandant arrived at his old station on September 18, 1789.

In the years of Bodega's absence, the waters of the Pacific shore had become turbulent with international rivalry. The presence of Russian fur traders in the Aleutian Islands was reported by the

---

[16] During his command of supply vessels to Alta California, Bodega visited San Diego and Santa Barbara. On the *Sonora* in 1775 and the *Favorita* in 1779 he was resident at Monterey and San Francisco.

[17] Manuel Antonio Flórez to Antonio Valdés, Nov. 26, 1788, in AHN, Estado, 4289. The glaring weakness of the Spanish defense of Alta California has been described by Maj. Terence M. Allen, USMC, in his thesis, "A Comparative Analysis of the Military Occupation of Alta California, 1768–1776," University of New Mexico, 1966.

[18] Revilla Gigedo to Antonio Valdés, April 14, 1789, in AHN, Estado, 4290 (reservada). Bodega's appointment was approved by Valdés, the Spanish minister of marine.

Frenchman, Comte de La Pérouse, during his visit to Monterey in 1786. Upon hearing this alarming news, Ensign José Martínez of the *Princesa* returned to San Blas and reported immediately to Viceroy Flórez.[19] His reward — and subsequent ignominy in Spanish naval history — was the command of exploring expeditions in 1788 and 1789, the second of which brought Spain to the brink of war with England in the diplomatic controversy over Nootka Sound. The crisis at Nootka came in the summer of 1789 while Martínez was acting as commandant of the Department of San Blas. It will suffice here to note that Martínez took positive control and prevented England from gaining a toehold in either military or commercial affairs at Nootka. In a strictly military sense, therefore, the ensign was acting within the limits of his orders, but as a representative of the Crown he endangered Spain by his rashness. Certainly he was ill-suited to so important an assignment as the commandancy of the Department of San Blas,[20] and Captain Bodega y Quadra arrived to replace him none too soon.

The first permanent Spanish garrison at Nootka was organized by Bodega at San Blas late in 1789, and a flotilla of warships was hastily dispatched to the north the following February under Lieutenant Francisco Eliza.[21] Bodega's long trip from Spain and further journeying across Mexico had not placed him in any advantage for study of the situation and implementation of a new laboring force; yet all major preparations, as well as the detailed outfitting of both vessels and crews, had been personally supervised by the new commandant. Not a flaw or hitch was observed in the process. "I labored in all matters of preparation, including the effort of collecting artillery and fresh provisions," Bodega reported to the viceroy, "and

[19] Martínez to Manuel Antonio Flórez, aboard *Princesa* at San Blas, Dec. 28, 1786, in AHN, Estado, 4289.

[20] While this judgment is a conjecture by the author, the hot temper of Martínez is proven out both by his malicious treatment of his pilots during the 1788 expedition and by his confrontation with James Colnett in Nootka Sound. Petitions from Pilots Serantes, Verdia, and Narváez, with letters of González López de Haro, to Viceroy Flórez, San Blas, Oct. 28, 1788, in AHN, Estado, 4289; and "Diario de José Martínez," July 3, 1789 (732), MS in MN, for insults to Colnett.

[21] Salvador Fidalgo, "Extracto de los más esenciales del Diario del Teniente de Navío Salvador Fidalgo . . ." (271), MS in MN; and "Salida de Los Tres Buques . . . para la obligación de Nutka . . ." (331), MS in MN.

thus it has been possible to launch the relief expedition for Nootka in a period of thirty-six days."[22]

Lieutenant Eliza, on board his flagship *Concepción*, arrived at Nootka Sound on April 5, 1790. In compliance with his orders, he took precautions to insure that the garrison of seventy-six Catalonian troops under Colonel Pedro Alberni would not suffer hunger or privation.[23] Eliza's sailors began at once to cut and haul wood, sometimes using native labor, and to lay in supplies and barter for fresh produce with Chief Maquina and his tribe.[24] Two subordinate officers, Salvador Fidalgo and Jacinto Caamano, were assigned to reconstruct the barracks and outbuildings along the fringes of Friendly Cove. By summer the northernmost outpost of New Spain had assumed modest military proportions. The new fortress, San Miguel Castillo, stood as it had earlier on Hog Island, and Eliza's crewmen had re-positioned the cannon. Barracks and supply houses were now going up on Hog Island and at Friendly Cove; and an elaborate two-story quarters had been erected for Colonel Alberni, along with a bakery shop, a milling room, and storage sheds for perishable goods brought up from Monterey.

After three months of activity at Nootka, Lieutenant Eliza was able to report some notable progress to his superior at San Blas. The remaining artillery, six cannon of 24-caliber, had now been placed; and the regular overhaul of an English prize ship, renamed *Princesa Real,* had been accomplished in twenty days. This sloop, under the command of Manuel Quimper and with Gonzalo López de Haro as pilot, had then sailed on May 31 on a reconnaissance of the Strait of Juan de Fuca with nine soldiers aboard. On May 4 Salvador Fidalgo had taken the *San Carlos* north for reconnaissance

---

[22] Bodega y Quadra to Revilla Gigedo and to Antonio Valdés, San Blas, Feb. 4, 1790, in AHN, *Estado,* 4289.

[23] Alberni was appointed "commandant of arms" at Nootka in October, 1789, by Viceroy Revilla Gigedo. His original company consisted of eighty men. "Relación de la Fuerza con que se halla dicha Compañía hoy día de la Fecha, Puerto de San Lorenzo de Nootka," Aug. 23, 1790, MS in MN.

[24] For details on Maquina, see Oakah L. Jones, Jr., "The Spanish Occupation of Nootka Sound, 1790–1795" (Master's thesis, University of Oklahoma, 1960). Descriptions are found in the MSS of Eliza, Fidalgo, and Alejandro Malaspina.

of the Gulf of Alaska. Finally, Eliza had launched a new ship of thirty-two tons within the short space of five weeks. Between May 26 and July 3 he unloaded the shell of a schooner from his flagship and supervised its rapid construction.[25] This vessel, christened *Santa Saturnina,* remained in service at Nootka and on the California coasts for two years. Thus was shipbuilding begun at Nootka, and while the total tonnage was not significant, the Spaniards did outstrip other nations in this work until the arrival of Kendrick, Gray, and other "Boston men" from the United States.

At about the same time as the Spanish reoccupation of Nootka, the globe-circling expedition of Alejandro Malaspina was moving up from Chile to Mexico. In March, 1791, his two corvettes *Descubierta* and *Atrevida* anchored at Acapulco and took on provisions and new personnel for the long trip northward to Mulgrave Sound, on the Alaskan coast, and back by way of Nootka and Alta California late in the same year. The stopover at Nootka between the 14th and 28th of August proved a busy time for Captain Malaspina's officers; longitudinal and latitudinal observations were completed there, as well as recordings for weather and magnetic variations. Malaspina's was the last full-scale naval and scientific expedition to be sent out from Spain, and his northern voyage was consonant with the latest flurry of discovery and mapwork northward from the Californias.[26]

An entirely new concept of sovereignty was promulgated under Malaspina's leadership. He advanced the theory that true sovereignty was the product of possession-taking, appropriate map-making, and adequate publication of the results of discovery. Thus, according to the authoritative student of this voyage, it reduced symbolism to "the simple, practical expedient of burying a bottle with an enclosed coin to serve the same purpose of dating as the previous written testimony of possession."[27] Moreover, since the international arbitration over Nootka Sound was then proceeding

---

[25] Eliza to Bodega y Quadra, July 5, 1790, in AHN, Estado, 4289.

[26] See Donald C. Cutter, *Malaspina in California* (San Francisco, 1960), for a scholarly summation.

[27]*Ibid.,* 7.

apace and the Spanish Crown was coming to realize that a token force could not possibly defend the entire coastline from San Francisco to Alaska, Malaspina was confirmed in his opposition to earlier views of the importance of military control at Nootka. He firmly believed in the assignment of spheres of commercial influence, and his presence at Nootka in 1791 extended these ideas and brought about a general agreement that the northern limits of Alta California should be drawn at the Columbia River or more preferably at the margins of the Strait of Juan de Fuca.

Malaspina's emphasis on scientific data and a fuller knowledge of new terrains made a dramatic impact upon the officials of New Spain. From Acapulco and San Blas three expeditions were now sent to Nootka to explore and chart the Inland Passage, the Strait of Juan de Fuca, and the surrounding regions,[28] although the garrison at Nootka had few tools and supplies to spare for scientists and explorers.[29] The officers in command of these expeditions were aided by Tomás de Suría, the Mexican artist whom Malaspina had taken north with him in 1791, and several other artists who contributed to the production of native portraits, landscapes, coastal profiles, and sketches of plant and animal specimens. The extent and significance of these activities has only recently been appreciated and assimilated.[30]

The Department of San Blas by now had been sufficiently staffed and equipped to carry out such explorations. The several junior officers who had come with Captain Bodega y Quadra from Spain were assigned to his command at San Blas,[31] and two new warships were soon added to the West Coast fleet: the *Concepción*

---

[28] See Henry R. Wagner, *Spanish Explorations in the Strait of Juan de Fuca* (Santa Ana, Calif., 1933), for an account of these voyages of Dionisio Alcala Galiano and Cayetano Valdés in the *Mexicana* and the *Sutil*, Quimper in the *Princesa*, and Narváez in the *Santa Saturnina*.

[29] Malaspina made this clear in his "Viaje en limpio de las corvetas Descubierta y Atrevida" (181), MS in MN.

[30] Two Spanish archival collections are pertinent: the Malaspina and Bauzá materials in the Museo Naval, and the materials in the Archivo del Ministro de Asuntos Exteriores. Professor Donald C. Cutter has pioneered this investigation.

[31] Oficiales: Asuntos Particulares (1163), MS in MN. These officers were Jacinto Caamaño, Francisco Eliza, Salvador Fidalgo, Manuel Quimper, Ramón Saavedra, and Salvador Meléndez Valdés.

from Realejo and the 213½-ton *Activo,* the largest vessel to be built at San Blas in the Spanish era. Restitution of two prize ships to the Englishmen James Colnett and Thomas Hudson had deprived the department of valuable tonnage,[32] but upon Malaspina's recommendation Viceroy Revilla Gigedo ordered construction of the schooners *Mexicana* and *Sutil.*[33] Bodega was vitally involved in all such projects,[34] but of more immediate importance to the theme at hand was the special commission as senior officer of the "Expedition of the Limits" awarded to him late in 1791. It was this commission which took him personally to the northwest coast the following year to negotiate with the representative of Great Britain on the practical aspects of the Nootka Sound question.

The Expedition of the Limits was ordered by the court in Madrid and executed by Viceroy Revilla Gigedo, who named Bodega as commanding officer and called him to Mexico City for planning conferences in November, 1791.[35] The nominal purpose of the expedition was to settle claims with Great Britain which had resulted from the Spanish seizure of the merchantmen owned by Colnett and Hudson; a second purpose was the exploration and scientific mapping of the Straits of Juan de Fuca and Rosario "behind" Nootka, with a final reconciliation of the jurisdictional differences between England and Spain as the ultimate political objective. A team of scientists, headed by the brilliant Mexican botanist, José Mariano Moziño, was appointed by the viceroy to accompany the expedition. Lieutenant Fidalgo would act as interim commandant at San Blas while Bodega was on the northwest coast.[36]

---

[32] The two prize ships, *Argonauta* and *Princesa Real,* had been used for more than a year at San Blas before being returned to their owners. See Thurman, *The Naval Department of San Blas,* 310–317.

[33] "Noticias del Departamento de San Blas" (127), MS in MN; and "Expediente" for *Mexicana* in AGN, Californias, 42. Details on the *Sutil* are in Francisco Hijosa to Revilla Gigedo, San Blas, Jan. 5, 1792, in AGN, Historia, 42.

[34] "Reglamento provisional para el Departamento de San Blas," Dec. 7, 1789, Colección Guillén, Tomo VIII (1211), MS in MN.

[35] Details and logistics are found in the Revilla Gigedo Collection, vol. 14, Bancroft Library, University of California, Berkeley. The formal instruction was Revilla Gigedo to Bodega y Quadra, Oct. 29, 1791, in AHN, Estado, 4289.

[36] Bodega y Quadra to Revilla Gigedo, Nov. 23, 1791, and José María Monterde to Revilla Gigedo, July 5, 1792, both in AGN, Historia, 42.

After six months of preparations at Acapulco and San Blas, which included the building of the *Activo* under Bodega's direction, the Expedition of the Limits sailed from San Blas on March 3, 1792. Bodega was on board the *Santa Gertrudis,* a new warship which had been sent up from Peru at the viceroy's request,[37] and convoyed by the *Activo* and the *Princesa.* Even though the *Activo* required repairs after being damaged in a high wind at Las Islas Marías, the expedition reached Nootka by midsummer, well ahead of the English commissioner whom Bodega was to meet. Upon landing, Bodega made an inspection of the military fortifications while the scientists set up an observation post.

The English representative, Captain George Vancouver, finally arrived in Friendly Cove late in August aboard his flagship *Discovery,* escorted by the tender *Chatham.* A veteran of Cook's famed voyage of the 1770's, Vancouver had sailed from England with an exploring force the year before and was assigned to the Nootka negotiations as an afterthought. The trust placed in his diplomatic abilities was not wasted, for he proved a wily antagonist at Nootka and then spent two additional years cruising up and down California waters as a spy.[38]

Vancouver's approach to the outpost at Nootka on August 28, 1792, brought forth a thirteen-gun salute from the battery at San Miguel Castillo,[39] and for the next three weeks the English captain basked in the hospitality provided by his Spanish counterpart. Meeting together on board the *Activo* or the *Discovery* or ashore in their permanent quarters, Bodega and Vancouver spent much time in joint inspections of the Spanish settlement at Friendly Cove and in ceremonial visits to Chief Maquina's interior village. Detailed, vivid sketches by the Spanish artists depict the lavish meals and

---

[37] Revilla Gigedo to Antonio Valdés, Nov. 17, 1791, in Revilla Gigedo Collection, vol. 14, Bancroft Library.

[38] Revilla Gigedo to Duque de la Alcudia, Feb. 18, 1793, and same to same (No. 154) in AHN, Estado, 4290; Bodega y Quadra to Revilla Gigedo, Monterey, Dec. 30, 1792, in AHN, Estado, 4290.

[39] Jones, "The Spanish Occupation of Nootka Sound," 78.

native entertainment enjoyed by the two commissioners.[40] Bodega and Vancouver became close friends, highly respectful of one another, and Bodega happily accepted the English captain's suggestion that this insular site be named Quadra and Vancouver Island.[41]

On September 20, following one of his last trips to the interior, Bodega wrote his final letters to Vancouver;[42] two days later he set sail from Nootka on board the *Activo*. Thus ended Bodega's only visit to Nootka as commandant. The Expedition of the Limits had been successful in the realm of natural science, as José Moziño's *Noticias de Nutka* would attest,[43] but had failed in its vital diplomatic mission. The northwestern boundary of New Spain had not been fixed, and the Spanish retreat from Nootka was inevitable.

After a stop at Núñez Gaona, a tiny station on the Washington coast, Bodega handed over his command to Lieutenant Fidalgo, who was northward-bound out of San Blas.[44] Vancouver remained briefly at Nootka, greeted Fidalgo upon his arrival on October 2, and then apparently followed Bodega south to San Francisco Bay where both captains stayed out the winter. Viceroy Revilla Gigedo meanwhile was anxious for news from Bodega, but not until January 19, 1793, did the *Santa Saturnina* reach San Blas with letters from both Bodega and Vancouver. On the 1st of February, perhaps a bit tardily, Bodega returned to San Blas to resume his role as commandant of the department.[45]

---

[40] Revilla Gigedo Collection, vol. 30, Bancroft Library. This exquisite assemblage of line drawings, portraits, coastal profiles, and charts is a priceless heritage for the modern historian and anthropologist. I am deeply grateful to Irving Robbins of Atherton, California, for his exhibit of this volume and other materials during the meeting of the Pacific Northwest History Conference in April, 1967. Professor Cutter has identified duplicate copies of the portraits of Maquina, Bodega, and Vancouver in the Spanish archives.

[41] Letters of Bodega y Quadra to Vancouver, Sept. 12–20, 1792, in AHN, Estado, 4290. Cartographic works showing the northwest coast in these years are found in the Edward W. Allen Collection, Seattle, Washington. "Quadra and Vancouver Island" appeared on those maps, but by 1852 the name of the Spanish captain had been dropped from usage.

[42] Bodega y Quadra to Vancouver, Sept. 20, 1792, in AHN, Estado, 4290.

[43] A copy of Moziño's work is in the Revilla Gigedo Collection, vol. 31, Bancroft Library.

[44] Bodega y Quadra to Revilla Gigedo, on board the *Activo* at Núñez Gaona, Sept. 25, 1792, and Salvador Fidalgo to Revilla Gigedo, Nov. 26, 1792, both in AHN, Estado, 4290.

[45] Revilla Gigedo to Bodega y Quadra, Feb. 17, 1793, in AHN, Estado, 4290.

On February 12, six months after the Bodega-Vancouver conferences at Nootka, the final convention between Spain and England was signed. In essence, this agreement called for enforcement
of the earlier convention of October 28, 1790, whereby Spain
promised to pay 200,000 dollars in Spanish coin for restitution while
at the same time recognizing England's right to navigate, fish, and
conduct commerce within those northern waters which had once
been a special preserve of the Spanish king.[46] In theory as well as
in practice, Spain was admitting to a hasty retreat from her position
of exclusive control of the Pacific Coast.

What had gone wrong with the Spanish plan to maintain the
outpost at Nootka by supplying it from Monterey and defending
its approaches through the straits with the small station at Núñez
Gaona? First, Vancouver was able to learn that the attempts of the
Spaniards to keep up a good front at Nootka were somewhat empty.
He cleverly parlayed his personal friendship with Bodega into an
inspection of the California ports and bases on the pretext of need-
ing repairs and awaiting further instructions, and thus he saw at
first hand that the garrisons were weak and the presidios defenseless.
When word of Vancouver's spying tactics was circulated in 1794,
he was screened away from Monterey; but many local officials were
censured for permitting the Englishman to see what Viceroy Revilla
Gigedo had called "the deplorable state of our presidial defenses."[47]

Second, Bodega clearly felt — and recommended as much to
the viceroy early in 1793 — that the most important thing to be
done was to assign more ships and men specifically to duty in
California for patrol and for apprehension of foreigners. Third,
Spanish hopes of participation in the fur exchange of the northwest
coast had been dashed by formal orders, and Spain could no longer
expect to isolate her northern domains from aggressive English and
American traders.

A new viceroy was appointed in 1794, but Revilla Gigedo did
not leave office without rendering a full report on the practical
aspects of withdrawal from Nootka. In his long *informe* of April

---

[46] Manning, *The Nootka Sound Controversy*, 466–468.
[47] Revilla Gigedo to Bodega y Quadra, Feb. 8, 1793, in AHN, Estado, 4289.

12, 1793, he stated categorically that to maintain Nootka from California was simply too expensive.[48] His recommendation was for abandonment of the distant outpost in favor of strengthening the stations of Alta California.[49] This was the counsel of both Malaspina and Bodega, and this was what Revilla Gigedo finally recommended to Madrid.

The last assignment of Captain Bodega y Quadra was to direct plans for the occupation of Bodega Bay just north of San Francisco.[50] An expedition was organized at San Blas in March, 1793, but command was given to a junior officer, Juan Bautista Matute, because Bodega's health had broken. Grievously ill by June of that year, the commandant requested sick leave and designated Manuel Quimper as his replacement at San Blas.[51] With his personal chaplain, Alejandro Jordan, he went into seclusion at Guadalajara and suffered a seizure. He died in Mexico City on March 26, 1794, at the age of fifty-one and at a time when most of his naval associates had gone back to Europe.[52] Vancouver's *Discovery* was sojourning in Monterey Bay when the news reached him that Bodega was gone. "He was my intimate friend," the Englishman wrote, "whose death grieves me to the soul."[53]

San Lorenzo de Nootka did not survive Bodega for long. Late in 1793 Colonel Alberni had sailed away with his Catalonian troops, a number of whom were sick, and a general dismantling of accoutrements took place the next year. The few soldiers and the station ship *Princesa* at Núñez Gaona likewise retired to California in 1794.[54] The last Spanish commandant of Nootka, Brigadier

---

[48] Manning, *The Nootka Sound Controversy,* 468–469.

[49] Revilla Gigedo to Conde de Aranda, Nov. 30, 1792 (124 Reservada), in AHN, Estado, 4290.

[50] Revilla Gigedo to Bodega y Quadra, Feb. 13, 1793, in AHN, Estado, 4290; Juan Bautista Matute, "Reconocimiento del Puerto de la Bodega por el Teniente de Fragata D[o]n Juan Bautista Matute" (332), MS in MN.

[51] Bodega's request and the designation of Quimper are in AGN, Provincias Internas, 3.

[52] Revilla Gigedo to Duque de la Alcudia, April 30, 1794, in AHN, Estado, 4290.

[53] Vancouver to Branciforte, aboard the *Discovery* in Monterey Bay, Nov. 23, 1794, in AHN, Estado, 4290.

[54] General Alava's instructions for disbanding are detailed in Revilla Gigedo to Duque de la Alcudia, April 30, 1794, in AHN, Estado, 4290.

General Manuel Alava, met with Lieutenant Thomas Pearce of Great Britain on March 23, 1795, to arrange the final evacuation and abandonment of the port. After the two commissioners had paid their respects to the national ensigns of Spain and England with gun salutes and troop maneuvers, Spanish interests at Nootka came to an end. Ships of the Royal Navy seldom made close approach to 49° N. latitude, and Nootka Sound ceased to be of significance in the annals of Spanish exploration.

The "Last" Frontier

CALIFORNIA'S ECONOMIC
IMPERIALISM: AN HISTORICAL ICEBERG

by

W. H. HUTCHINSON

The iconoclastic "Hutch" grew up in Goldfield, Nevada, southern Arizona, and Oxford, Mississippi, where William Faulkner was once his scoutmaster. A professor of history at Chico State College since 1964, he was previously a horse wrangler, fireman, harvest hand, sailor, labor negotiator on the San Francisco waterfront, and free-lance writer. His biography of Eugene Manlove Rhodes, *A Bar Cross Man* (1956), and *Oil, Land, and Politics* (1965) won special awards. He has written a column on Western Americana for the *San Francisco Chronicle* for almost twenty years and has served as a contributing editor to *The American West* since 1966. Six times in a row he has taught in the summer session at San Francisco State College, and in the spring semester of 1968 he was at the University of Texas as a visiting professor of history.

CALIFORNIA'S CURRENT IMPERIALISM, an unceasing water quest of increasing magnitude, should be a clear and a present issue — four-dimensional, obviously ominous, and congressionally militant. California's precedent imperialism was a business one. It was not so clearly visible as today's and most certainly it has not been measured truly. Hence our titular iceberg — a truly majestic berg gliding athwart the history lanes and posing a titanic threat to the foolhardy and the careless.

Our berg has visible mass, and this mass seems to me to be composed of the mining frontier and the Central-Southern Pacific complex. This visible mass comes to its eroded peak in that one-time sovereignty of sagebrush-and-silver known as Nevada, that so-called "Great Rotten Borough," which now appears destined to become one of Howard Hughes' smaller real estate holdings. The work of Rodman Paul and William S. Greever, of Stuart Daggett and Oscar Lewis, to name but a few, has established this visible mass to my own satisfaction. What I presently propose is to bounce some echoes off our berg's submerged and vaster bulk in the hope that these will yield a rough outline for the guidance of future mariners.

Three Septembers past, I made a pilgrimage to a spot I had not seen since 1917 and found a querulous pack rat ensconced amidst the brittle shingle fragments that marked my father's house. I stood there, where the insistently restless desert wind once had made melodic theme for the unceasing beat of an hundred-stamp mill, and I realized that what I had been doing for many years past was acquiring some measure of meaning for my memories. In my father's years there, Goldfield, Nevada, made the last bibulous Babylon of the last mining frontier. Its chief producer in those years, and the mainstay of its payroll-based economy, was the Goldfield Consolidated Mines Company, the ostensible property of that agate-eyed quondam jockey for a Cantonese chef in Winnemucca, George Wingfield.

Let me stand *in locoed parentheses* once again. A recent work on this era in Nevada mining gave credit for solving the metallurgical mysteries of Goldfield's complex ores to Wingfield. My father would not have appreciated this conveyance. And I have yet to see an account of the Western Federation of Miners in Goldfield which stated that one of the sacred rights of Labor for which they struck was the right to steal highgrade out of the Mohawk and other shafts. These remarks display my weakness for dancing the tangential schottische without invitation.

Wingfield and Goldfield long have been linked with the late Bernard M. Baruch, and there is no doubt, because of personal knowledge, that funds from Denver and from sanguine Corn Belt purchasers of assessable shares in non-existent mines played their parts in Goldfield's heyday. Notwithstanding all these, my father's bi-monthly trips to San Francisco were to report on the operations of Goldfield Con to the Crocker interests on Montgomery Street. Whether the Crockers and their bank were acting for themselves or for other investors, or as fiscal conscience for Wingfield, is beyond my competence. For whomever they acted, their linkage with Nevada mining makes a part of the *visible* mass aforementioned.

What is not a part of this mass is the yet unplumbed relationship between the Crockers and Wingfield's later Nevada banking empire which had ramifications in Utah, Idaho, and Arizona. What is not a part of this mass is the amount of dynamite exploded in Goldfield, virtually all of which came from California manufacturers. (Those who know the mining West should well remember the empty "Hercules" boxes that made both stools and cupboards in many a rainbow-chaser's shack.) What is not a part of this mass is the amount of goods and commodities consumed by Goldfield's human thousands. These came from California, by and large, and a goodly portion of them came from Los Angeles, not San Francisco, which bears remembering in view of southern California's growth which has spawned and sustained today's water imperialism.

Worth remembering, too, is the amount of lumber used annually in Goldfield. This lumber came from the Sierra forests of California and from the Douglas Fir stands of California's Redwood Coast. In both these regions, the whole process of converting standing timber into stulls and lagging and mill timbers, into floor-joists and rafters and shingles, was controlled by California capital for most of Goldfield's productive life. This leads me to note that the lumber foundation upon which Robert Dollar built an international shipping and trading firm was headquartered in San Francisco and to point out that as early as 1877 the Sierra Lumber Company, a product of California quartz-mining capital, had developed an export lumber trade with Australasia and the China Coast. This California export trade has endured to the present.

Now another personal recall with a slightly different flavor. Forty years past this month, a frying-size boy who claimed to be a horse wrangler was getting in the way of the work being performed on a cattle ranch in the southwest quadrant of the northwest quarter of Arizona. (This deliberately nebulous geography is to impede further researches into my equine ineptitude.) It was an open range operation — using school sections, Santa Fe lands, and public domain without bothering to lease or buy it — and you could ride from Date Creek to the Colorado River, via the Big Sandy and Hualapai Valley, without too many detours due to "bob wahr."

We branded some 1,200 calves that year, in the middle of what became a too-long drought even for the Bank of Arizona. Using that range's rule-of-thumb, 1,200 calves branded equated to some 5,500 head of cattle, plus whatever bulls still were functioning. This figure was down almost fifty per cent from the last good year of 1923, when the owner had sold the ranch to investors in San Diego. Southern California sent us supplies in carload lots: everything from horseshoe nails to canned tomatoes, not forgetting sun-and-sulphur-cured dried fruits in boxes made from California pine. Coal oil came from California: two five-gallon tins to a wooden box that made our pack-boxes later. And rolled barley for horse feed came in sacks sufficient to total tons twice a year. With rare exceptions during the three years I rode there, we sold our cattle to California for finishing and slaughter.

North of this range was another California investment, that of the Perrine family. Whether they held by freehold or lease, or simply by opportunistic fencing, they controlled some hundreds of square miles and ran more cattle in their Bar Cross iron than we did. (I should note that this was not the same Bar Cross that made a part of the life of 'Gene Rhodes.) Beyond them, from the Santa Fe tracks to the Canyon between Williams and Seligman, was what, to a kid's imagination, was a real cattle ranch — the Three V's — where they ran a wagon, sometimes three of them, not a greasy-sack pack string. This, too, was another California outfit.

Twenty years after this youthful time, I began serious work on Eugene Manlove Rhodes, thanks to the confidence supported by cash of Leslie E. Bliss and the late Robert Glass Cleland. In this work I enlarged, although not by design, my awareness of several things, including the notion that New Mexico made a fluid frontier between California's nineteenth-century economic imperialism and that century's Texas imperialism of people and cattle and folkways. This is a primrose path I cannot walk today.

The largest cow outfit in 'Gene Rhodes' early years in the Rio Grande Valley of New Mexico was the J-Half-Circle-Cross, the "John Cross," which I found to have been financed by California capital accrued from the Comstock Lode. This company once ranged upwards of 30,000 head, then overstocked, and was drouthed out in the 1890's. Such fate did not befall the other California investment I found in 'Gene Rhodes' home parish around Engle, New Mexico. This was the 7TX, using the Armendáriz Grant, which was acquired as part of a far-flung California investment in Southwestern lands and livestock. How many head, how many acres, made up its maximal holdings, I do not know.

I do know that the Three V's that caught my boyish fancy were and are a part of it. I know that it began as a venture of Lloyd Tevis and James Ben Ali Haggin, California bankers and risk-takers even before the Comstock enlarged their sphere. I know that their corporate descendant, the Kern County Land Company (KCL), today operates more than 1,400,000 acres in Arizona and New Mexico for livestock production. So their last corporate report made clear; and their letter to me, which gives me the semblance of a document, indicates that Tevis and Haggin began acquiring this acreage in the latter 1870's. An interesting sidelight to this is simply that an elderly widow died recently in San Francisco, bequeathing some hundreds of thousands of dollars to the University of California at Davis in memory of her father. He had been for more than thirty years the cow buyer for, and manager of, KCL's great grasslands empire in the Southwest.

Given KCL's cow-and-calf operations in the Southwest and their vast agricultural acreage in the San Joaquin Valley, you may link these into the rise of Bakersfield, California, as a great feeding center for slaughter cattle. Then consider that the increments of profit from production to butcher shop enhanced California's reservoir of investment capital. To KCL's operations must be added the Southwestern and Mexican ranching operations of George

Hearst and, inevitably, the far-flung investments of Miller & Lux. Henry Miller had "good hands," as reinsmen put it, and a seat of proven durability. Nonetheless, you need not accept uncritically the legend that he could drive from Mexico to Oregon and sleep every night on his own land.

You should consider, if nothing more, a legend that has yet some currency in southeastern Oregon. This legend holds that Henry Miller's range boss in that region was wont to amble over to Salem every two years to negotiate with the governor of Oregon about the tax rate in Malheur and Harney counties over the next biennium. It seems feasible, as well, to consider other nineteenth-century California investments in eastern Oregon land and cattle — such as Pete French of Frenchglen and sudden death fame — as well as the Gill Cattle Company of this century. In this century, too, a wealthy Californian invested large quantities of his capital gains from California petroleum fields in Arizona cattle and ranches, presumably to keep his several sons-in-law gainfully employed.

What I have been suggesting here is that California increased its supply of investment capital by bringing in and finishing raw materials for its own consumption from its economic outposts, while selling these outposts the processed products that they needed. And they needed lumber and grain and flour and powder and air-tights and hardware and coal oil and dried fruits, to name those I have touched upon *en passant,* and to say nothing of Levi Strauss products.

It would be useful if we knew the interaction between such mercantile firms as Hellman, Haas & Company of Los Angeles — the Hellman name being prominent in Wells Fargo's affairs today — and such firms as the Central Commercial Company of northern Arizona and Lindauer & Company of Deming, New Mexico. It would be enlightening to examine the effects of these commercial relationships upon California politics. For example: I found some evidence (*Oil, Land and Politics*) that Thomas Bard's stand against Arizona's statehood produced an anti-Bard reaction in Los Angeles commercial circles which felt that his stand, as a United

States Senator from Southern California, jeopardized their customer relations. I suspect that it would be most illuminating to explore the role of taxpayers resident in California in the political affairs of their economic colonies. For example: given the state of New Mexican politics in the latter years of the past century, if not later, it seems logical that the owners of multiple thousands of acres would be interested in county politics, at least, and have some effect upon them. Like finding a drowned cat in a cream jug!

These echo soundings have been bounced off some major outcroppings of our iceberg's underwater bulk. What follows may be harder to read aright, because the echoes are absorbed by the invisible aspects of economic imperialism — banking, shipping, insurance and the like. I turn perforce to the equipment I know best, the biographer's kit, to calibrate my findings. In the process, it just may come about that in but two-thirds of one man's life, we can in some measure gauge California's own transition from economic colonialism to the imperial role I attribute her.

For a quarter-century, until failing health curtailed his pace, John Parrott's massive frame made a familiar sight along Montgomery Street, the major artery in the Far West's financial heart. Three firms keep his name alive in that heart's beat today. Two are investment companies representing divergent segments of his descendants; the third perpetuates the firm name he began, without his family's participation but in the same pursuits. A short distance from these chambers, a stub alley bears his name, and a long block-and-one-half beyond the Palace Hotel (the Sheraton prefix be damned) New Montgomery Street comes to an end because of John Parrott's unflagging opposition to one of William C. Ralston's schemes.

John Parrott's name is touched upon in every worthwhile record of the Golden years of the city inside the Golden Gate. Yet these visible signs but compound the frustration that has come to me from trying to sound the vast mass of his years. This mass has its own above-water peak in the fact that he died, near the end of his seventy-third year, leaving almost $8,000,000 in United States bonds and even more gilt-edged California real estate. This peak remained after he had raised and married off seven daughters, three of them to well-born Europeans, which indicates that it once was much larger. Like James Lick, he reached San Francisco with ample funds, which makes him a Gold Rush rarity and makes the acquisition of his initial investment capital germane.

This had its beginnings in the operations of his older brother, that William Stuart Parrott who served as John-the-Baptist for Slidell's mission to Mexico and whose estimate of Mexican affairs in 1845 probably prompted that mission. There is far more to W. S. Parrott's Mexican career than the Slidell affair, and he deserves better than he received at the pens of Waddy Thompson and Anthony Butler, whose remarks form the basis for most appraisals of him yet today. From Virginia via War Trace Creek in Tennessee, the breastworks at New Orleans, and Havana, W. S. Parrott reached Mexico City in February, 1822. He apparently had some skill in dentistry, inasmuch as Stephen F. Austin's followers called him "Doctor," as did James Buchanan, and he parlayed his prac- tise into extensive mercantile operations and land holdings. He also was a power in organizing a line of stages, using Troy-built coaches and imported American Jehus, which ran from Guadala- jara to Vera Cruz via Mexico City as early as 1835. When he was forced to leave Mexico in 1839, his claimed losses neared $700,000.

Why he had to leave Mexico is too extensive to discuss here, except to note that he was an ardent exponent of *federalismo,* and to note that he, not Joel R. Poinsett, probably deserves credit for establishing the York Rite of Masonry in Mexico. He once wrote Stephen F. Austin, for whom he acted in Mexico at a critical time in Austin's affairs. Ten years before he left Mexico, his younger brother, then eighteen, had joined him there. Despite John Parrott's gravestone, despite his family's belief, despite the Census of 1880, he was not born in Virginia but in the canebrake country of Jackson County, Tennessee, near the town of Carthage, on April 26, 1811.

In 1835, after six years of his brother's tutelage, John Parrott established himself on Mexico's West Coast, doing business as

Parrott, Talbot & Company in Mazatlán, which is an overlooked port of call in our commercial climb up the ladder of the latitudes from Cape Horn to California. What has become today's Mazatlán appears on Castillo's map of 1541; Drake knew its potential, as did Cavendish, and Vizcaino noted it in 1602. Despite these notices and usages, it slumbered down the centuries, an unprepossessing sand spit used by pearlers and pirates, until about 1806 when, as field work in Mexico two years ago indicates, it was settled by a "company of mulattoes." This makes it suitably ethnic by today's standards. Over the next thirty years it grew to about 6,000 people for two good reasons: it was the last port with direct access to open sea before Baja California intervened, and behind it, in the wrinkles of the Sierra Madre, were silver mines which allegedly included one of the richest in all Mexico.

Whether the silver was mule-backed three hundred miles across the spine of Mexico to be minted at Durango and then returned, or whether it went into commerce simply as lumps of amalgam called *platillas*, Mazatlán had an ample supply of funds. This is supported by the fact that *HMS Samarang* lifted $1,250,-000 in specie for England in 1834; that *USS Congress* took $200,-000 in specie and bullion in 1838; that the Howland & Aspinwall brig *Cayuga* lifted $250,000 in 1840; that the Boston brig *Griffon* plied regularly between Mazatlán and Canton, with outward cargoes of Brazil-wood and bullion and with inward cargoes of quicksilver and China silks valued at $200,000 more than once. Finally it bears noting that $130,000 in hard Mexican coinage came up from Mazatlán in 1848 to pay the United States forces in California.

Mazatlán was a far cry and many miles from the seat of authority in Mexico City. It was addicted to the sacred Federalist Constitution of 1824. It was dedicated to using the revenues from its Custom House for its own ends. It had a whole-souled passion for evading the governmental export tax on silver. It was a brawling, smuggling, international port almost from birth, and it attracted the attention of the world's traders.

The Tepic-based English firm of Barron, Forbes & Company

did business there. Jecker, Torre & Company represented French interests and later financed a French filibustering expedition into Sonora. Hamburg apparently was represented by Uhde & Pini on Mexico's West Coast. The first American consulate on this coast was established there November 1, 1826 and was filled by James Lennox Kennedy — of New York, not Boston. Kennedy, for an opinion, represented the New York firm of Howland Brothers, later Howland & Aspinwall, and it would be worthwhile to explore what part Mazatlán played in enabling the Howlands to survive the depression of 1837 and thus have a major role in New York's rise to commercial eminence.

Whether John Parrott, using his brother's funds in all probability, bought out Kennedy or founded his own firm about 1835 remains unclear. And I hope I may be permitted to remark that trying to do documentary research in Mazatlán is physically pleasant, but is otherwise as rewarding as shouting down an empty well. Revolutions, French occupation, and two burnings of the town to combat bubonic plague and cholera have taken their toll. It is of record that Parrott was posted as consul there on December 26, 1837, and our archives show that he served as such for most of the next twelve years. He also became the port's leading American merchant, the firm name changing to Parrott & Company in 1841.

Many years later the *San Francisco Chronicle,* in the impertinent blackguard stage of its journalistic development, spun some wondrous tales of Parrott's youthful physical prowess. This perhaps helped him to survive the vicissitudes of life in lusty Mazatlán. His commercial shrewdness plus his political connections in Washington — the latter stemming from his brother's friendship with William L. Marcy — enabled him to survive the trade rivalries of his competitors and an 1841 effort by Howland & Aspinwall to oust him from his consulship.

Parrott traded both inward and outward ladings between Mazatlán and Guadalajara, Durango, and Sonora. He was buying hides from Thomas Oliver Larkin as early as 1840, and soon was selling Larkin more on credit than he bought from him. The strength of their trade relations is evidenced by the fact that Parrott chartered and sent two vessels to California in 1845 at Larkin's urging, and upon Larkin's promise to arrange the essential Custom House chicanery at Monterey. One of these was the brig *Matador* out of Hamburg, which paid duties of $60,000, thus enabling Larkin to recoup his advances to the last Mexican governor of California. The other was the schooner *Star of the West,* out of Liverpool with a cargo at invoice of £25,000, which was wrecked off Monterey for a total loss to Parrott and a substantial salvage profit to Larkin. The loss did not grate against Parrott's sensibilities nearly so much as did Larkin's levying of niggardly consular fees for recording the disaster. The fact that Parrott could absorb such a loss without financial faltering supports my belief in his prosperity.

In his consular capacity, Parrott also contributed to his country's approach toward California. I find it interesting to speculate upon his part in Larkin's appointment as consul at Monterey, inasmuch as Parrott was in Washington, en route to Europe, when it was made. His despatch to Commodore Thomas ap Catesby Jones at Callao triggered that fiery officer's ill-timed seizure of Monterey in 1842. Archibald Gillespie, the peripatetic lieutenant of Marines, obtained a loan of $300 from Parrott before sailing for California via Honolulu in 1846. And it was Parrott's schooner *Hannah* that brought to Commodore Sloat Larkin's frantic request for a man-o'-war to offset Frémont's theatrics on Gabilan Peak. Finally, it was a despatch from Parrott, then travelling across Mexico toward Vera Cruz, that stirred Sloat's sluggish blood sufficiently to make him quit fretting about marine borers in his ships' planking and make sail for Monterey.

Parrott's letters to Secretary of War Marcy during Scott's advance on Mexico City make interesting reading, but our concern here is with the losses Parrott absorbed, which further buttress my claim to his solvency. He apparently wholesaled tobacco to American sutlers accompanying Scott's troops, and claimed a loss through misfeasance by the Mexican government of $110,000 on the three hundred tons of tobacco he had imported. He also purchased more than 400 horses and mules in Mexico to go overland to the American forces in California, and lost them through confiscation in Chihuahua for another loss of $120,750. Even so, he is said to have reached San Francisco in 1849 with some $300,000 in minted Mexican money. Whether in whole or in part, his possession of coin in a coinless land gave him a source of profit at once: what George P. Hammond has recently and most aptly termed *Digging For Gold Without A Shovel* in editing the letters of Daniel W. Coit, who had the same advantage.

Parrott's possession of funds is supported by his purchase of an interest in the New Almadén quicksilver mine from James A. Forbes for $33,000. What is of merit to my major premise in this transaction is the scattered evidence of New Almadén's production that was exported. In 1851 it appears that the bulk of the mine's 9,400 flasks, seventy-five pounds each, went to Mexico at sixty dollars per hundredweight. Twenty years later, out of 91,000 flasks produced, more than 34,600 of them went to Mexico, South America, and China. Parrott and his fellow investors got out of New Almadén to Philadelphia capitalists, presumably at a profit, but this did not end Parrott's connection with quicksilver. He and his son from Mexico, Tiburcio, operated producing properties in Lake County for many years. I have no figures on their production or its consumptive destination.

Parrott's arrival in California with ample funds stands out in his investment of $232,000 in Montgomery Street real estate and construction by the end of 1852. Had he not done so, Fisherman's Wharf might have become San Francisco's commercial center. Following the series of fires that wracked the city in 1851, its commercial heart seemed destined to beat along its North Beach. Harry Meiggs — "Honest Harry" was his sobriquet — gambled that this would transpire. Instead, Montgomery Street pulsed with renewed life, and Honest Harry began a new career in South America, leaving behind a legacy of unpaid debts and unauthorized city warrants.

Parrott's initial holdings place us today at the apex of an isosceles triangle, and if it be true that buildings then reflected their owners more accurately than can be the case in this day of corporate and condominium erections, the Granite Block on the northwest corner of Montgomery and California streets certainly reflected John Parrott. It has been said that he was the first in San Francisco to use granite imported from China, but it appears to me that Ebbetts & Company used China granite some months earlier to face a block they built on California Street between Front and Battery. Using indentured artisans from Hong Kong at one dollar per day plus rations of rice and fish, using Chinese granite for the facing and Chinese brick for interior walls, the Granite Block was begun August 1, 1852 and completed for occupancy by December 4 of that year.

Those unbelievers who may be astonished by the bamboo scaffolding used in erecting Hong Kong's high-rise buildings today will understand the attention devoted to this construction device by the San Francisco press in 1852. Parrott had acquired the lot from William Heath "Kanaka" Davis for $19,500, and construction costs brought his total investment to $117,500. He rented its three floors at once for a monthly income of $3,000. The banking firms of Page, Bacon & Company and Adams & Company were its first occupants, and this is said to have been the crucial factor in making Montgomery Street the city's financial center. When these firms failed in the local crash of 1855, Wells Fargo made it their office for twenty years, and the Hongkong & Shanghai Banking Corporation used it thereafter. It survived the earthquakes of 1856, 1859, 1865 and 1868, as well as the more noted quake of 1906. It also survived the horrendous explosion — ten killed and some fifteen injured — that resulted when a Wells Fargo employee sought to open an unmarked case of Dr. Nobel's Patent Blasting Oil with a hammer. Incurably sentimental San Franciscans have sworn that the Granite Block visibly resisted the wrecker's ball when it was razed in 1925-26.

Just up California Street from the squat massiveness of the Granite Block was reared the four-story Iron Building at a cost of $23,000, land included, which Parrott promptly rented to the U.S. Land Commissioners for $1,200 monthly. On the northwest corner of Montgomery and Sacramento streets, Parrott erected three three-story brick edifices at a total cost of $86,000, which brought him a monthly revenue of $2,500. This latter site was where he maintained the offices of Parrott & Company. It now is occupied by the Pacific Department of the National Union Insurance Company. The site of the Granite Block and Parrott's contiguous holdings supports today's headquarters of the United California Bank.

There is evidence that Parrott also conducted a private banking business in these first hectic years, lending to such as Mariano Vallejo at five per cent per month. He also financed trading voyages to southeast Asia, to the China coast and to his old port of Mazatlán for spices, sugar, coffee and rice — all commodities not so subject to such violent fluctuations as accompanied imports of less exotic wares from the Eastern seaboard and from Europe. His banking and import businesses became a formal operation with the formation of Parrott & Company in September, 1855, after the crash of that year which provided a foundation of economic unrest for the second Committee of Vigilance in 1856.

Parrott's feelings about the state of affairs in San Francisco during the Committee's heyday may be of interest to students of the Vigilantes' sanctity or lack of it. These made an addendum to his letter of July 4, 1856 to D. D. Page of St. Louis, for whom Parrott acted as agent in San Francisco:

> If I could find a purchaser at 50¢ on the Dollar for all my property in California, I would take it and abandon the country forever. I at times am so much disgusted at the turn things have taken in the State, to say nothing about the thieves and corruption and insecurity of life and property, that I deeply regret ever having invested my all in it. I am the only one [sic] of the Old School that can say he has gained anything, and there is no telling how soon I may be robbed or assassinated for what I have. There is really no pleasure in living in a country like this and there is less hope of ever getting the villains out of the country.

While Parrott's mercantile business continued after his death, and that profitably, he sold his private banking business in 1871 to the London & San Francisco Bank, of which Milton S. Latham was president. I venture the opinion (one supported by Latham's small estate) that Latham was the political and promotional front for the Bank, while "Old John" Parrott continued to supply the financial acumen and the funds for ventures attributed to Latham. If this supposition be true in any part, then Latham's railroad and ferry conflicts with the Central Pacific need to be re-examined.

A question requiring its first examination is that of Parrott's relations with the Comstock crowd, "Ralston's Ring," which included such as D. O. Mills and William Sharon, the latter of whom boasts the distinction of having been sued for adultery while a widower. In this regard, a published list of the income taxes paid by San Franciscans in 1864 shows that Parrott paid more than twice as much as either Mills or Ralston, and more than three times as much as George Hearst.

It is evident to me, if no one else, that the Comstock created a second pool of San Francisco investment capital to compete with the original pool of mercantile and real estate capital represented by such as John Parrott. The Central Pacific, of course, created, in time, a third such pool, while the Bonanza Kings made a fourth. It is the first two that are my concern, for their conflict may have had more to do with Ralston's ultimate downfall than heretofore has been envisioned. This conflict, if I am correct, was not born solely from Ralston's formation of the Bank of California, under-cutting his former banking associates in the process, but found another ancestor in a battle over a California-financed insurance industry. I am indebted to my officemate at Chico State, Professor Clarence McIntosh, for his research-based conclusions regarding the domination of California insurance by Eastern and foreign firms during the state's first decade. In this period, Parrott & Company were agents for such firms as the Royal Insurance Company of London and the Canton Insurance Company, Ltd.

When Ralston secured legislation in Sacramento imposing a tax on foreign, meaning non-California, insurance firms and formed the Pacfic Insurance Company, he was countered by Parrott and his associates with California Lloyds. This evolved into the Union Insurance Company which paid some $2,250,000 in dividends, three times its capitalization, in twenty years. Other insurance firms in which Parrott and the non-Comstock crowd were associated included the California Home Insurance Company, the Merchants Mutual Marine Insurance Company, and the National Insurance Company. Parrott's co-venturers in these firms included such as Lloyd Tevis, Haggin, W. S. Selby of the smelter and shot tower, A. B. McCreery, and Alvinza Hayward after he split away from the Comstock crowd. In these insurance ventures, Parrott played another part in making San Francisco the financial center of the Far West, and in increasing its and his reservoir of investment capital.

In support of my conflict contention, it is germane to note that Parrott shunned the Comstock as the Devil would a Baptist preacher. He did, however, play a part on the mining frontier by forming the Reese River Mining Company at Austin, Nevada during the excitement there and involving the New York firm of Duncan, Sherman & Company in it. There is a Parrott Claim in the annals of Montana's transition from an investment by silver-seeking Californians to a copper satrapy of the financial East. And until four summers past, a substantial building still marked the site of Parrott City, a few miles west of Durango, Colorado.

As was noted earlier, Parrott's mercantile business remained operative after his death, and he had augmented its operations in 1861 by acquiring the 17,700-acre Llano Seco ranch in Butte County, near Chico. His payment was less than five dollars per acre and the seller was Caleb T. Fay, one of his insurance company associates, who had acquired his capital start as a merchant in Gold Rush Sacramento. Parrott was perhaps the first, certainly one of the first, to import Durham cattle into California from England, but the ranch in his lifetime was basically a wheat-sheep operation. The shatter loss in wheat harvesting was about one hundred pounds per acre on which the sheep got fat until the autumnal rains brought new grass. Thus Parrott & Company had its own wool to sell on the world's markets, as well as mutton wethers for San Francisco's tables.

This brings me to make the point that we have at best inadequate data on the cross-movement of sheep between California and the West, and that we have less than this on the economic apsects of this livestock ebb-and-flow. When it comes to wheat and its role in California's economic growth, we have no solid examination known to me of what wheat meant to this growth. For example: the names of Friedlander and Dresbach are prominent, perhaps dominant, in the early wheat days, but they have no economic meaning. In the wheat year of 1880-81, Parrott & Company despatched twenty-eight of 356 full cargoes sent from San Francisco Bay to overseas ports, primarily England, while G. W. McNear sent eighty-one and Starr & Company sent thirty. This may be interesting, but it has no economic meaning. The same is true of barley. I know that Parrott shipped barley cargoes to Australia, but I know not their effect. By the same token, the barley that fuelled the freight teams in Arizona after the Southern Pacific provided linkage, came from southern California, and all we know is that this resulted in a rise in the growers' price per bushel.

Finally, I would note that Parrott & Company were joint venturers with Captain R. H. Waterman in sending one, possibly two, sealers onto the Pribilof rookeries ahead of the Alaska Commercial Company. These were tarred as rum traders and poachers by that company, and Parrott became embroiled with the law thereby. The end result was that John Parrott became a shareholder in the monopoly company, and his several daughters each wore new sealskin coats whenever they needed or, more likely, wanted them.

In a time when cheap emotional contentions and equally spurious visceral concepts seem to have slopped over from the political into the historical field, I stand committed to the premise that the business history of California's economic imperialism affords a singular opportunity for solid, prolonged, rewarding, and much-needed historical accomplishment.

THE PASSAGE TO INDIA REVISITED:
ASIAN TRADE AND THE DEVELOPMENT
OF THE FAR WEST, 1850–1900

by

THOMAS R. COX

A native of Oregon, the author taught in secondary schools for seven years before joining the faculty of San Diego State College in 1967. He has done graduate work at the University of Hawaii, then at the University of Oregon for his doctoral dissertation on the Pacific lumber trade, under the direction of Professor Earl Pomeroy. Previous publications include articles and reviews in the *Oregon Historical Quarterly,* the *Pacific Historical Review,* and *Forest History.*

AMONG THE many results of James Marshall's discovery of gold in California was a revitalization of trade between the west coast of North America and the Orient. Both British and American observers were heartened by the development. In England a writer for *The Economist,* noting the surge of activity which the revived trade had caused in Hong Kong, commented that, "the fairest hopes of the colony are founded on the new trade which is springing up between it and California. . . . In these circumstances there is some prospect of Hongkong becoming a useful settlement."[1] In

---

[1] *The Economist,* Mar. 8, 1851, reprinted in Hong Kong *China Mail,* May 29, 1851. The journal noted that in the first six months of 1850 some 10,776 tons of shipping loaded in the British colony for the West Coast of the United States. Exports thence included coarse silks, lacquerware, matting, camphorwood ware, tea, sugar, molasses, wrought granite, and various other items. Granite seemed one of the most promising exports. Noting the shortage of building materials in San Francisco, the author of the article offered the opinion that the "cities of the new El Dorado may not improbably be built out of the hills of Hong Kong." See also the June 17, 1852, issue of *Friend of India,* reprinted in *China Mail,* July 22, 1852.

San Francisco the editor of the *Alta California* noted: "Each day adds to the value and amount of our China trade, and each month shows new sources of profit to those who embark in this adventure."[2]

Traders in the Pacific Northwest were also stirring. Early in 1851 the brig *Emma Preston*[3] stood out from the bar of the Columbia River bound for Hong Kong with a cargo of masts and spars. Six months later the little vessel was back, laden with sugar, tea, rice, and assorted China goods. The brig *Amazon*, with a similar cargo, had crossed from Whampoa to Portland a few weeks ahead of her. Other vessels soon followed in their wakes.[4] Trade between the Pacific Northwest and China, quiescent since the death of the maritime fur trade, was once again under way. It would continue throughout the century. Too small to have any real impact on the national economy, this trans-Pacific commerce nonetheless was important in shaping and promoting the development of the Far West.

The mid-century revival of trade between the Far West and the Far East was but an incidental result of the demand, created by the Gold Rush, for tonnage to carry passengers and freight to California. Many of the vessels that flocked in through the Golden Gate were too valuable to be left riding idly at anchor or rotting on the mud flats of San Francisco Bay. Since few cargoes for the

---

[2] San Francisco *Alta California,* May 16, 1851. In his annual message to the legislature Governor Peter Burnett called the attention of the lawmakers of the state to California's growing commerce, especially that with China. *Legislative Journals, 1851,* 806–807.

[3] Sometimes referred to as a schooner.

[4] *China Mail,* April 3, May 22, Sept. 25, and Oct. 2, 1851, May 18, April 1, and Dec. 16, 1852; Hong Kong *China Overland Mail,* May 23, 1851, Dec. 27, 1852; Oregon City *Oregon Spectator,* Jan. 16, July 3, and Sept. 30, 1851; Portland *Star Marine Journal,* Jan. 23, 1851; Portland *Oregon Weekly Times,* June 26, 1851. See also consular despatches, Hong Kong, July 1, 1851, Eldon Griffin, *Clippers and Consuls: American Commercial and Consular Relations with Eastern Asia, 1845–1860* (Ann Arbor, 1938), 451 and *passim;* and E. W. Wright (ed.), *Lewis and Dryden's Marine History of the Pacific Northwest* (Portland, 1895), 36–39, 53. The *Oregon Spectator,* Sept. 30, 1851, expressed high hopes for the trade: "Already the trade of China has been directed, to a small extent, to this new Territory. It has been the result of enterprise. Just let that spirit become a little more generally diffused among our commercial men, and it will be easy to divine the advantageous consequences that will follow."

East Coast or Europe were being offered in California, many owners — rather than have their vessels brave the dangerous Cape Horn passage in ballast — had them dispatched to China to pick up cargo to carry from there around the Cape of Good Hope to London, Boston, or New York. To cut losses on the Pacific cross-ing, they had whatever cargo could be obtained in California put aboard for the trans-Pacific leg of the journey. It may be said, then, that these crossings generated the trade — not the reverse.[5]

The situation soon began to change, however. At first agricul-turists and lumbermen had been able to sell all they could produce for almost unbelievable profits right on the Coast, but by 1854 they found themselves faced with falling prices and glutted markets. A search for new outlets quickly developed, agents for vessels found freight being offered, and some producers — eager to move surpluses — even dispatched cargoes as ventures on their own account.[6]

In July, 1854, Nathaniel Crosby, Jr., a sea captain and entre-preneur resident in Portland, wrote to Joseph Lane, the territorial delegate for Oregon. This letter, and a second written three weeks later, clearly revealed the new state of economic affairs. Crosby had been engaged in trade between Oregon and California since 1846; but now, he calculated, the trade with San Francisco was "about don[e]." The captain announced that he was loading the bark *Louisiana* with lumber from the Columbia River country and

[5] John G. B. Hutchins, *The American Maritime Industries and Public Policy, 1789–1914* (Cambridge, Mass., 1941), 265–69; William Armstrong Fairburn, *Merchant Sail* (Center Lovell, Maine, 1945–55), II, 1534–37; IV, 2159–2296, 2454–61. See also consular despatches and returns of trade from Hong Kong and Shanghai, and com-mercial intelligence from *China Mail* and Shanghai *North China Herald*. These make it clear that the majority of vessels continued to arrive in ballast for some time after the first cargoes began to arrive.

[6] Edwin T. Coman and Helen M. Gibbs, *Time, Tide and Timber: A Century of Pope and Talbot* (Stanford, 1949), 75–77; Rodman W. Paul, *California Gold: The Begin-ning of Mining in the Far West* (Cambridge, Mass., 1947), 116–23; Owen C. Coy, *The Humboldt Bay Region, 1850–1875* (Los Angeles, 1929), 119–21; Edmond S. Meany, Jr., "History of the Lumber Industry of the Pacific Northwest to 1917," (unpublished thesis, Harvard University, 1935), 115; Fairburn, *Merchant Sail*, II, 1535; Carl Cutler, *Greyhounds of the Sea: The Story of the American Clipper Ship* (New York, 1930), 276.

would soon be off to China in quest of new markets for the products of the Pacific Northwest. He would visit all the ports of China that had been opened to trade, Crosby declared, and then stop off in Japan on his return voyage to canvass its potential as well.[7]

Once in the Far East, Crosby was so impressed with the potential of the markets there that he decided to stay in Hong Kong and act as agent for additional cargoes of lumber that he planned to bring from the Northwest. He put his first mate in charge of the *Louisiana* and sent him back to the West Coast with instructions for continuing the trade.[8] Crosby's example was seized upon by others, and lumber-laden vessels were soon being dispatched to China from Humboldt Bay and Puget Sound as well as from the Columbia.[9]

There is other evidence of decline in importance of trade with San Francisco. The Port Gamble sawmill of A. J. Pope and Frederic Talbot, one of the first of the giant mills that were to dominate the economy of the area around Puget Sound for the rest of the century, had been built for the express purpose of supplying lumber for San Francisco and its hinterland. In 1854, its first full year of operation, some 3,600,000 board feet of lumber were shipped from the mill, but, contrary to expectations, it was found necessary to ship well over a third of the cut to foreign ports.[10] Records do not make it clear just how much of this lumber went to the Far East, but it was probably a substantial portion. Three years later, when W. J. Adams and his associates in the newly established Washington Mill Company sought to send lumber to China, A. J. Pope

---

[7] Nathaniel Crosby, Jr., to Joseph Lane, July 22 and Aug. 13, 1854 (Crosby MSS, Oregon Historical Society, Portland).

[8] Mrs. George E. Blankenship (comp. and ed.), *Early History of Thurston County, Washington* (Olympia, 1914), 267–71; Harvey W. Scott, *History of the Oregon Country* (Cambridge, Mass., 1924), II, 247; Portland *Oregonian*, Aug. 5, 1854; *China Mail*, May 17, 1855, Jan. 31, Nov. 11, 1856.

[9] *China Mail*, Dec. 7, 1854, Mar. 22, June 21, Aug. 23, Sept. 13, Oct. 11 and 25, 1855, Jan. 31, May 22, Oct. 9, 1856, Jan. 1, 1857, July 8, Aug. 26, 1858, Jan. 27, April 21, July 21, 1859; Uniontown (Arcata) *Humboldt Times*, Dec. 28, 1856, and May 1, 1858; San Francisco *Herald*, May 4, 1857. See also Coy, *The Humboldt Bay Region*, 123–24. Cargoes were also being trans-shipped from San Francisco. *China Mail*, Oct. 4, Nov. 9 and 29, 1855, May 27, 1858.

[10] Coman and Gibbs, *Time, Tide and Timber*, 51–62; Olympia *Pioneer and Democrat*, Feb. 17, 1855.

did all he could to prevent these would-be competitors from entering the field. In spite of Pope's efforts, Adams was able to sell a
cargo to a firm in San Francisco which, Adams explained to his
partners, intended "doing quite a business in China" and would
be "wanting cargoes of lumber quite often."[11] The Washington
Mill Company sold many cargoes for shipment to the Far East
in the years that followed, though it appears never to have been as
active in the foreign trade as were the Pope and Talbot interests.
Unlike the latter, Adams and his associates do not appear to have
sent ventures there on their own account. However, to both firms,
as well as to the other large mills on Puget Sound, the trans-Pacific
markets proved an important outlet.[12]

What was true in Washington Territory was equally true
in California. Statistics for the years 1860-1865 show large quantities of lumber being exported from the state. China was by far
the most important foreign market during this period.[13]

Forest products were only a portion of the exports sent to the
Far East. California's governor, John Bigler, had complained in
1852 that the people of his state paid little attention to agriculture
and that "nearly all the necessaries of life" had to be imported; but
by 1860 the state was producing nearly six million bushels of
wheat per year, stood fifth among the states in the production of
that grain, and had a surplus for export.[14] Some 25,000 barrels
of flour and 24,000 sacks of wheat were shipped to China in that
year. By 1863 shipments of flour to China had doubled, and wheat
shipments exceeded 186,000 sacks. The upward trend was especially encouraging since the demand in Great Britain and Australia

---

[11] Adams, Blinn and Co. to [Washington Mill Co.], Apr. 6, [1858] (Washington Mill
Co. MSS, University of Washington library, Seattle). Other pertinent letters were
dated Oct. 16, 1857, and Feb. 24, Mar. 9, 12, and 20, 1858.

[12] The importance of these varied from time to time and from mill to mill. Of the
Puget Sound mills, Pope and Talbot appear to have been most dependent on the trans-
Pacific markets.

[13] California State Agricultural Society *Transactions, 1864–65* (Sacramento, 1866),
382–89, cited hereafter as CSAS *Transactions*. See also Eliot G. Mears, *Maritime
Trade of the Western United States* (Stanford and London, 1935), 113.

[14] Governor John Bigler, "Special Message to the Legislature, January 30, 1852," in
Journal of the Senate, 1852 (San Francisco, 1852), 77–78; U.S. Bureau of the Census,
Agriculture of the United States, Tenth Census, 1880 (Washington, 1882), 17, 22.

declined during the early 1860's. By this time California barley, oats, beans, hay, potatoes, and wool were also going to Oriental ports.[15]

Not all the shipments to the Far East were bound for Hong Kong and the ports of China. News of Perry's success had hardly reached the West Coast before entrepreneurs in San Francisco were planning a station in Japan to outfit whaling vessels and dispatching provisions to supply the post. Others were reported to be trading in Japan even before Townsend Harris had arranged a treaty of commerce with that nation.[16] Northwesterners shipped flour from Oregon to Japan as early as 1857, though trade with the island kingdom remained relatively unimportant until the importation of Japanese tea began some two decades later.[17]

Shippers sent their first cargoes to the Far East to supply foreign communities there and to furnish goods needed for the provisioning and repair of vessels calling in Oriental waters. Penetration of the native market came slowly but, in spite of competition from inexpensive Asian products, a demand eventually developed in that sector of the economy as well as in the foreign. Though it was low-grade and inexpensive by American standards, flour from the West Coast sold in the Chinese market for more than twice as much as the native product. In spite of this, significant quantities apparently were consumed by the wealthier Chinese, thus making possible far larger shipments.[18] In the 1870's, while

---

15 CSAS *Transactions, 1863,* 266–67; *1864–1865,* 384.

16 Arthur Abel, "How Trade with Japan Began," *The Pacific Historian,* XI (Winter 1967), 42–52. This trade is hardly surprising in view of announcements such as appeared in the *China Mail* stating, incorrectly, that Perry had opened Japan to trade. *China Mail,* Oct. 5, 1854.

17 Mears, *Maritime Trade of the Western United States,* 114; Fred Lockley, *A History of the Columbia River Valley from the Dalles to the Sea* (Chicago, 1928), I, 545.

18 *West Shore,* IV (October 1878), 58; Tientsin *The Chinese Times,* Feb. 25, 1888; Tientsin *Peking and Tientsin Times,* Feb. 12, 1898. See also D. K. Lieu, *The Growth and Industrialization of Shanghai* (Shanghai, 1936), 41; and U.S. Bureau of Foreign Commerce, *Consular Reports,* LVI, no. 209 (Washington, 1897), 314. The Bureau of Foreign Commerce will hereafter be cited at USBFC. The sale of foreign flour in China did not mean that native mills were forced out of business. For a thorough study of the impact of foreign goods on the economy of China, see Chi-ming Hou, *Foreign Investment and Economic Development in China, 1840–1937* (Cambridge, Mass., 1965).

the grain trade to England was getting the attention of most commentators, large quantities of flour were being shipped to the Far
East. Between 1877 and 1879, in fact, the amount was larger each
year than that sent to the United Kingdom.[19] This trade continued
to be important for the rest of the century. In 1895 the American
consul at Amoy reported: "American flour still controls the market."[20] The *Peking and Tientsin Times* reported the same situation
in North China, while a Japanese commentator noted that the
United States had a monopoly on the flour trade with Manchuria.[21]
The Far Eastern sales were doubly welcome since the grades of
flour sold there were in little demand on the West Coast or in
England.[22]

The situation was similar in the lumber industry. Most of
the early sales which North Americans made in Asia were to buyers
in the foreign settlements. At first Chinese and Japanese forest
products, less expensive but lower in quality, dominated sales to
the native population, but with the passage of time increasingly
large quantities of imported lumber were sold to Asian buyers.

The circumstances which kept the initial demand low in
China were different from those which led to the same result in
Japan. In China little wood went into the construction of native
dwellings, and what wood was used could be supplied from the
limited but adequate forests of southern China. Not until Shanghai began the mushrooming growth that was to raise it from a
regional marketing center to a focal point of international trade,

---

19 CSAS *Transactions,* 1878, 146–50; 1880, 246. As was noted in the *Pacific Rural Press,* the flour trade led to profits on milling "and the 'feed' in bran and middlings is left here for our dairymen and stock fatteners. . . . This is much better than shipping wheat abroad." Quoted in *West Shore* IV (October 1878), 58.

20 USBFC, *Commercial Relations of the United States . . .,* 1898 (Washington, 1899), I, 983. See also CSAS *Transactions,* 1895, 165; USBFC, *Consular Reports,* LIX, no. 221, 284–85; USBFC, *Commercial Relations,* 1898, I, 1063; 1894–1895, 577, 583; *West Shore,* VII (May 1886), 168; XIV (May 1888), 234–35; XIV (August 1888), 407.

21 *Peking and Tientsin Times,* Feb. 12, 1898; Kiyoshi K. Kawakami, *United States-Japanese Relations* (New York, 1912), 36–37, 132–34.

22 *West Shore VII* (February 1881), 42, put it well: "Hongkong has been a sort of reservoir into which all our offal and low grade flour has been poured, and highly advantageous prices have been realized."

and the nation as a whole belatedly undertook modernization, were demands created that could not be met from domestic stands.[23] Railroad construction was especially important; it created a need for bridge timbers of sizes and ties in quantities that Chinese forests could not supply. Large shipments of these items, both Douglas fir and redwood, were imported from the West Coast to meet the demand.[24]

In Japan, one of the most extensively forested nations in the world, the situation was different. The various *daimyo* of Tokugawa Japan had carefully husbanded the forests of their domains. The result was that the nation entered upon the hectic modernization that followed the Meiji Restoration of 1868 with abundant forest resources upon which to draw. Through most of the nineteenth century, as a result, Japan was a lumber exporter, and therefore a source of competition rather than a market for millmen of the Far West. By the 1890's however, the Japanese had severely overcut their accessible timberlands, and a growing quantity of forest

---

[23] As the prices of domestic Chinese lumber rose in the face of timber depletion and added *likin* taxes, some penetration of the native sector by American lumber was possible. Most important was the demand for larger dimensions which could generally not be obtained at any cost from the forests of the Far East. Information on the forests of China in the nineteenth century is scattered. Valuable information is to be found in *The Chinese Times,* Feb. 19, June 11, Oct. 8, 22, and 29, Nov. 5, 1887, Feb. 11 and 25, March 3, April 14, June 23, 1888, Aug. 3, 1889, Oct. 4, 1890; *Peking and Tientsin Times,* Sept. 15, 1894; and in [China] Imperial Maritime Customs, *Decennial Reports on Trade, 1892–1901* (Shanghai, 1904), I, 266-68; II, 99, 116; [China] Imperial Maritime Customs, *Returns of Trade and Trade Reports,* various years [for figures on imports and domestic shipments from port to port]. On the growth of Shanghai the best work is Rhodes Murphy, *Shanghai, Key to Modern China* (Cambridge, Mass., 1953).

[24] USBFC, *Commercial Relations, 1898,* I, 1056; USBFC, *American Lumber in Foreign Markets: Special Consular Reports,* XI (Washington, 1896), 84–93; *The Chinese Times,* June 11, Sept. 24, 1887; May 19, 1888; *Peking and Tientsin Times,* Sept. 15, Oct. 27, 1894, Jan. 4, Aug. 8, Oct. 10 and 17, 1896, June 12, Oct. 16, 1898; *The Chinese Times Supplement,* July 9, 1898; Farnham and Co. to Renton, Holmes and Co., Aug. 10, 1885 (Pt. Blakely Mill Co. MSS, University of Washington library, Seattle, Box 40, hereafter cited as PBMCo MSS); Stimson Mill Co. to Pt. Blakely Mill Co., June 18 and 20, July 6, 9, 12, and 14, 1898 (PBMCo MSS, Box 69); Pacific Export Lumber Co., information on charters (Pacific Export Lumber Co. MSS, Oregon Historical Society, Portland); Pope and Talbot to Puget Lumber Co., June 14, 1899 (Incoming correspondence, Ames Collection, University of Washington Library, Seattle).

products, including the soon-to-be-famous "Jap squares," were being imported from the West Coast of North America.[25]

As in the case of flour, the fact that the demand in the Far East was for grades of lumber hard to dispose of elsewhere enhanced the value of these sales.[26] Without a market for the lower grades, those for which there was a good demand would have had to carry the cost of production and thus be more expensive. This would have created major problems, since competition with producers in other areas was keen and the margin of advantage enjoyed by millmen of the Far West generally a narrow one. Even with the outlet for the lower grades that was supplied by China, mill managers found themselves burdened with an excess of low quality lumber.[27] Shippers often resorted to overgrading cargoes in an attempt to move some of this poorer material, but the amount that could be disposed of in this fashion was limited. A typical reaction was that of a buyer in Hawaii who angrily wrote to J. A. Campbell, manager of the Port Blakely Mill Company, that a shipment sent to The Islands was "rubbish," and added, "You had better sell this

----

[25] USBFC, *Commercial Relations, 1898,* I, 135, 991; *1894–1895,* I, 612; *1896,* I, 172, 835–36; USBFC, *American Lumber in Foreign Markets,* 94–97; *The Chinese Times,* June 11, Oct. 15, Nov. 19, 1887, April 14, June 2, and 16, 1888, July 27, 1889; *Peking and Tientsin Times,* Sept. 15, 1894, Oct. 10, 1896. See also Johannes Hirshmeier, *The Origins of Entrepreneurship in Meiji Japan* (Cambridge, Mass., 1964), 276. Small shipments had begun earlier, however, for which see CSAS *Transactions, 1877,* 148; *1879,* 220. One of the few good accounts of Japanese forestry in the nineteenth century that is available in English is [Japan] Imperial Commission to the Louisiana Purchase Exposition, *Japan in the Beginning of the Twentieth Century* (Tokyo, 1904), 224–82.

[26] Japanese markets did not take low-grade lumber but, by ordering Japanese squares which took almost the entire log, helped prevent the accumulation of such lumber in the yards. The Pacific markets continued to provide outlets for low-grade lumber even after railroads had opened new markets to the east. See *Export and Shipping Journal* III (March 1922), 40. Cf. USBFC, *Commercial Relations, 1897,* I ,1036–37.

[27] The problem became so acute that some millmen such as Eugene Semple, owner of the Lucia Mill in Vancouver, Washington, were forced to tell prospective customers that prices would be increased on orders of high-grade lumber unless the order also included some of the lower grades that were filling their yards. Eugene Semple to Norman Merrill, April 22, 1884; Semple to A. L. Stokes, April 28, 1884; Semple to Proebstel Bros., June 23, 1884 (Letterpress book, Eugene Semple MSS, University of Washington Library, Seattle).

kind of lumber to the Chinese Lumber yard[s] — we won't have it."[28]

Even had low-grade lumber presented no problems, the trans-Pacific markets would have been needed. When marketing abroad became impossible for one reason or another, the production of the mills quickly glutted the domestic markets and shut-downs soon followed.[29]

Lumber carriers often returned from the Far East in ballast, especially in those frequent cases where the vessels were owned by the mill companies whose lumber they transported. The rapid disposal of the lumber sawed by the mills, not freights earned by the vessels, was the primary source of profits for these companies. Lumber often went directly from the saws to the holds of waiting carriers. Under these circumstances a rapid return in ballast usually would lead to greater long-run profits than could be turned by delaying to find and load a return cargo.[30]

The situation was different with vessels hauling flour to the Far East. These were generally chartered vessels. Shipowners' profits were dependent upon the freights the vessels earned; thus return cargoes were a necessity. Rice was the primary item in this eastbound traffic; but a wide variety of Chinese products — and, in many cases, Chinese emigrants — were also carried. When the lumber business was slow, even company-owned vessels would sometimes seek employment in this fashion rather than hasten back in ballast. In such instances they generally carried the return

[28]J. C. Allen to J. A. Campbell, Nov. 22, 1898 (PBMCo MSS, Box 35). It might be added that, inasmuch as redwood was relatively high-priced, there was less demand for that item in the markets of China than for Douglas fir. See California State Board of Forestry, *Biennial Report, 1885–1886* (Sacramento, 1887), 147–48.

[29]Pope and Talbot to C. Walker, Dec. 22, 1888 (Walker correspondence, incoming, Ames Collection, University of Washington Library, Seattle). W. H. Talbot to C. Walker, June 3 and 18, 1887 (Correspondence, incoming, Pope and Talbot, Ames Collection, University of Washington Library, Seattle), also indicates that the demands of foreign markets sometimes took precedence over those of domestic ones. Cf. Richard C. Berner, "The Port Blakely Mill Company, 1876–1889," *Pacific Northwest Quarterly,* LVII (October 1966), 167.

[30]Returns in ballast also helped maintain the region's generally favorable balance of trade. See California Board of Railroad Commissioners, *Third Annual Report, 1880–1882* (Sacramento, 1882), 556.

cargo to San Francisco, the largest West Coast market, where they picked up provisions and equipment to carry northward along the coast to the sawmill communities.[31]

A different sort of triangular trade developed with Australia. Lumber shipments from the West Coast to the colonies on the Island Continent were large throughout the last half of the nineteenth century.[32] Among the vessels hauling forest products thence were many chartered craft. Since few cargoes for the United States could be obtained in Australia and owners of vessels hauling lumber there did not wish to have the long return voyage made in ballast, they often had their agents load erstwhile lumber droghers with coal and dispatch them to Hong Kong, Shanghai, or Japan. There the coal was discharged and Oriental goods were taken on for the crossing to North America. This triangular trade lessened the freight charges that would otherwise have been laid to lumber shipments to Australia and, in so doing, helped keep North American wood products competitive with those imported from New Zealand, Southeast Asia, and the Baltic.[33]

In the 1870's a regular commerce of a different sort sprang up between Portland and Hong Kong. John Ainsworth, the foremost entrepreneur in the Oregon city, purchased three vessels for the

[31] Hong Kong *China Overland Trade Report,* March 14 and Oct. 28, 1959. *Coloma* and *Alden Besse* folders, journals, and ledgers (John C. Ainsworth MSS, University of Oregon library, Eugene) contain data which give good insights into the eastbound traffic.

[32] California State Board of Forestry, *Third Biennial Report, 1889–1890,* 72; *Fourth Biennial Report, 1891–1892,* 51; *CSAS Transactions, 1864–1865,* 382–89.

[33] *Kate Davenport* folders, charter folders, and vessels' journal, vol. 1 (Ainsworth MSS), taken together, give a rather complete picture of the problem of trade to Australia. See also Wright, *Lewis and Dryden's Marine History,* and Joseph Collins Lawrence, "Markets and Capital: A History of the Lumber Industry of British Columbia, 1788–1952," (unpublished thesis, University of British Columbia, 1957), 11–29, 113. Pertinent manuscripts include John Booth and Co. to Renton, Holmes and Co., Oct. 4, 1882, Aug. 12, 1885, Jan. 28, 1886, and A. Burns to Renton, Holmes and Co., June 18, July 16, Aug. 13, 1885, April 21, 1886, July 11, 1888, Jan. 22, 1890 (PBMCo MSS, Box 37); H. R. Carter to Renton, Holmes and Co., Oct. 4, 1886 (PBMCo MSS, Box 38); Cowlishaw Bros. to Renton, Holmes and Co., June 10, 1895, Oct. 11, 1899 (PBMCo MSS, Box 39); Dempster and Keys to Renton, Holmes and Co., Dec. 11, 1878 (PBMCo MSS, Box 40). Prior to the opening of the deposits in the Pacific Northwest, vessels sometimes returned directly from Australia with cargoes of coal. Fairburn, *Merchant Sail,* IV, 2313–14.

specific purpose of engaging in Hong Kong trade.[34] Lumber, scrap iron, provisions, and passengers to China filled the vessels on their outward voyages; rice, granite, curios, chow chow cargo, and Chinese laborers were carried on the return. For all this diversification, however, Ainsworth's financial records show clearly that it was the combination of lumber and coolies that made the trade a profitable one.[35] This two-way commerce continued through the 1880's and '90's though much of it shifted to Washington and British Columbia as railroad construction increased north of the Columbia and attracted Chinese laborers there. As late as the 1890's, however, the arrivals from Hong Kong of the old coolie-lumber trader *Coloma* were still what the *Oregonian* described as "the events of the year" in Portland.[36]

Ships loaded with Chinese laborers were bringing to the Far West the one factor of production in which the region was conspicuously deficient: labor. Regardless of how Westerners eventually came to look upon them — and it is interesting to note that regional spokesmen at first welcomed the Chinese for the inexpensive labor they supplied[37] — it seems clear that their presence was a factor of great importance in regional economic development. Western railroads, for instance, were often under-capitalized. Without cheap labor, construction schedules would probably have been set back and some projects abandoned altogether. Although railroads in the Far West opened no significant new markets in the years immediately following their completion, they did supply

---

[34] Studies of Ainsworth's career tend to ignore his interests in deep-water trading vessels. Ainsworth had become extremely wealthy as a result of the sale of his interests in the Oregon Steam Navigation Company. Apparently he invested in deep-water traders as a part of his efforts to "carefully invest this money, so that it will be of greatest advantage to my children...." John C. Ainsworth, "Autobiography of John C. Ainsworth, Oregon Capitalist," entry dated Feb. 9, 1881 (Ainsworth MSS, Box 1). On the China trade, see also U.S. Customs House, Astoria, "Marine List and Memoranda," (Oregon Historical Society, Portland), II.

[35] *Coloma* and *Alden Besse* folders, vessels' journals and ledgers (Ainsworth MSS). See also USBFC, *Commercial Relations, 1894–1895, 576–86.*

[36] *Oregonian,* Jan. 24, 1903.

[37] *Ibid.,* Mar. 22, 1868, Feb. 20, Aug. 2, 7, 1869; *Alta California,* May 12, 31, Aug. 7, 1851.

improved means by which the produce of the hinterlands could reach the ports of the region for export by sea. The coolie traffic speeded the economic development of the Far West by speeding railroad construction and thus encouraging the expansion of exports.[38] Chinese laborers also contributed to the growth of exports by supplying much of the labor in the salmon canneries along the Pacific Coast and by working in lumber mills, logging camps, and many marginal mining areas.

There were other items in trans-Pacific trade besides lumber, flour, and coolies. For a time in the 1860's, quicksilver was among the most important exports to China. In the late 1870's lead shipped from San Francisco was "laid down in China at prices defying all competition." In addition to the major agricultural products, cargoes of butter, hops, leather, and bones were sent from California to China and Japan, as were beer, whiskey, and wine. Hopgold brand beer, produced in Oregon, was heavily advertised in the Tientsin press in the 1880's. Dried abalone and preserved salmon were also sent. Of all these items, however, none except quicksilver even temporarily reached the level of importance enjoyed by the long-term mainstays of the trade between Far West and Far East.[39]

But of what significance was this trans-Pacific trade? For all its diversity it was a far cry from that of which John Gilpin, Thomas Hart Benton, and a host of other Americans had dreamed. The West became no great commercial freeway over which passed goods traveling between the eastern United States and Europe, on one

---

[38] Not until the twentieth century did revised rate structures and changed marketing conditions make it possible for significant quantities of lumber, wheat, and other Far Western products to penetrate markets east of the Rockies to any major extent. In the meantime, the primary markets were those within the region or accessible by ocean transportation. See James N. Tattersall, "The Economic Development of the Pacific Northwest to 1920," (unpublished thesis, University of Washington, 1960), esp. 137; Tattersall, *The Importance of International Trade to Oregon* (Eugene, 1961), 3; and the articles in *Oregon Historical Quarterly* LXVII (June 1966), an issue devoted to measuring the economic impact of the coming of railroads on the Northwest.

[39] Consular despatches, Amoy, July 13, 1878, Nov. 15, 1894; CSAS *Transactions*, 1863, 265; 1864–1865, 384; 1879, 221; and USBFC, *Consular Reports*, LVI, no. 209, 345.

hand, and Asia, on the other. Nor did this trade go far toward opening the seemingly limitless Asian markets to the products of Occidental factories. The dream of spindles and foundries kept busy to supply the masses of Asia was a will-o'-the-wisp after which Americans were to quest in vain. Asian trade remained a mere five per cent or so of the total foreign commerce of the United States throughout the nineteenth century. Only part of this passed through the ports of the West Coast. Trans-Pacific trade was clearly too limited to have any great impact on the economy of the nation as a whole.[40]

On the other hand, trans-Pacific trade was of real importance to the residents of Washington, Oregon, and California. The Far West was not integrated into the national economy in the last half of the nineteenth century. However much Westerners may have thought and acted as Easterners, however much they may have tried to recreate along the shores of the Pacific what they had known elsewhere, the fact remained that their economy was dependent upon other markets, had different wage and price structures, and rested upon a foundation made up of a different combination of productive activities than those enjoyed by other sections of the country.[41] To the economy of this isolated region the trans-Pacific markets, however small, were of vital importance. When gold was discovered in Australia, when Shanghai boomed, when Hawaii shifted from dependence on whaling to a plantation economy, when railroad construction was undertaken in North

---

[40] Tyler Dennett, *Americans in Eastern Asia* (New York, 1922), 578–606, esp. 580; and Paul Varg, "The Myth of the Chinese Market, 1890–1914," *American Historical Review*, LXXIII (February 1968), 742–58. There were, of course, some goods bound for the East Coast that entered through Pacific ports. See *West Shore* XI (August 1885), 228; XI (September 1885), 262; XII (November 1886), 322; XIV (February 1888), 87–96; XV (Dec. 14, 1889), 430. Cf. Earl Pomeroy, *The Pacific Slope* (New York, 1965), 254–55.

[41] Harvey S. Perloff *et al., Regions, Resources, and Economic Growth* (Baltimore, 1960), 109–221, 284–92. This is not to say that the Far West had no financial connections with the rest of the United States. It did. Credit, entrepreneurial talent, and manufactured goods all moved to the settlements along the Pacific Coast from sources to the east and helped to tie the business cycles of the Far West to those of the older portions of the country. See Arthur Throckmorton, *Oregon Argonauts* (Portland, 1961), and Pomeroy, *The Pacific Slope*, 83–119 and *passim*.

China, or when the forests in Japan became depleted, the effects were felt on the Pacific Slope.[42]

The direct value of goods shipped to the Far East was only the most obvious benefit from trade with the Orient.[43] Other values derived from trade with the markets of Asia may have been of even greater importance than returns from the sale of goods sent there. As has already been pointed out, Far Eastern markets tended to be complementary to those found in other quarters, supplying outlets for otherwise unmarketable grades of products and thus lowering the cost of production that had to be carried by goods shipped elsewhere. Since the flour and lumber trades were highly competitive and the demand elastic, this was of real importance. So, too, has it been pointed out that the trade in Chinese coolies, which speeded the building of the railroads of the region, did a great deal to maximize the regional development that could be achieved with the investment capital that was available.

There were other ways in which Asian trade had indirect influences on Far Western development. Trade out of Pacific Coast ports was important as a generator of secondary sources of income. Reports of the California State Board of Harbor Commissioners for Humboldt Bay show, for instance, that the freights earned on cargoes shipped from the bay were roughly as great a source of wealth as the income from the sale of lumber produced in the area.[44] Shipments to ports far distant, such as those in China, obviously

---

[42] This is not to say that these were the only places involved in Pacific trade; there were also ports in Latin America, Asiatic Russia, the Philippine Islands, and the South Pacific with which residents of the Pacific Slope had commercial relations.

[43] If proponents of the export-base theory of regional economic development are correct and exports are the main determinant of regional development, then the importance of these to the region is very great indeed. See Tattersall, "The Economic Development of the Pacific Northwest to 1920"; Douglas C. North, "Location Theory and Regional Economic Growth," *Journal of Political Economy*, LXIII (June 1955), 243–58; G. M. Meier, "Economic Development and the Transfer Mechanism: Canada, 1895–1913," *Canadian Journal of Economics and Political Science*, XIX (February 1953), 1–19. A brief explanation of the theory is in Perloff, *Regions, Resources, and Economic Growth*, 57–58.

[44] California State Board of Harbor Commissioners for Humboldt Bay, *Annual Report*, 1898 (n.p., n.d.), and the reports for 1899 and 1900.

earned larger freights than the same quantity of lumber shipped to markets nearer at hand. Not all of this income stayed within the region, for many of the ships involved in the lumber trade were transients owned by outsiders, but, after the first few years, the majority of the vessels were owned on the West Coast. Since freight charges were passed on to the consumer, the earnings of vessels owned on the West Coast was thus a profit for the area. In effect Far Westerners were exporting a service — the carrying capacity of their merchant vessels — and outsiders were paying the bill.

The potential for profits through the ownership of merchant vessels generated other activities. Initially the vessels used on the Pacific Coast were built elsewhere, usually in New England. However, increasing numbers came to be built on the West Coast. As local shipyards became more active, the drain of capital from the region that was attendant upon the hiring or buying of outside merchantmen diminished. Over one hundred sailing vessels were turned out at H. R. Bendixson's yard on Humboldt Bay. A. M. Simpson's large fleet of lumber droghers was built, for the most part, at his yards at North Bend, Oregon, and Hoquiam, Washington. The Hall Brothers turned out many of the vessels that worked out of Puget Sound. Other yards dotted the coast.[45] Though Eastern experts might deprecate these specially designed schooners as "freaks" — and Lloyd's of London might label them soft-built, poor insurance risks — they were probably better suited to the peculiar needs of West Coast commerce than were the Down Easters and clipper ships turned out in Atlantic yards. The four-, five-, and six-masted schooners developed for the long passages

---

[45] Robert E. Johnson, "Schooners Out of Coos Bay," (unpublished thesis, University of Oregon, 1953); Stephen D. Beckham, "Asa Mead Simpson, Lumberman and Shipbuilder," *Oregon Historical Quarterly,* LXIII (September 1967), 259–73; shipyard record book (Hoquiam Mill Co. MSS, University of Washington Library, Seattle); Wright, *Lewis and Dryden's Marine History, passim;* Jack McNairn and Jerry MacMullen, *Ships of the Redwood Coast* (Stanford, 1945), 78–81, 129–36; U.S. Works Progress Administration, *Ship Registers and Enrollments of Marshfield, Oregon, 1873–1941* (Portland, 1941; mimeo); U.S. Works Progress Administration, *Ship Registers, Port of Eureka, California, 1864–1940* (San Francisco, 1941; mimeo); *West Shore* I (May 1876), 10; VII (March 1881), 63; VIII (February 1882), 26, 35; Gordon Newell (ed.), *The H. W. McCurdy Marine History of the Pacific Northwest* (Seattle, 1966), 21, 80.

through the tradewind belts to Australia and China were among the highest achievements of West Coast shipbuilders.[46]

The lumber and grain trades not only helped to generate these secondary activities; they also encouraged the development of areas whose resources hitherto had been largely untapped. Puget Sound, Grays Harbor, Coos and Willapa bays, and the Redwood Coast would have been of little importance in the nineteenth century had it not been for the lumber trade. The grain trade opened the way for a more intensive utilization of much of the land in the Inland Empire of Oregon, Washington, and Idaho as well as in the Sacramento, San Joaquin, and Salinas valleys of California. Not just the immediate areas of production benefited. Since much of the Far West was, in one degree or another, economically tributary to San Francisco, much of the profit from the shipping and handling of exports accrued not to the producers but to businessmen in the bay city.[47]

Nor did goods actually have to be dispatched in order for benefits to be felt. Mere potential for exportation helped lure outside investment capital. The Gold Rush, with bullion as the potential export, provided an attraction of this sort. As with gold, oil products of California also drew outside attention and capital before the exportation of such items was much advanced. Kerosene had long been a major American export to the Far East, but little was shipped from the Far West to Asia until around the turn of the century. However, entrepreneurs trying to attract outside development capital stressed the potential of Oriental markets for California oil products as early as 1864. When Standard Oil finally entered pro-

---

[46] *West Shore* I (May 1876), 10; Fairburn, *Merchant Sail,* III, 1621–26, 1657–89; IV, 2605–2607, 2621–22; Howard I. Chapelle, *The History of American Sailing Ships* (New York, 1935), 264–67.

[47] Northwesterners did not accept their position as residents of San Francisco's economic hinterland without complaint. Yet they could hardly have developed as they did without the capital and business talent which they found available in their southern neighbor. See *Oregonian,* Aug. 23, 1865; Olympia *Pioneer and Democrat,* June 10, 1854; Olympia *Columbian,* Dec. 10, 1853. Donald Hathaway Clark, "An Analysis of Forest Utilization as a Factor in Colonizing the Pacific Northwest and in Subsequent Population Transitions" (unpublished thesis, University of Washington, 1952), 54–55, restates the old complaint.

duction on the Coast, it came in large part in order to strengthen its competitive position in the Far East. Prior to this time Standard had shipped its kerosene to Asia from New York and other Atlantic coast ports, but company representatives were finding it increasingly difficult to compete with Russian and Dutch products which were produced nearer the Asian consumer.[48] Even an area as richly endowed in mineral wealth as the Far West needed to attract outside capital and the know-how that went with it if the area was to grow. The dream of great Asian markets made the job of attracting such capital to the Far West easier than it otherwise might have been. The trade that did exist between the Far West and the Far East, though hardly what the more sanguine expected would emerge in the near future, made the dream appear all the easier of realization.

Thus, however inconsequential and mundane Pacific trade during the last half of the nineteenth century may have appeared when viewed from the vantage point of New York or Boston, the people of the Pacific Slope had, after their own fashion, developed a Passage to India. These Westerners looked out across the vast stretches of the Pacific and found markets for the surpluses of their region. To them the frontiers of trade lay across the waters to the west, not the lands to the east. Their region became not a gateway to the Orient, not an artery through which trade passed, as so many had predicted that it would, but one terminus in a two-way trade between the Far West and the Far East. As residents at one of the termini, those living in the Far West benefitted far more than they would have as mere handlers of goods in transit. Pacific trade, of which commerce with the Far East comprised a key element, was, in other words, a major force in shaping and encouraging the economic development of the Far West during the last half of the

---

[48] USBFC, *Commercial Relations, 1894–1895,* I, 591; *1898,* I, 1063; Gerald T. White, *Formative Years in the Far West: A History of Standard Oil Company of California and Predecessors through 1919* (New York, 1962), 6, 41, 45, 57–58, 73, 271–72, 281–82; Ralph and Muriel Hidy, *Pioneering in Big Business, 1882–1911* (New York, 1955), 123–54, 260–68; *Peking and Tientsin Times,* Oct. 27, 1894.

nineteenth century.[49] Its effects extended into the new century. Even after the region was integrated with the national economy and goods from the area moved inward by rail more often than they moved outward by ship, the eyes of residents along the Pacific shore continued to be turned more than those of the rest of the nation toward the Orient. They remain so today.[50]

---

[49] Since this paper has focused on trade between the Far West and the Far East, it seems worth emphasizing that the author does not mean to imply that this facet of Pacific trade was all-dominant. A thorough study of Pacific trade during the last half of the nineteenth century is yet to be made, when it is, this writer expects that it will show a pattern similar to that depicted for the Atlantic-Caribbean in Richard Pares' excellent little volume, *Yankees and Creoles: The Trade Between North America and the West Indies before the American Revolution* (London, 1956), *i.e.,* a many-sided trade, each of the facets of which helped to complement and buttress the others.

[50] For a detailed exposition of this view see Pomeroy, *The Pacific Slope,* 253–92.

PIVOT OF AMERICAN VIGILANTISM:

THE SAN FRANCISCO VIGILANCE

COMMITTEE OF 1856*

by

RICHARD MAXWELL BROWN

A professor of history at the College of William and Mary and formerly of Rutgers University, the author is a native of Mobridge, South Dakota, a graduate of Reed College, and received his A.M. and Ph.D. at Harvard University. In 1963 the Harvard University Press published his book, *The South Carolina Regulators,* following which he turned to developing a history of American vigilantism.

OCTOBER 1967 marked the two hundredth anniversary of American vigilantism.[1] The long history of this ancient if not honorable American institution divides into two major phases: the old vigilantism and the new vigilantism. The old vigilantism occurred mainly before the Civil War, was directed primarily against frontier lawlessness, and focused chiefly upon horse thieves and coun-

---

*Grateful acknowledgment is given to the Huntington Library for a grant-in-aid for July-August, 1966, which allowed research on this subject.

[1] The first vigilante movement in American history was that of the South Carolina Regulators beginning in October, 1767. Richard Maxwell Brown, *The South Carolina Regulators* (Cambridge, Mass., 1963), 39.

terfeiters in the far-flung Mississippi Valley.[2] It was a frontier
phenomenon of the agrarian era of American history. The new
vigilantism was a much broader and more complex thing. Not
confined to frontier or countryside, it was a function of the transition from a rural to an urban America. The new vigilantism found
its victims among Catholics, Jews, immigrants, Negroes, laboring
men and labor leaders, radicals, free thinkers, and defenders of civil
liberties.[3]

The San Francisco committee of 1856 is pivotal in the history of American vigilantism because it signals the transition from
the old to the new vigilantism. The two phases overlapped, but the
change began to occur in the mid-nineteenth century. The San
Francisco vigilantes blended the methods of the old with the objectives and victims of the new. Not only was the committee of 1856
the largest and best organized vigilante movement in American
history, but it was by far the best known. It received publicity on a
worldwide scale and attracted the editorial approval of the Eastern
press.[4] The performance of the San Francisco vigilance committee
was widely copied and even more widely admired[5] and had much
to do with creating the favorable image of American vigilantism in
the nineteenth century. It marked a turning point in American
vigilantism from a concern with rural frontier disorder to a grop-

---

[2] Richard Maxwell Brown, "American Regulators and Vigilantes: An Hypothesis"
(unpublished paper read at the annual meeting of the Mississippi Valley Historical
Association, Cleveland, Ohio, May 1, 1964).

[3] The terms "old" and "new" vigilantism are my own. On the new vigilantism see, for
example, John W. Caughey, *Their Majesties the Mob* (Chicago [1960], 1–25, 100–205.

[4] See Hubert H. Bancroft, *Popular Tribunals* (San Francisco, 1887), II, 548–559,
where many Eastern and European editorials are reprinted, most of which (including
such journals as the *Tribune, Herald,* and *Times* of New York and the Boston *Journal*)
favored the vigilance committee. This second volume of Bancroft's massive two-volume
Popular Tribunals is devoted entirely to the vigilance committee of 1856. Its 748-page
text amounts to practically a primary source on the movement because of Bancroft's
friendship with, and access to, many old vigilante leaders, including the greatest of
them all, William T. Coleman. Despite Bancroft's strong and open bias in favor of the
vigilantes, the book remains not only the largest but the best published treatment of
the 1856 vigilance committee.

[5] Perhaps the most notable example of a vigilance committee outside of California,
which modeled itself on the San Francisco committee of 1856, was that of Virginia
City, Montana in 1863–1864.

ing — and unsuccessful — quest for solutions to the problems of a new urban America.[6]

Ethnically, there was perhaps no more cosmopolitan city anywhere in the Western world of the 1850's than San Francisco. Virtually all strains were represented in the population. Old-stock Americans; English, Scotch, and Irish; French, Germans, Italians, and Scandinavians; Mexicans, South Americans, Polynesians, and Australians; Jews, Negroes, Chinese, and many more were present. Many ethnic and religious groups had their own special societies and newspapers.[7] The French had not merely one newspaper but four, and shortly after the height of the vigilante movement even a Negro newspaper hit the streets.[8]

In official pronouncements and editorials there was much ethnic tolerance and good will,[9] but under the surface ethnic hostility was rife. To a great extent, the political alignments of San Francisco represented the ethnic tensions of the fast-growing city. The Democratic Party was split into two wings. One faction was

----

[6] In San Francisco in the 1850's the contrast between the old and the new vigilantism is graphically revealed. The San Francisco vigilance committee of 1851 arose mainly in response to an orthodox crime problem stemming from Australian ex-convicts and other ne'er-do-wells. The vigilante movement of 1856 was in its objectives much more typical of the new vigilantism.

[7] Harris, Bogardus, and Labatt (comps.), *San Francisco City Directory for the year commencing October, 1856* ... (San Francisco, 1856), 129–132.

[8] *The Daily Town Talk* (San Francisco), Sept. 13, 1856. The four French newspapers were *Bibliotheque Populaire, Echo du Pacifique, Le Phare,* and *De La Chapelle.* Harris, *Directory,* 127; *Town Talk,* May 22, 1856. The *Town Talk* was founded in the spring of 1856 shortly before the vigilante movement got underway. Contrary to the implication of its title, the *Town Talk* was not a scandal or gossip sheet. Instead, it was a regular four-page daily, similar to the other leading dailies of San Francisco of the era. The *Town Talk* gave excellent coverage to the vigilante movement. Its editorial policy, like that of all the dailies of the city except the *Herald,* favored the vigilance committee.

[9] The vigilance committee itself gave lip-service to the ideal of brotherhood. Thus its motto was: "No creed. No party. No sectional issues." Bancroft was technically correct when he said that the vigilance committee was "composed of all classes and conditions of men" with every nationality, political and religious sentiment, trade, occupation, and profession represented. *Popular Tribunals,* II, 84–85 ,110. This was true, not surprisingly, in a movement of from 6,000 to 8,000 members; but the important point is that the movement was strongly dominated by merchants and old-stock Americans of Northern origin and of Whig, Know Nothing, or Republican politics with relatively few Irish or Catholics among the membership.

Southern-oriented, but the dominant wing was the machine of
David C. Broderick. Broderick was an aggressive political operator
from New York City who introduced the system of New York
ward politics into San Francisco.[10] The Broderick machine dominated the city by ballot-box stuffing, manipulation, and the strong-
arm election efforts of Irish Catholic "shoulder strikers" from the
East.[11] It ran roughshod over the opposition of the Know Nothings
who had inherited much of the old-stock appeal of the fading Whig
Party. There is no doubt that the Broderick faction looked to the
Irish and the Catholics, and to the black-leg and laboring elements
of the population, for the nucleus of its strength.

San Francisco was a seething cauldron of social, ethnic, religious, and political tensions in an era of booming growth. In the
short space of seven years — from 1849 to 1856 — the city had bal-
looned to a population of 50,000.[12] Streets were built, municipal
services established, the shoreline improved, and wharves constructed. But all this was done at the cost of enormous payments to
the Broderick machine. Huge salaries, rampant graft, a soaring
municipal debt, depreciating city scrip, and rising taxes were the
signs of fast approaching municipal bankruptcy.[13] By 1855 the
municipal budget had skyrocketed to $2,500,000.

It was against this background that the vigilance committee
of 1856 arose. The story begins in October, 1855, with the launch-

---

[10] John Myers Myers, *San Francisco's Reign of Terror* (New York, 1966), 35–36,
68–69.

[11] Bancroft, *Popular Tribunals*, II, 1–21. Professor David A. Williams of Long Beach
State College, who is preparing a badly needed biographical study of Broderick, has
told me that he feels that Broderick had a good deal of social consciousness in regard
to his Irish Catholic and mainly lower class adherents in San Francisco. From my own
knowledge of Broderick I believe that this was probably so, and it is not incompatible
with the sort of ward tactics Broderick used to dominate San Francisco politics in
the 1850's.

[12] Myers, *San Francisco's Reign of Terror*, 80. J. P. Young, *San Francisco: A History
of the Pacific Metropolis* (San Francisco, [1913]), I, 216.

[13] See the exposé in the form of a front-page, three-column report from the executive
committee of the vigilantes: "Official Corruption," San Francisco *Daily Evening Bulletin,* July 14, 1856. This is one of the key documents in the vigilante episode. See also
Young, *San Francisco,* I, 216.

ing of the San Francisco *Daily Evening Bulletin* under the excited editorship of James King of William.[14] King gave his readers one sensational editorial after another in which he blasted the alleged conditions of crime and corruption in the city.[15] Then, on November 17, 1855, an Italian Catholic gambler named Charles Cora fatally shot the U.S. Marshal, William Richardson.[16] When Cora's trial ended in a hung jury in January, 1856, King's flaming editorials in the *Bulletin* roused San Franciscans to a white heat. King had been a San Francisco vigilante in 1851, and the threat of vigilante justice frequently appeared in his columns.[17]

By the spring of 1856 King had created a near-panic psychology in San Francisco with his fulminations against the Broderick machine. Laying claim to a martyr's halo in advance, King predicted time and again that his enemies would get him. Finally on May 14, 1856, his prediction came true when he was shot and fatally wounded by James P. Casey, an Irish Catholic political manipulator and erstwhile inmate of Sing Sing prison.[18] The shooting of King hit San Francisco with sledge-hammer impact. The very next day the vigilance committee was organized by William T. Coleman and other leading merchants of the city, who were determined that Casey would not escape retribution as Cora had thus far.[19]

---

[14] The Huntington Library has a complete file of the *Bulletin* for the years 1855–1856 which the writer used. The *Bulletin,* especially the editorials of King, are crucial for an understanding of the fears and anxieties which gave rise to the vigilance committee of 1856. Had his newspaper career not been cut short before it had fairly gotten started, I am confident that King would have become one of the famous journalists in American history. King had been a failure in business but had found his metier in journalism. He was a remarkably trenchant, even demagogic, editor, and he took San Francisco by storm in the months before his death. Although it is a favorable treatment, *Villains and Vigilantes: The Story of James King of William and Pioneer Justice in California* (New York, 1961) by Stanton A. Coblentz does not adequately explain the martryred editor.

[15] For examples, see especially these issues of the *Bulletin:* Oct. 13, 16, and Dec. 27, 1855; Jan. 4, 8, 22, Feb. 2, and Apr. 1, 3, 1856.

[16] *Bulletin,* Nov. 19, 1855.

[17] See, for example, *Bulletin,* Nov. 20, 22, 24, and Dec. 12, 1855; Jan. 8, 17, 1856.

[18] On Casey's background see *Bulletin,* Nov. 5, 1855.

[19] Bancroft, *Popular Tribunals,* II, 69ff. *Bulletin* and *Town Talk,* May 15, 1856.

Within a matter of days the vigilantes tried and hanged both Casey and Cora. Two months later they hanged two more;[20] altogether they expelled twenty-eight men. Meanwhile, thousands of San Franciscans flocked to join the vigilance committee. Soon its membership was approaching its peak figure of 6,000 to 8,000.[21] It was well understood at the time, and cannot be emphasized too strongly, that the vigilance committee was dominated lock, stock, and barrel by the leading merchants of San Francisco who controlled it through an executive committee.[22] In this body, William T. Coleman, one of the leading importers of the city, had near-dictatorial powers as president of the organization.[23] The papers of the vigilance committee have survived today in the manuscript collection of the Huntington Library, and countless documents testify to its strongly mercantile ethos. It was a highly rationalized movement with everything organized to the last degree. Nothing was overlooked by the directing businessmen, who had the same passion for order and system in the running of a lynch-law movement as they had in their own commercial affairs.

It was this passion for order and system that caused the vigilantes to use printed forms for membership applications. Out of a total membership of 6,000 to 8,000 some 2,500 applications have survived in the Huntington Library collection.[24] These constitute an unique file in the history of American vigilantism and provide a

---

20 *Town Talk,* July 30, 1856.

21 In the *Century Magazine* of November, 1891, Coleman put the membership at about 8,000 (p. 145). The 1856 sources on the vigilance committee estimated its military force as being about 6,000. The file of applications for membership documents the frequent contemporary assertion that each vigilante was assigned a number. The highest number that I have seen in the Committee of Vigilance Papers in the Huntington Library is 5,757.

22 Bancroft, *Popular Tribunals,* II, 80–81, 117–118, 121, 125–126, 418. Letter from "Cosmos" in *Bulletin,* June 6, 1856. All contemporary sources attest mercantile domination.

23 Bancroft, *Popular Tribunals,* II, 86–87 and *passim.* See also James A. B. Scherer, *"The Lion of the Vigilantes": William T. Coleman and the Life of Old San Francisco* (Indianapolis and New York, 1939).

24 Box labeled "Applications for Membership, 1856," Committee of Vigilance Papers, Huntington Library.

rather complete picture of the make-up of the 1856 committee. In addition to his name, each applicant was required to state his age, occupation, where he was from, and where he lived in San Francisco. On the basis of the data in these applications, it can be said, in general, that the vigilance committee was composed of young men in their twenties and thirties. Virtually every ethnic strain, American state, and country of Europe was represented, but the American membership was predominantly from the northeastern United States from Maine to Maryland. There were also strong contingents from Germany and France. Significantly, few Irishmen were members. The fact that the bulk of the membership was drawn from the North Atlantic basin — that is, from the coastal states of the northeastern United States and from such western European countries as France, Germany, England, and Scotland — seems to reflect the maritime orientation and origin of so much of San Francisco's population. As to occupation, the vigilantes came largely from the ranks of the city's merchants, tradesmen, craftsmen, or their young employees. Laborers were in a scant minority, and gamblers were forbidden to join.[25]

The mercantile complexion of the vigilance committee is the key to its behavior. The merchants of San Francisco were dependent on Eastern connections for their credit.[26] Like most businessmen, the San Francisco merchants had a consuming interest in their own credit ratings and the local tax rate. In the eyes of Eastern businessmen, San Francisco economic stability was being jeopardized by

---

[25] These generalizations are made upon the basis of my analysis of each one of the approximately 2,500 applications. Internal evidence indicates that virtually all of the applications were accepted. Only one was marked as rejected. It is likely that most of the rejected applications were not retained in this file. Thus the approximately 2,500 applications represent the same number of members or from about 30% to 40% of the entire membership, depending upon whether 6,000 or 8,000 is accepted as the figure for the total membership. For statistical purposes, the 2,500 applications represent a more than adequate sample of the vigilante membership.

[26] For the anxieties which this could cause, see the article, "Steamer Day," in *Town Talk*, Oct. 5, 1856. Steamers left San Francisco every two weeks for the East with remittances for Eastern creditors. The attempt of San Francisco businessmen to raise money for the Steamer Day sailings had economic reverberations throughout the entire city.

the soaring municipal debt, rising taxes, and approaching bankruptcy under the Broderick machine. The spectre of municipal
bankruptcy made Eastern creditors fearful that the city was on the
verge of economic chaos. The restoration of confidence in San Francisco's municipal and financial stability was a *sine qua non*. It had
to be accomplished — and in such a way that would let Easterners
know that conservative, right-thinking men had definitely gained
control.[27] Fiscal reform at the municipal level was thus basic to the
vigilante movement. But in order to bring about fiscal reform it was
first necessary to smash David C. Broderick's machine.

Vigilante violence was the means used to destroy the Broderick
organization. Consider the hanging of James P. Casey: Casey had
recently broken with Broderick, but he had formerly served him as
a hard-hitting election bully and manipulator. The execution of
Casey not only had done away with the assassin of James King of
William, but it put Broderick's Irish Catholic political henchmen
on notice of the sort of fate that might await them. Even more
important was the banishment of the twenty-eight men, for it was
their expulsion that really broke the back of Broderick's power.
After the hangings of Casey and Cora, the vigilance committee
organized sub-committees and methodically went about collecting
evidence of ballot-box stuffing, election fraud, and municipal corruption.[28] The Irish Catholic "shoulder strikers" and bully boys
who had bossed elections were rounded up, jailed, tried, and sen-
tenced to expulsion from California. Broderick himself was called
before the committee. There were rumors that he would be hanged
or banished, but this the committee did not quite dare. Broderick
was released, but he had the wisdom to leave quickly for sanctuary
in the mountains.[29]

---

[27] Following the executions of Casey and Cora, the effects of further vigilante actions
were anticipated in *Town Talk*, May 28, 1856: "The 'reign of terror' is working our
redemption, and California stocks will rise in the market when this news reaches
the Atlantic."

[28] Extensive testimony and evidence are in "Papers relating to Ballot Box Stuffing and
Fraudulent Elections, 1854–1856," a box of 112 pieces in Committee of Vigilance
Papers.

[29] *[*James O'Meara*]*, *The Vigilance Committee of 1856* (San Francisco, 1887), 46–56.

Broderick would come back to San Francisco another day, but when he returned his chief lieutenants would be gone — put aboard ships for foreign or Eastern ports with the warning never to re-appear. To understand what happened, it is only necessary to consider the names of those expelled. A Celtic tinge is unmistakable. Among the twenty-eight banished were Michael Brannegan, Billy Carr, John Cooney, John Crowe, T. B. Cunningham, Martin Gallagher, James Hennessey, Terrence Kelly, James R. Maloney, Billy Mulligan, and Thomas Mulloy.[30] The most famous of all — Broderick's trusted aide, Ned McGowan — ran for his life.[31] Thought to be implicated in the shooting of James King of William, McGowan was sought for hanging by the vigilantes. He escaped to Santa Barbara with neck unstretched but would no more turn out the vote for Broderick.[32]

With the Broderick machine in ruins, it was time to put something in its place. On August 11 the leaders of the vigilance committee initiated a political reform movement which they called the People's Party.[33] The People's Party represented the consummation of the movement that began with hangings and banishments. The violent, illegal phase of the vigilance committee lasted only three months, from its organization on May 15 to its disbanding with a grand review and parade on August 18.[34] The legal, political phase of the movement, on the other hand, lasted for ten years — until

---

[30] *Town Talk*, Oct. 5, 1856; Bancroft, *Popular Tribunals*, II, 590–609.

[31] The colorful story of Ned McGowan is ably told by John Myers Myers in *San Francisco's Reign of Terror* (New York, 1966) on the basis of good research. Despite the deceptive title, this book is really a biography of McGowan with heavy emphasis on the vigilante period. Myers grossly overrates McGowan as a writer and at times exaggerates his importance, but Myers' anti-vigilante interpretation, in contrast to that of the predominant pro-vigilante historians, is refreshing and realistic.

[32] A prominent "shoulder striker" and election manipulator, Yankee Sullivan, would have undoubtedly been banished had he not died, allegedly by suicide, while in vigilante custody. *Town Talk*, May 31, 1856. Bancroft, *Popular Tribunals*, II, 649 states that it was "roughly estimated" that eight hundred of the "worst characters" voluntarily left San Francisco because of the vigilante action. Included were "thieves, murderers, corrupters of public morals, gamblers, prize-fighters, ballot-box stuffers, loafers, and vagabonds."

[33] *Town Talk*, Aug. 9, 12, 1856.

[34] *Bulletin*, Aug. 18, 19, 1856.

1866 — during which time the People's Party controlled the politics of San Francisco.

The call for the mass meeting that founded the People's Party and the resolutions adopted at it, although mentioning crime, put the emphasis on municipal financial reform. Great complaint was made of "heavy taxes filched from honest industry," of the near prostration of city and county credit, and of the vast sums that went into the pockets of office-holding drones. The plea was made that the best men of the city give their attention to levying taxes and making public appropriations. An "economical administration of the public funds" was demanded. Close control of salaries and fees was stipulated.[35]

The call for the meeting had been signed by virtually the entire corps of San Francisco merchants. The "Committee of 21," which was chosen to make People's Party nominations, was firmly dominated by merchants. On September 16 the committee published its slate of candidates. It was a large list but chosen very carefully so as to give full representation to the business enterprises, trades, and professions of San Francisco. The appeal of the slate was to the commercial occupations of the city rather than to religious or ethnic groups.[36]

It was unmistakably a vigilante-dominated ticket. In the first place, support of the vigilance committee was demanded of the entire list of People's Party candidates. Beyond that, some of the leading vigilantes were put at the head of the ticket. Charles Doane, the commander of the vigilance committee's 5,000-man military force, was nominated for sheriff. Other prominent vigilantes ran for chief of police and the state legislature.[37] The People's Party forbore making a choice in the Presidential race between Buchanan, Fremont, and Fillmore, but its sympathies were clearly Republican. In fact, the opportunistic young Republican Party of San Francisco made its support of the vigilance committee a principal appeal

[35] *Town Talk,* Aug. 9, 12, 1856.

[36] *Daily Alta California* (San Francisco), Aug. 9, 1856; *Town Talk,* Aug. 12, Sept. 16, 1856.

[37] *Town Talk,* Sept. 16, Nov. 4, 1856.

in the election. The Republicans endorsed all People's Party municipal and county candidates, and in return gained endorsement of
their state and national candidates who greatly benefited from vigilante votes.[38] In time, most of the leading vigilantes became Republicans in state and national politics.

The result of all of this was a smashing victory for the People's
Party in the November general election. It buried the weakened
Democratic opposition by margins that often ran as high as two to
one. Not a single People's Party candidate was defeated. The
reformers carried the entire city with the exception of the waterfront first ward. Even the sixth ward — formerly a Broderick
machine stronghold — went heavily into their column.[39]

In terms of a lower tax rate and lower municipal expenditures,
the People's Party delivered on its promises. It drastically slashed
municipal expenditures from a height of $2,500,000 in 1855 to
$353,000 in 1857.[40] For ten years the People's Party held the gov-
ernment, mainly on the basis of its platform of keeping the tax rate
down.[41] In proudly reviewing the history of the vigilance committee
from the vantage point of 1891, William T. Coleman was in no
doubt as to the significance of its offspring. The People's Party, he
said, introduced a "new era" into San Francisco life by lowering
taxation and introducing "economies" which "radically reduced"
the municipal debt. "The credit of the city, State, and people, which
before all was uncertain," wrote Coleman, "soon after took a foremost rank, which has since been finally held and maintained."[42]
Coleman's statement emphasizes that vigilante action and People's
Party fiscal reform raised the credit rating not only of the city but
of the "people." By "people" Coleman meant San Francisco's businessmen — such as himself — who were crucially dependent on
Eastern lenders and suppliers.

---

[38] *Bulletin,* Oct. 9, 11, 1856.

[39] *Bulletin,* Nov. 25, 1856.

[40] Young, *San Francisco,* I, 216.

[41] *Ibid.,* 104.

[42] *Century Magazine,* XLIII (November 1891), 145.

To what extent did conditions of crime lead the businessmen of San Francisco to employ the traditional penalties of hanging and banishment that were often used by frontier vigilantes? In their rhetoric both James King of William and the vigilantes in the early stages of their movement made much of a supposed crime problem. Did the reality support the rhetoric? The crime news in the San Francisco newspapers of 1855–1856 indicates that the regular organs of law and order had crime fully under control.[43] The main thrust of the vigilante movement was not against crime but was directed toward smashing the political machine of Broderick and the Irish Catholic Democrats and establishing one of its own.

This raises another question. If political reform was fundamentally the main concern of the vigilantes, why did they not try that in the first place? The answer of the vigilantes to contemporaries who asked that very question was that there was no possibility of political reform at the polls, since the corrupt element simply stuffed the ballot boxes and counted out the opposition. Hence, the vigilantes claimed, they were forced to take the law into their own hands.[44] That was their answer, but it is too simple.

---

[43] Despite King's fulminations in the editorial columns, my survey of the police news columns in the *Bulletin* and *Town Talk* during the fall, winter, and spring of 1855–1856 has convinced me that the San Francisco crime problem was under control. King was outraged at the hung jury in the murder trial of Charles Cora, but the circumstances surrounding Cora's killing of Richardson leave the real possibility that it could have been in self-defense. That Cora went free does not seem to be a reflection on San Francisco justice. At another level, King's crusade against wide-open houses of prostitution in San Francisco showed a commendable regard on his part for the general conditions of morality in the city, but the news of arrests and convictions indicate that any overt crime stemming from the latitude of life in a wide-open city was kept well under control. Vigilante leaders had sufficient confidence in the regular system that in the summer of 1856, while the vigilance committee had an iron grip on the city, they allowed the police officers and courts to enforce law in a regular way. The vigilance committee restricted itself to four hangings, investigation of the Broderick machine, and banishment of its leading operatives. For some examples of regular law enforcement in San Francisco during the height of the vigilante period, see *Town Talk*, May 28, 29, 30, 31, 1856. See also Joseph L. King, "The Vigilance Committee of '56," *Overland Monthly*, LXVIII (July-December 1918), 519.

[44] *Town Talk*, June 10, 15, 1856. The vigilantes made much of their discovery of a ballot box with false bottom which had been used for stuffing purposes by Yankee Sullivan in the interest of Ned McGowan, Charles Duane, and other Broderick stalwarts. See Bancroft, *Popular Tribunals*, II, 6–8 where the false ballot box is described and sketched.

Implicitly, the reason why the reform-minded businessmen of San Francisco first resorted to vigilante violence rather than political action stemmed from the perennial problem of reformers: the difficulty of organizing apathetic and indifferent voters against an organized and entrenched political machine. Yet in the fall of 1856 the vigilantes did triumph at the polls by a two-to-one count. No amount of skullduggery by Broderick's henchmen could have overcome such an overwhelming majority.

The final question, then, is why did not the vigilantes invoke that overwhelming sentiment for reform in the first place and save themselves the trouble of the hangings and banishments? The answer, of course, is that it took the vigilance committee itself to break through the crust of apathy and bring about a mass movement for reform.

Before the founding of the vigilance committee there simply was no reform organization in San Francisco. In order to carry out the banishments and executions, the vigilance committee enrolled thousands of members. Since they had to control a large city and since they feared that the governor might raise a militia force against them,[45] the vigilante leaders felt it necessary to fashion a tightly organized movement with military discipline. Thus vigilantes were enrolled in military companies of fifty to one hundred members which, in turn, were organized into battalions and regiments. The companies, battalions, and regiments all had officers.[46] The rank and file of the vigilantes elected representatives to an Assembly of Delegates of about 150 members, and the president of the vigilance committee in turn named an executive committee of about forty members.[47] The military establishment was headed by a grand marshal,[48] the president and the executive committee exer-

---

[45] *Town Talk,* June 4, 5, 1856.

[46] Bancroft, *Popular Tribunals,* II, 87–111. The names of vigilante officers were printed in the newspapers. A convenient listing of the officers, down to the level of the captains who commanded the companies, is in Samuel Colville, *Colville's 1856–1857 San Francisco Directory: Volume I: for the year commencing October, 1856* . . . (San Francisco, 1856), 226–227.

[47] Bancroft, *Popular Tribunals,* II, 113.

[48] *Colville's Directory for 1856,* 226–227.

cised autocratic control over the movement, and the Assembly of
Delegates functioned merely as an organ for voicing rank and
file opinion.[49]

Thus the vigilance committee — organized in pyramidal,
chain-of-command fashion and based on primary units of fifty to
one hundred members — was ideally constituted for success in an
election campaign. To win a smashing victory at the polls, all the
People's Party leadership had to do was to draw upon the vigilante
apparatus — and that is exactly what it did.

Seen superficially, the San Francisco vigilantes were faced with
the familiar problem of a corrupt Irish Catholic Democratic political
machine. Their solution was to crush it. But in Broderick's approach
to government, and in his appeal to the voters and his concept of
municipal life, there was something more basic than boodle. At
issue in the San Francisco of the 1850's were the same unresolved
questions that came to typify American cities. Could gigantic urban
improvements be made only at the cost of wholesale corruption?[50]
In ethnically mixed cities, would newcomers of minority-group
status — Irish, Italians, Catholics, Jews, and others — be fully
absorbed into American life, or would they be permanently condemned to economic degradation and social inferiority?[51]

To complex problems such as these the vigilance committee's
starkly simple response of hanging and banishment was tragically
inappropriate — tragic for the victims, of course, but tragic also for
the vigilantes who thought they were solving something when they
really were not. From his viewpoint of 1891 William T. Coleman

---

[49] Bancroft, *Popular Tribunals,* II, 109–113; *Town Talk,* Aug. 8, 1856.

[50] Seymour J. Mandelbaum in *Boss Tweed's New York* (New York, [1965]), 46–47,
has pointed out that this was a major problem in New York City after the Civil War.
The similarities between the problems of San Francisco in the 1850's and New York
after the Civil War are striking. The Tammany machine in New York, like the
Broderick machine in San Francisco, produced similar reactions although in New York
incipient vigilante movements never got to the point of taking the law into their
own hands.

[51] This problem has been of major concern in important studies by Oscar Handlin,
John Higham, Barbara Miller Solomon, Stephan Thernstrom, Moses Rischin, David
Brody, Gunther Barth, and others.

complacently believed that the vigilance committee of 1856 had left San Francisco a permanent legacy of civic virtue and fiscal integrity. But he spoke too soon, for San Francisco was at that very time on the eve of the most turbulent period in its history: the era of the monumentally corrupt regime of Boss Ruef and Mayor Schmitz and the reform crusade of Fremont Older, Francis J. Heney, and Hiram Johnson.

The vigilantes of 1856 were on the right track when they abandoned the rope for the ballot box, but their People's Party reform movement was much too narrowly concerned with fiscal matters to achieve any lasting solutions to San Francisco's problems. The vigilantes never had a real understanding of the fundamental issues involved.

The new vigilantism, of which the vigilance committee of 1856 was a harbinger, was one of the birth pains of urban America. But for the problems of the new America it was a symptom rather than a solution.

THE PROSPECTORS:

SOME CONSIDERATIONS

ON THEIR CRAFT*

by

OTIS E. YOUNG (JR.)

Professor of history at Arizona State University since 1963, the author earned the A.B., M.A., and Ph.D. degrees at Indiana University. His publications include *The First Military Escort on the Santa Fe Trail, The West of Philip St. George Cooke, How They Dug the Gold,* and several articles on the military and mining frontiers.

PROSPECTING on the old frontier was an art — an art which was learned by apprenticeship, discussion, and experience, but seldom from documents. It is my purpose to present here some idea of the rudiments of that art — to show the frontier prospector at work, as it were — to give some idea of the devices by which he looked for gold, silver, or whatever else Nature might provide — to tell how he knew what he had found and how he occasionally improved upon Nature's bounty when it came to selling what he had discovered.

---

*This paper is an abridgement of the first chapter of a book approaching completion and tentatively titled *Western Mining*. Annotation is omitted here, but the author would be glad to supply references to anyone desirous of learning his authorities. The paper has been checked for technical accuracy by Robert Lenon, P.E., of Patagonia, Arizona.

[121]

Prospecting is, by definition, as old as the Bronze Age and considerably older than written history. From ancient times to nearly the modern, its principles were not only unwritten but actually kept as trade secrets. We have some ideas as to how the ancient prospectors worked, but virtually no idea of what they thought about their methods. Prospectors and miners were usually slaves, but always socially impossible, and the classical writers were invariably gentlemen who seldom drank out of the same jug with the men with mud on their boots. What is written by the philosophers about mineral-finding is usually clap-trap, though now and then some writer like Agatharchides actually observed miners at work and recorded what he saw. But he also usually made a sad mess of interpreting what it was he had seen.

We do know that prospecting goes better in some places than in others. Climate has a great deal to do with the matter. Where there is rain, snow, permafrost, or ocean, the ground is concealed from the eye, and effective survey prevented, unless it be streambank placering. This leaves chiefly desert, and it is not a coincidence that until recently most of the great mineral strikes have been made in deserts or veldt country. On this account, the ancient writers supposed that abundant sunshine somehow created mineralization, not realizing that they were engaged in *post hoc* rationalization.

Not just any desert will do. The prospector knows instinctively that he will stand a better chance of finding something in up-and-down country where subterranean forces have been actively at work, both to bring up mineralization and to exhibit it. But not just any rugged desert terrain is suitable, either. Where the activity has been basic — that is, where the rocks are brown-black, and show the characteristics of basalt or free-flowing lava — the prospector goes quietly away. He knows that he will find little there. What he seeks is *acidic* country — places where the mountains shine white, as evidence that large percentages of silica have been deposited. Silica is a very efficient trap of mineralization, and a prospector can no more pass an exposed quartz outcrop without a close look than a small boy can walk past a candy store with his eyes averted.

In this sort of country, the rock is colorful. It has all the hues of the rainbow in striking primary colors, and the rocks are shot through with veins and shoots and innumerable threadlets of quartz. Its shapes are jumbled and irrational, and there is an indescribable "burned" appearance caused by the presence of iron. To be sure, mineralization can be found in the flat strata and dull pastels of sedimentary rock — it can be found literally anywhere, for that matter — but the finding is difficult and requires special techniques.

This much was known to prehistoric man. It was disseminated throughout the known world by the Phoenicians, and the tradition preserved by the Greeks and Romans. A medieval repository of such knowledge was Spain, and the Spaniards brought with them to the New World a considerable body of prospecting tradition. This was passed on to the American mineral frontier, as witnessed by the large vocabulary of Spanish terms used by Americans. Another great, but almost ignored, source of prospecting tradition was the Appalachian South, particularly Georgia, where low-grade gold placers and soft lodes had been worked since Revolutionary times. The theme of Georgia runs like a thread through the history of early Western prospecting. John H. Gregory and William Green Russell of Colorado were Georgians by birth; Georgians discovered Butte; Isaac Humphreys of Georgia introduced the American-style placer pan to the California diggings. A third source of prospecting lore was Cornwall, where by repute the pure Phoenician canon was introduced in early Classical times and improved by the Cornish. They in turn swarmed to America by the thousands during the 1850's, and such mining and prospecting terms as are not Spanish will almost certainly have Cornish roots.

Armed with these traditions, the American prospector went forth to seek what he could find. As a rule, the first mineral discovery in a given district would occur by accident. An Indian — and the Indians were great mineral-finders — might trade a gold nugget, usually for whiskey, and prospectors would start poking around the territory. As a rule, the prospector kept three sets of criteria in mind: terrain forms, which indicated quartz veins; "blossom," or the color of metallic salts "painted" upon an outcrop; and "float," or mineral particles eroded from an outcrop and concentrated in a wash by stream action. Each was sought in its own way, and it is not too much to say that the prospector should have a soldier's eye for terrain, an artist's sense of color, and a gopher's ability to dig. Luck also helped considerably, but this could be neither taught nor learned.

Such terrain forms as white mountains of quartz can be seen for miles, shining like snow. There is one a little north of Phoenix, Arizona, on the road to Pinnacle Peak — but it has no values, alas! But another one is found a few miles south of Tonopah, Nevada, where there stands alone and conspicuous among the dreary basalt ranges one hill which shines white from afar. It is almost pure vitreous quartz, and with such a beacon to mineralization the wonder is that Tonopah's silver and nearby Goldfield's gold were not discovered until the turn of the twentieth century.

But smaller terrain anomalies were the first to be investigated, since these hinted that the rock therein was either harder or softer than the surrounding country-rock and hence probably of differing composition. These have been systematized as (1) a trench or ditch that does not run directly down the slope of the hill or mountain; (2) a sudden change of slope: (3) a sharp notch that crosses a ridge which has a rather uniform altitude on both sides of the notch; (4) several springs of water in a line with each other; (5) a sudden change in kind or quantity of vegetation; and (6) a change in the nature of the rock fragments. The prospector lifted his eyes to exposed rock walls, where the formations were obligingly laid bare to provide a geological cross-section which could be surveyed at a glance. Free-standing dikes of rock, winding about the flanks of the hills, were of interest. He did not like uniformity in the country-rock, no matter what its composition, but preferred instead the confused, commingled varieties displaying igneous quartz threads adjacent to metamorphosed sediments.

The prospector was particularly interested in color, and his heart beat faster when he found the "blossom" of mineral salts "painted" upon a ledge or outcrop. Such blossom was usually of

deep, bright primary shades: the brown-to-yellow of iron, the blue
or green of copper, the black of manganese, the light yellow of
molybdenum or lead, and the lilac of cobalt. The color not only
indicated mineralization but was frequently a good clue to the sort
of values in the lode. The rusty brown of hematite (iron oxide) was
usually regarded as a signpost of gold, for gold is quite often associated at depth with the iron pyrites (iron sulphide) which weathers
down into hematite. The Tough Nut silver lode at Tombstone,
covered entirely by rubble, was traced nonetheless by the deep
brown fan of hematite which had spread downward from its outcrop. The blue and green of copper chlorides and carbonates hinted
at silver; wicked old Panamint was discovered by observation of
a cliff glowing with their peacock shades.

  Indeed, any intense color *except* metallic yellow called for
investigation. For the most part, a lemon yellow was but the salt
of the useless laboratory metal, uranium. If metallic in glint, it was
almost certainly copper pyrite or iron pyrite, the "fool's gold" of
legend, unless it were the even more worthless sheets of mica.
When in doubt, eye, hand, and teeth could instantly discern the
difference between the false and the real article. Pyrite "blinked";
that is, if the sample was rotated slightly in the light, its plane crystal
surfaces would wink or change their reflective pattern. Gold specks,
on the other hand, were rounded and had a steady, less brassy
shimmer. Another test was to place a crumb of the suspect substance
on a hard, flat surface and tap it lightly with a hammer or knife
handle. The extraordinarily malleable gold would merely flatten,
whereas pyrite would shatter into dust. Finally, a bit of the dust
taken between the teeth would feel distinctly gritty if spurious;
gold felt "softer" and produced no gritty sensation. Still and all, the
very presence of pyrite indicated *some* mineralization, whereas mica
was no indication at all.

  If nothing tangible could be discerned by a visual survey of
otherwise promising country, the prospector was still by no means
at a loss. Feeling in his bones that something worthwhile ought to
be about, he would hunt up a suitable camp site, make himself and

his burro comfortable, then lay out his tools in preparation for a search for "float." This term embraced mineral particles and scales eroded from a lode and carried away by water action. By finding float and tracing it back to its point of origin, the prospector might well discover some sort of lode. In dealing with float (from one viewpoint, all placering was nothing but dealing with float), one either found it by accident — in drab outwash gravel, mineral float tended to stick out like a sore thumb — or sought it with deliberation. When found, its physical condition was significant. Round, smooth float hinted at much abrasion by wind and water, and hence a long journey from the point of origin. If the float were rough and angular, there had been little abrasion; hence the source might not be far from the point of discovery. The obvious next step was to estimate the direction and distance of that travel.

If float was sought with deliberation, the prospector commenced operations at the head of a promising wash or arroyo because any heavy minerals there would be nearer the surface and because heavy float tends to "dig itself in" the farther it travels downstream. With pick and shovel, he dug his "prospect hole" down to the bedrock, saving soil specimens from the lower layers. If water was absent, he subjected his gleanings to "dry washing"; that is, he spread out a sheet, then gently picked and puffed at the sample upon it until the lighter constituents had been blown away, leaving only the heaviest fragments behind. If water was handy, he was content to pan a shovelful of dirt, washing away the light soil over the edge with circular, gently flipping movements until perhaps half a spoonful of residue was left. Either way, the prospector was most often rewarded with nothing. Now and then, however, he would be encouraged by a procession of gold specks, or the black granules of silver chlorides, in the "drag" of the pan.

The residue on the sheet or in the pan determined the next course of the prospector's action. Should the particles be other than free gold, it was essential to determine whether they were metallic, and if so, what metal or metals were present. In other words, a qualitative determination was in order even though specific colors might convey some strong hints. The prospector collected sufficient particles to fill a spoon, dried them, and scraped them into the cavity of a charcoal block. He covered the sample with a layer of bicarbonate of soda, then used a blowpipe and candle flame to smelt the batch. (Somewhat the same process could be approximated by burning the sample with damp gunpowder in a closed container, or just edging it into close proximity to a campfire's coals.) This reduced the mineral by driving off sulphur, chlorine, or carbonate, and left a metallic "bead" or "button" behind. The acid test, as it came to be called, would rapidly distinguish the white base metals from silver or gold. It is interesting to note that the silver wealth of the Comstock Lode was first encountered as an aggravating "black sand" which clogged the sluiceboxes of placermen in the vicinity; then later, when its volume grew so great in proportion to the free gold dust, this pale dust was christened "bogus gold." The prospectors knew so little of field assay work that none thought to apply the blowpipe and acid tests to see what it was they had actually encountered.

Some chemistry necessarily enters the picture at this point. Gold is usually found in the pure metallic form as "free-milling" gold, occasionally as tellurides or "black gold." Silver, on the other hand, is ordinarily found below-ground in a vein of sulphurets or "silver glance." Where such a vein crops out into the air, the atmosphere goes to work on it, gradually converting the metallic sulphurets into chlorides. These silver chlorides are detached by erosion, tumble away, and constitute float. The miner, of course, sought the vein or lode, but in the old West a class of men made a living of sorts scavenging the washes and dumps below the lodes for silver chlorides which they exhumed and sold to the mills. These people were called "chloriders," and it was not exactly a complimentary term.

Should the drag of the prospector's pan display a promising procession of gold specks, and should enough water be present to make placering worthwhile, the search often ended right there. But should the "color" be sparse, be covered with the ferric "rust" that inhibited efficient placering, show physical indications that it had come from a nearby vein, or be mixed with other heavy minerals, it might be best to abandon the prospect hole and go looking for the lode. Size and shape of the "color" was determined by scrutinizing the drags of several pansful, concentrated in the "horn-spoon" or its replacement, a small iron skillet sawed in half. Largish, rough dust indicated that the source was near at hand; flattened and "frayed" grains, or flour-like lenticular dust, proclaimed much peening on stream bottoms, and hence a long trip down and a prolonged search.

Should the point of origin not be immediately apparent, or should the country not afford a good hint as to lines of wash, the prospector employed statistical sampling methods, invented by his profession thousands of years before mathematicians thought of it. He began to dig like a gopher, taking dozens of scattered soil samples from as many upstream prospect holes and carefully washing or winnowing portions from each. After great labor, his mentally tabulated results showed that the holes within a given area held mineral float, and the holes to either side of the area did not. More digging amplified these findings, and at the end he could lay out an imaginary triangle in three dimensions. The apex ought to lie on the point of origin, even though it be concealed by talus or brush.

Out on the flat desert or up the cut-banks of a wash, the samples would narrow the area of search and, as one approached the lode, the gold might cease to be free, but instead be held in bits of gangue. Given luck, there it would be at the apex of search. Most often, it would be a greater or lesser ledge of perfectly conventional ore, none of which would appear at all attractive to the inexperienced eye unless, as occasionally happened, water and weathering had purified and concentrated chunks of pure "native" metal on the surface. Some of the best gold-bearing quartz is rusty in appearance; "silver glance" is dingy yellow or greyish-white, much resembling a Chicago street pigeon.

Now and then, however, the strike would be something astounding and completely contrary to the prospector's understanding of nature. In Arizona Territory in 1863 the Peeples Party found a graveling of substantial gold nuggets exposed on the flat top of Rich Hill mesa, sometimes inelegantly known as the Potato Patch. As a rule, of course, nuggets are found next to the bedrock of watercourses, or at any rate in declivities, not roosting about on the tops of mesas. Nevertheless there they were, and the Peeples Party made off with the lot, scarcely pausing to give thanks. A reasonable explanation was presently vouchsafed, but the odds of the phenomenon being repeated are very, very slender.

Having found a mineralized lode of some potential, the first thing the prospector did was to knock off a chip, apply his wetted tongue to the raw surface to remove dust and highlight the contents, and look long and hard (in later days, with the help of a pocket magnifying glass) at the indications revealed: the specks of gold or thin black line of sulphurets. Indeed, the stigmata of the prospector might well have been a calloused tongue, since this organ was most prominent within his armentarium. When prospectors met, they did not exchange the Kiss of Peace but rock specimens, to which each clapped his tongue and peered intently before exchanging mutual congratulations and mental reservations.

If the saliva test augured well, the prospector set in train a rough field assay for the purpose of determining whether the ore would be worth working, always beginning with an egg-sized sample which experience showed would weigh so near one pound as to make no difference. (Incidently, prospectors seldom if ever encumbered themselves with balances and weights; if a weight was necessary one could make-do with fluid-ounce glasses of the heavy and durable construction which were readily obtainable in any settlement large enough to support a saloon.) To determine gold content alone, the sample was pulverized in an iron mortar or tubemill, then boiled vigorously with mercury, salt, and soda. The liquid was poured off, and the mercury amalgam washed free of the residues. The amalgam pill was then wrapped in a twist of paper or parchment, roasted on an iron shovel to drive off the mercury, and the bit of sponge gold remaining estimated with a knife-gauge.

To make a general determination of either gold or silver content, the prospector likewise began by pulverizing the ore sample.

He panned out the gangue, collected the drag, and dried it. If the only acid he had along was hydrochloric, he then had to smelt the sample with his blowpipe before dissolving it; if his acid was nitric, he could dispense with this step and proceed directly to add sample to the reagent, heating gently. All metals present except gold reacted to form soluble nitrates or chlorides. If nitrates, the prospector then added brine or salt to form metallic chlorides. This produced a reaction in which insoluble silver chloride instantly precipitated as a white, milky cloud which rapidly turned purple-black in the presence of sunlight — the critical test for silver. Should this be the case, the black precipitate was filtered out, dried, and reduced by the blowpipe to form a bead or button of metallic silver. The bead was then gauged by a silver table-knife, whose blade tip had been sawed or filed into a very acute V-shaped angle. Cupel-buttons of various known weights, borrowed from the local assayer, were fitted into the angle to calibrate it. Rough marks were then scribed onto the blade, with appropriate legends for fast estimation of unknown beads.

Lead and copper content could also be determined by a few simple additional tests. Lead chloride would refuse to turn the dramatic black of silver, but would remain as a white suspension which could be slowly dissolved in twenty times its volume of water. Copper could be estimated by one of two methods, the older of which was to dip a bit of clean iron into the test-glass for a few minutes. If copper were present, it would reveal itself by coating the iron in a clearly distinguishable manner. Otherwise, crude ammonia poured into the solution would react with the copper present to turn the contents a theatrically bright blue.

Much has been made of the accidental discovery of rich lodes by animals. The stories take two general forms, of which the first is the uncovering of rich ore by an animal pawing or grazing about. The second involves the throwing of a rock, usually at a recalcitrant stray, which reveals intriguing contents upon being picked up or broken open. There is in fact little enough to such stories. Among the few which survive close scrutiny, some common points appear. The incidents almost without exception occur in early morning at the camp site of the prospector or traveler, not while wandering in the open or while making camp at dusk. A camp site would usually be chosen with regard for vegetation, water, and shelter, that is, close up to an elevation or outcrop and a spring or running creek. In well-mineralized country, this is just the sort of place to go a-prospecting, particularly since ground water follows geological discontinuities every time. The suspicion grows, therefore, that if the animal's antics had not resulted in discovery, the morning's systematic search would have had the same results.

Normally a prospector only prospected; once he found a promising lode, he desired only to sell his claim to a mining syndicate, take his money, and go on a prolonged spree at some "hog ranch" near his base of operations. In some cases, of course, prospectors knew — worse, employed — ways of "improving" assay results. This was known as "salting." The prospector who was reasonably honest, however, simply measured the size of the vein, and with a geologist's hammer (or prospect pick, or a poll-pick of two-handed size) detached small chips clear across its face to form a representative sample. These chips were then bagged, carried back to what passed for civilization, and submitted to a professional assayer's attentions and presumably disinterested report.

With registration patent in one hand and assay certificate in the other (and, usually, a consuming thirst in between), the prospector now went in search of a buyer at the central oases where such persons congregated. When the two met, the proceedings were of a nature to shame a Levantine rug-peddler. The prospector inflated the value of his claim with all the art and forensic cunning in his power; the buyer automatically deprecated his words and his assay. That the assay was professionally certified was a fact to be gently waved aside. The buyer who did not personally visit the lode to get his own samples, plus an independent assay report thereon, would be regarded by the community as a cretin: any discovery was considered "salted" *per se* until proved otherwise beyond reasonable doubt.

"Salting" ranged from fairly harmless propaganda to operations such as the Great Diamond Hoax which were really imaginative and large-scale confidence games. In its least obnoxious form it consisted of taking for assay a single high-grade specimen of ore, rather than random samples, to be represented as "typical" of the discovery. This was understood and allowed for. On a more deceptive level, it involved deliberate sophistication of the quality of the ore, since it was virtually impossible to increase the apparent size of the face of the lode or outcropping. One method was to buy a wagonload of respectable ore from a going mine, and scatter it about the face of one's own property. A better effect could be had by loading a shotgun with gold dust and firing it into the face. Various gold solutions could be purchased and applied; one story tells of a salter who, while taking a patent kidney medicine containing gold chloride, regularly transferred his own assay content to that of his vein. For that matter, an honest assay of good tenor could be taken from an entirely different lode. Assayers themselves could be suborned, though this was a risky and one-shot operation.

The buyer avoided a great deal of trouble by going out personally to the claim, and insisting that the face be shot down and mucked out, making certain that he was on the spot during these operations, and that only he himself gathered the chips from the cleaned-off new face. But these specimens had to be guarded closely during their trip to a reputable assay office. One buyer thought he was well away with honest ore, not realizing that the drunken stranger who had stumbled and smashed a whiskey bottle over his sample bags was not intoxicated; nor did the bottle contain whiskey. Such *post facto* trickery could be avoided, however, by quietly including "blind" or clearly worthless samples; if these showed substantial values later, something was obviously amiss. Surprisingly enough, salted lodes were occasionally worked by the victims and made to pay well. The geological "indications" which had helped to fool them sometimes actually expanded into real values.

In its historical evolution, prospecting in a newly-discovered mineral region proceeded naturally from the low country to the back-country highlands, and in methodology from placering to hard-rock mining. Lowland placer diggings were easier for the first-

comer to work, since so much of the preliminary labor had already
been accomplished for him by Nature. Yet the temptation to press
upstream was great. When the prospector found a big nugget of
gold, he could barely stay long enough to eat lunch; he was sure
that the lode of origin was both near to hand and richer than the
proverbial "yard up a bull's throat." Neither assumption was necessarily correct. Nuggets could "grow" in a stream bed by a process of
melding and accretion, for one thing. For another, a thin lode could
erode off over the years to produce by natural concentration a high-
grade placer at its foot. Similarly, a "stockwork" vein system, such
as that at Rich Hill in Arizona, shot through with threadlets of gold,
might assay hundreds of dollars to the ton and yet not pay to work
because of the vast quantity of gangue present; still it might provide
good placering-ground at the point where it crops out. As a placer
district grew, however, it inevitably expanded upstream toward the
foothills, and it was never very long until someone was led to the
lodes from which the placer colors originated.

Employing the art he had mastered, the frontier prospector
combed the West in the second half of the nineteenth century. His
pursuit of the treasures of the earth was relentless; he left virtually
no stone unturned in his quest. Out of his storied searches grew
a myth that has persisted to this day: that of the prospector's con-
cealment of rich lodes — and their subsequent loss from the ken of
man — by covering them with rock or shooting down the adit. The
presumption here is that such lodes are lost for good, and will never
be recovered save by a person in possession of the appropriate map.
Quite to the contrary, this would not deceive for ten minutes any
prospector of experience. Given the slightest hint of the inevitable
downstream float from the original outcropping, he would head
for the "lost mine" like a bear for a bee-tree — and would have it
located and salted before the sun went down.

THE UMBRELLA AND THE MOSAIC:
THE FRENCH-ENGLISH PRESENCE
AND THE SETTLEMENT OF THE
CANADIAN PRAIRIE WEST

by

LEWIS G. THOMAS

Born near Okotoks, Alberta, the author received the bachelor's and master's degrees at the University of Alberta and the doctorate at Harvard. Except for wartime service in the Canadian navy, he has taught at the University of Alberta since 1938 and was head of its department of history for six years. His major work, *The Liberal Party in Alberta,* was published in 1958, following which he turned to work on a history of the province of Alberta. He also edited the notes for the re-publication of A. S. Morton's classic *History of the Canadian West to 1870–1.*

THE SETTLEMENT of Canada's prairie west coincides, though not exactly, with the century of Canadian development that has elapsed since Confederation in 1867. Confederation served two major purposes. The first was to create out of a number of British North American colonies a political entity capable of an existence separate from the United States. The second was to accommodate within that entity the presence of two major groups, one French-speaking, the other English-speaking. The purpose of this paper is to suggest that the arrangements necessary for this accommodation of the French-English presence, and the national policies and attitudes that grew out of these arrangements, influenced the Canadian pattern of prairie settlement.

The "mosaic" of the title is, of course, the pattern of prairie settlement; the "umbrella" is the French-English presence. The implication is that the "umbrella" has protected the "mosaic" from the fading, blurring, chipping, breaking and scuffing that would have reduced its pattern and its color to a dull and unexciting homogeneity, without either aesthetic interest or physical durability.

If this suggestion is acceptable, it seems to indicate a direction that research in the history of Canadian prairie settlement might profitably take. Though much has been done for particular ethnic groups, less has been said of the impact on them of the national policies under which their settlement took place. National policies are obviously of the first importance, since immigration, railways, agriculture, and, for the most significant period, public lands were all matters of federal concern. Such policies have been extensively discussed, but more from the point of view of the creation and maintenance of a political and economic than a cultural entity. It is conceivable that out of the operation of national policies in relation to prairie settlement, cultural values have arisen that, though regional in origin, are significant for Canada not only in her internal but in her external relationships.

There is in Canada a widely held view that in the United States the processes of history have produced a national character that can be recognized as distinctively American, as distinctive as the national character of the English, the French, the German, or the Greek. While it is recognized, even by the naive, that there are regional differences — that the southern Californian is distinguishable from the Vermonter — these differences are seen as much less than the sum of the resemblances that constitute being an American. It is also held that the establishment of this American norm took place fairly early in the history of the United States; and that its existence permitted the assimilation of an exceedingly polyglot immigration, mainly of European origin, into the distinctively American community. The crudity of this view will be instantly recognizable, but the point is that something like it is held by many Canadians of varying degrees of sophistication.

Many Canadians also hold that the existence of such a national

norm is essential to national survival, and a great deal of time and
thought has been devoted to the search for a norm of Canadianism.
There are obvious difficulties, the most obvious of all the fact that
a very large minority exists with a history, a cultural tradition, and
above all a language that differs substantially from those — and the
plural is important — of the majority. This minority, although
widely dispersed throughout Canada and with an historical presence in every part of the country, has an extremely strong geographical base in the province of Quebec, a vitally important part
of the country from the point of view of physical and human
resources. There the minority becomes an overwhelming and even
an aggressive majority. The norm of Canadianism, if it is to have
any meaning as the core of Canadian nationhood, must be acceptable to this minority. It seems perfectly clear at present that a
Canadianism analogous to what many other Canadians regard as
the American norm, essentially assimilative as that is, is not acceptable to the vast majority of French-speaking Canadians.

Assimilation to a single Canadian norm poses other problems
than the obdurate, but entirely comprehensible, distaste of a substantial element in the Canadian population. Some Canadians,
outside the French tradition, believe that a single norm of Canadianism would be for all practical purposes undistinguishable from
that which they believe to exist in the United States, and that the
achievement of such a norm would make nonsense of the continued
existence of Canada as a separate political entity. Those who hold
these views differ as to whether this is desirable. Some Canadians
undoubtedly regard the swallowing up of Canada by the great
republic to the south as inevitable and, consciously or unconsciously,
do not look upon this as a fate worse than death. Others, while considering the disappearance of a political Canada as inevitable, still
hope, rather vaguely perhaps, that the whale will, when the time
comes, either be a more socially acceptable whale or perhaps benefit
in health and temper from its ingestion of the northern Jonah.

A third group regards the continued separate existence of
Canada as desirable and is consciously opposed to what is called
Americanization, although there are marked differences within this

group as to which aspects of the American way present the greater menace to Canadianism. This group is not necessarily made up entirely of aging Colonel Blimps and their ladies. At one time it surely would have included a majority of French-speaking Canadians; nowadays this is not so sure. Certainly, however, anti-Americanism in the sense of hostility to political absorption into the United States has been historically a very powerful force in Canadian development. There has nevertheless been a wide, and perhaps an increasing, recognition that such a negative sentiment is an uncertain foundation on which to build a sense of nationality — this in spite of the numerous and illustrious precedents which exist in other countries whose national identities are no way in doubt.

The process of settlement in the Canadian West, from the Bay to the Pacific, has been conditioned by the tensions suggested here. Prior to confederation the Hudson's Bay Company fought a skillful holding action against settlement, a holding action primarily economic in motivation but with important political overtones. To the Hudson's Bay Company the preservation of British sovereignty north of the Great Lakes and the forty-ninth parallel was a desirable, even an essential, condition for the preservation of its trade in furs. Settlement was inevitable in the future, as the Company fully realized, but it could scarcely be expected to encourage or hasten the process. The fate of the Company in the Oregon country after 1846 made obvious what it might expect elsewhere if the United States rather than Britain became sovereign throughout the western part of the continent. Insofar as the Company encouraged, or at least gave assent to, the processes of settlement, it was settlement that was as little as possible American in origin and continental in outlook.

The Dominion of Canada, as the heir of the great company, pursued after 1870 policies that differed radically as to the degree to which settlement was encouraged, but which were not unlike those of the Bay insofar as they sought to avoid the situation that arose in Oregon — or, if we wish to draw on the earlier history of the Canadian heartland, the situation which the Loyalist element feared was arising in Upper Canada prior to the War of 1812. It was consistent with the national purposes of the new Dominion in the first decades of its life that undue pressure should not be placed on immigrants to conform to any Canadian pattern. The resulting transformation might go too far and issue, not in Canadianism, but in Americanization.

The future of the new Canada depended not only on the avoidance of absorption by the neighboring republic but also on the rather more positive necessity of maintaining the cooperation between the French and English speaking elements, upon which the very existence of confederation was based. When the new Canada assumed control of the Northwest not quite a century ago, what settled society existed in the prairie region was not merely bi-cultural but multi-cultural. The Red River settlement itself showed a great variety of social patterns; but, and this was true generally of the tiny pockets of settlement that were growing up around the Hudson's Bay posts, they could be roughly divided into French and English speaking, Roman Catholic and Protestant. Both groups had a close relationship with the Indians through intermarriage, but even as late as 1871 racial mixture was less important than economic and educational status.

Indeed it may be suggested that by 1871, thanks to the comparative isolation which the *régime* of the Company had provided for nearly half a century and to the educational efforts of the missionaries, British Northwestern America had taken important steps toward the assimilation of the Indian to something like a settled pattern of living which was European in many respects but very much part of the new world. This western society had affinities with the two cultures of eastern Canada, but it was only tenuously linked with them. The majority of the English-speaking, of whatever racial mixture, looked generally to the United Kingdom; the slightly larger French group had, as far as those of mixed, white, and Indian race were concerned, come to think of themselves as *Métis*, the New Nation of Louis Riel.

The vigor of the reaction in eastern Canada to the disturbances of 1870–71, commonly called the first Riel rising, made apparent the dangers that would be involved in a rigorous policy of assimilation to a single Canadian norm, even assuming that such a norm existed. There were, of course, some eastern Canadians who assumed that it did. Among the English-speaking, the movement called "Canada First" saw assimilation to the patterns of Ontario, the old Upper Canada, as the happiest possible fate for all inhabitants of the Dominion. The French-speaking were more modest, putting forward the view that the bicultural nature of central Canadian society should be reproduced west of the Great Lakes.

The federal government, treading gingerly between the two positions, actually inclined toward the latter. The constitutional foundation it laid for the province of Manitoba and for the Northwest Territories was rather more appropriate to a new Quebec than to a new Ontario. The rights of the two languages and the two religious positions were entrenched, though it was apparent that it was the French and Roman Catholic position that was expected to need constitutional support.

The power of numbers, rather than constitutional safeguards, determined the issue, and Manitoba became, according to her most distinguished historian, not a new Quebec but a new Ontario. When Manitoba became a province, the balance of population inclined slightly towards the French and Roman Catholic element; but the boom of the early 1870's, and the substantial settlement upon which it was based, changed the picture. Not all the settlers came from Ontario, but the majority were English-speaking and Protestant and, even though they came from the United Kingdom, from the Maritime provinces, or from the United States, they identified themselves with the newcomers from Ontario and soon formed a majority.

In the next twenty-five years the new majority eliminated in Manitoba the constitutional safeguards for a bi-cultural society, though not until a French-speaking and Roman Catholic prime minister, Wilfrid Laurier, had fought and won a national election on a provincial rights platform that maintained the right of Manitoba as a province to take the action that she had. The French and Catholic element in the province nevertheless survived. It did not lose either its language or its faith. St. Boniface, in spite of its propinquity to the booming metropolis of Winnipeg, retained its distinctively and recognizably French flavor. What Laurier had won was actually an administrative compromise that permitted the minority to maintain its identity, even though it lost its legal safeguards. To have maintained these safeguards would have infuriated English-speaking Protestants, not only in Manitoba but in Canada at large. To have forced the French Catholics of Manitoba into the same mould as her English Protestants would have offended Quebec beyond endurance. Manitoba was not to be a new Quebec, but within her borders French-speaking Catholics could preserve, with some qualification, much of their cultural heritage. This may well mark the acceptance of a Canadian national policy that, whatever its uncertainties, did not equate assimilation with homogenization.

Meanwhile other elements had been added to the Manitoba mosaic. The first party of Icelanders arrived in 1875 and established themselves in what to others might have seemed the unpromising lands west of Lake Winnipeg. This region, however, bore some resemblance to their homeland — and they had come, after all, to establish a New Iceland. They had every intention of founding an exclusively Icelandic colony; misgivings which this may have aroused at Ottawa were stilled by Lord Dufferin, the governor-general.[1] When he visited the colony in 1877, Dufferin expressed a singularly unassimilationist point of view:

> ... I trust you will continue to cherish, for all time, the heart-stirring literature of your nation, and that from generation to generation your little ones will continue to learn in your ancient sagas that industry, energy, fortitude, perseverance and stubborn endurance have ever been the characteristics of the noble Icelandic race.[2]

Dufferin was an Irishman and the representative of the Crown. Two of his ministers, Mills and Pelletier, visited the Icelanders three days later and were most favorably impressed; they did noth-

[1] W. Kristjanson, *The Icelandic People in Manitoba: A Manitoba Saga* (Winnipeg, 1965), 26.
[2] *Ibid.*, 75.

ing, therefore, to contradict Dufferin's advocacy of Icelandic cultural survival.[3] Tacit assent to such doctrine by the ministers for the Interior and for Immigration — both directly concerned with western settlement, one English, the other French-speaking, one a representative of Ontario in the cabinet, the other of Quebec — supported the view that those responsible for federal policies were not likely to adopt a vigorously assimilationist position, with all its possible consequences for French-English relations. It is worth noting that Mills and Pelletier had heard bitter criticism of the Icelanders in Winnipeg.

Even before the Icelanders arrived, the more numerous Mennonite settlers had by an order-in-council of March 4, 1873 received assurance that the umbrella was in good working order. This order-in-council deserves special attention. The Mennonites were not interested merely in good farm land; they indeed chose to settle in Manitoba rather than on superior land available in the United States because the Canadian government was prepared to give more satisfactory guarantees for the preservation of their peculiar culture, especially in so far as this involved religion, language, education, and exemption from the obligation of military service. Though the order provided a convenient exit in the saving clause "so far as the law allowed," the Mennonites certainly intended to preserve their cultural identity; and the Macdonald government not only raised no difficulties but also gave positive encouragement.

Its assurances were an embarrassment when the Manitoba majority decided to use education as a means of creating a culturally homogeneous society and when Canada found herself involved in a world conflct, but the Mennonite communities developed under the shelter of these assurances a position of strength that did not readily melt away under the pressures of an alien and different society. The Mennonites changed, but they changed much less rapidly than they might have done without the bulwark provided by federal policy. Today the descendants of the Mennonite settlers may appear at first sight to differ little from their fellow Canadians,

---

[3]*Ibid.*, 76–77.

but it does not take much probing to discover a cultural deposit all the more important because it lies in such sensitive areas of human rights as religion, education, and the obligation or lack of it to assent to the taking of human life.

The highly permissive attitude of the Conservative administrations of Canada's first three decades arose, of course, from a variety of factors other than the need of accommodation to the realities of the French-English presence. The empty lands had to be filled if the national objective was to be achieved, and Icelanders and Mennonites seemed promising as settlers. My argument is that there was opposition in the west to the policy of encouraging them and that this opposition was met with bland indifference at the federal level. In view of the necessity of preserving some working arrangement between English and French, a policy of assimilation would have been, if not impossible, of such complexity that its administration, and perhaps even its conception, would have been rather beyond the modest resources commanded by the politicians and civil servants of post-Confederation Canada. Local opposition to the preservation of cultural identity by immigrant groups did develop, but at worst only provincial action could be taken and this, as in the case of the Manitoba schools, only in the teeth of a federal desire to avoid arousing racial and religious antagonisms on a national scale.

Conspicuous among the group settlements in the Canadian West is that of the Mormons. Though adherents of the Church of Jesus Christ of the Latter Day Saints are widely dispersed throughout Canada, the extreme southwestern corner of Alberta is still recognizably "the Mormon country." The Mormon identity differs from that of the Icelanders or the Mennonite in that ethnic origin and language do not enter into it. Mormon identity is conferred by religion, a religion that involves a very clearly formulated social and cultural organization. It may be noted that Mormons are overwhelmingly of northwest European origin and that the English language enjoys an unchallenged predominance. The Mormons came in part as refugees from persecution for religion's sake, in part as seekers after new land. Some were fugitives from the law of a neighboring country, but the Canadian government put no obstacles in their way though Sir John A. Macdonald's accustomed permissiveness did not extend to official approval of the practice of polygamy.[4]

Many of the earliest Mormon settlers had been substantial citizens in Utah; they had the full support of the Mormon Church; and they brought with them a knowledge of the techniques of irrigation likely to be particularly useful, given the physiographical circumstances of their chosen land. The Mormons had little difficulty in making a satisfactory economic adjustment, and their colony prospered, unhampered by difficulties over language or other outward appearances of peculiarity. The Mormon nevertheless retained an identity. Cultural ties with Salt Lake City remained very close, in spite of the fact that some of the early arrivals were from the British Isles. The Mormon pattern in the Canadian West is identifiably American; this in no way prevents Mormons from entering fully into western Canadian life, but the links with the United States remain unbroken. Thus it is by no means surprising to western Canadians when a prominent Alberta politician, widely regarded as a potential provincial prime minister, returns to Salt Lake City as apostle of the Church. It would be much more surprising if a western Canadian bishop, Roman Catholic or Anglican, were to be elected Pope or even Archbishop of Canterbury.

The Mormon newly arrived in Southern Alberta could not easily be distinguished from the immigrant from Ontario or North Dakota or Nottingham. Much more conspicuous in the railway stations and the shops of Winnipeg and Edmonton were the Ukrainians, one of the most important elements in the ethnic mosaic of the prairie west. Eastern European, speaking a Slavic language, using the Cyrillic alphabet, adhering to the Russian Orthodox or Greek Catholic churches, drawn largely (though by no means entirely) from peasant stock, the Ukrainians had no national base but possessed nevertheless a strongly held sense of national identity. They settled mainly in the park lands opened in the early years of

[4] Sir Joseph Pope (ed.), *Correspondence of Sir John Macdonald* (Toronto, 1921), 463.

the present century by the building of two new Canadian transcontinental railways, the Canadian Northern and the Grand Trunk Pacific, which were later fused into the Canadian National. Although Ukrainians arrived in Manitoba as early as 1891, their main migration followed the change in government of 1896 when Laurier and the Liberals replaced the tired Conservative administrations that held office following the death of John A. Macdonald.

Laurier's Minister of the Interior, Clifford Sifton, was a white Anglo-Saxon Protestant, a product of the wave of emigration from Ontario that had transformed the character of Manitoba. A lawyer and newspaper owner, founder of one of the notable Canadian fortunes, Sifton had played a part in the destruction of the bi-cultural basis of Manitoba society. He was to break with Laurier mainly over the question of separate schools in the newly emergent provinces of Saskatchewan and Alberta, though there were other strains in their relationship. A vigorous promoter of immigration at a time when conditions were ripe for a fuller settlement of the prairie west, Sifton, in spite of his background and his strongly held convictions, was an enthusiastic advocate of the East European immigration of which the Ukrainians formed so substantial a part. To quote again his much-quoted utterance:

> I think a stalwart peasant in a sheep-skin coat, born on the soil, whose forefathers have been farmers for ten generations, with a stout wife and a half-dozen children, is good quality.[5]

Many prairie Canadians disagreed with Sifton's immigration policies. Election results suggest, however, that these critics were by no means a majority, hotly though they denounced "Sifton's pets" as "the scum of Europe."[6] Others, accepting the view that the development of the prairie west would require a not too discriminating immigration policy, demanded that it be complemented by a vigorous program of assimilation. Opinion varied, of course, as to the pattern to which the new arrival was to conform. Even such a sympathetic and knowledgeable observer as Robert England took

---

[5] John W. Dafoe, *Clifford Sifton in Relation to His Times* (Toronto, 1931), 142.
[6] *Ibid.*

it for granted that the teaching of English was of paramount impor-tance,[7] and it was on the use of English as the language of instruc-tion in predominantly or almost exclusively Ukrainian communities that much of the controversy over methods of assimilation centered. Alberta adopted a vigorous program aimed at obtaining maximum results in a minimum time. There was strong and dogged resistance. Once again, as had so often happened in the educational systems of the prairie west, the policy was not pressed to its conclusion. The Liberal *régime* that controlled provincial politics in Alberta until 1921 had substantial support in areas where the French were a deci-sive influence, and they did well in ridings where non-English-speaking ethnic group settlements predominated. The Ukrainian group, like many others, was able to maintain itself. It was to some extent consolidated by its sense of isolation and of the danger of cultural aggression from outside. Simultaneously it was protected by the general reluctance of politicians and public servants to create a crisis over language, race, or religion.

So far attention has been directed only to the experience of groups which are easily recognizable in one way or another as substantially non-conformist in relation to the norms of either Ontario or Quebec. It should also be helpful to consider the fate under the umbrella of bi-culturalism of the settler from the United Kingdom, whether Irish, Scottish, Welsh, or English. Was he more likely to retain his cultural identity under the circumstances of the prairie west than he would have in a less permissive environment? Contact between the United Kingdom and what was to be Canada's prairie west was as old as the fur trade, and group settlement began with the arrival of Lord Selkirk's Kildonan Scots on the Red River in 1814. Certainly the Kildonan Scots were highly successful in retaining their cultural identity, as both the Hudson's Bay Com-pany and the Church of England missionaries were from time to time made painfully aware. Immigrants from the British Isles con-tinued to arrive, at a much accelerated pace after 1871 and in a

---

[7] See especially his *The Central European Immigrant in Canada* (Toronto, 1929).

positive flood during the great period of immigration to the Canadian West between 1896 and 1914.

Arrivals from the United Kingdom made up the most substantial portion of the body of newcomers to Canada in this period. Naturally they did not think of themselves as aliens, though employment signs saying "No Englishman need apply" may occasionally have aroused misgivings. As British subjects they enjoyed a preferred political position; there was no period of waiting to enjoy the privileges of citizenship. Language presented no serious problem. The society in which they found themselves was very different from that of the United Kingdom, but the maintenance of a political link and a strong predilection for various aspects of the British cultural tradition, not only in the west but also in Eastern Canada, eased the passage of the newcomer from "the Old Country" — a term very generally used in the west. Economic factors also operated; Britain was a natural market for prairie products, and the prairies could reciprocate by purchasing British manufactures. The Hudson's Bay Company had supplied its posts with British staples; account books of posts like Edmonton, when white settlement was beginning there, evidence the sale in the prairie west of commodities that today might be regarded as exotic luxuries. The Hudson's Bay department stores in western cities carried on the tradition, and their grocery divisions remained the first resort of those in search of such comestibles as Gentleman's Relish or superior China tea. The interaction between the cultural habits of the settler and the economic life of the prairies has not been closely studied, but it might well be a rewarding area of research.

Kildonan was the first, but by no means the last, attempt at group settlement by those of British origin. Lady Cathcart's crofters; the East London Artisans' Colony, in which that ubiquitous philanthropist Angela Burdett-Coutts was interested; Cannington Manor, an attempt to transport the life of the English shires to the prairies of Saskatchewan; and, best known and most ambitious of all, the Barr of Britannia Colony at Lloydminster, were not all as successful in retaining their identity as the Mennonites of Manitoba or the

Mormons of southern Alberta. They did not, however, disintegrate under any pressure to conform to local patterns of behaviour but rather as a result of the unreality of their economic bases.

It was more usual for the United Kingdom settlers to merge, as individuals or as families, into the general trend of development. Many established themselves in cities and towns, often playing a prominent part in the business and professional life of those communities. Still larger numbers established themselves in agriculture. In some areas — the foothills of southern Alberta, for example — they came in such numbers from 1885 to 1914 as to give a definite and pervasive flavor to the manners and customs of the region. Their pastimes, their ways of building and furnishing their houses, their cultural interests, and their political and social attitudes were to persist beyond the first generation. The foothills region was particularly favorable to the small-scale ranching which provided a congenial livelihood to those who liked an outdoor life and had brought with them sufficient capital to moderate the rigors of pioneering. Even such a society, well adapted to its physical environment though it was, might not so readily have survived in a region less culturally permissive than Canada's prairie west. It was permitted to continue to enjoy an easy confidence in its own superiority long enough to become part of the accepted cultural myth of the prairie west.

It would be to go far beyond the limits of reality to suggest that cultural patterns as diverse as those of the Scottish crofters of Benbecula, the foothills ranchers, or the Welsh miners (who made up such a substantial portion of the work force of Alberta's collieries) survived unmodified in the prairie air. Groups and individuals alike were profoundly changed by their new environment, an environment which to many must have seemed strange indeed. Not all were as fortunate as the Icelanders on the lands west of Lake Winnipeg, or the Ukrainians who found the parklands agreeably reminiscent of their old homes in the Carpathian foothills. To the town-dwelling, working-class Englishman, the dense bush and muskeg of the lands along the Grand Trunk Pacific and the Canadian Northern west of Edmonton were less attractive than might be the cozy valleys and rolling grasslands of the foothills to the younger son of a Leicestershire squire or rector. But however challenging the physical environment to those struggling for economic survival in a way of life that was always partly and sometimes totally unfamiliar, the human environment was less hostile than it would have been in a society dedicated to a single and clearly defined ideal.

Certainly for the immigrants generally, pressure to conform was not wholly absent. In the matter of language there were obvious strains: the majority used English, and the majority of the majority was inclined to view other tongues and those who spoke them with some suspicion. Few communities were sufficiently sophisticated to see skill in the use of a variety of languages as a positive advantage, though there were plenty of individuals who echoed the views Lord Dufferin had so eloquently expressed to the Icelanders. The teaching of French and German, not to mention Latin and Greek, was entrenched in the curricula of all the prairie provinces, and the semi-legendary command of languages by early settlers in many western communities enjoys a place in the cultural myth second only to the gaiety and style of their entertainments. Though the daily use of languages other than English yielded inevitably to the demands of convenience, the pressure to abandon the culture which they symbolized was less intense in a society where many, especially those in positions of influence, were aware that the conflict over language could develop into a national tug-of-war. In these circumstances a program of really vigorous suppression of linguistic variety was unthinkable and, though there were moves in this direction, they were tempered by official discretion which was sometimes difficult to distinguish from official inertia.

Religious diversity in the prairie west was even more marked than linguistic, for many of the ethnic groups were themselves sharply divided in matters of theology. Gone were the old simplicities that allowed Sir George Simpson to equate English with Protestant and French with Roman Catholic, though even in his day such an equation was questionable. Indeed by 1880 devout Anglicans could be found who resented the suggestion that they were Protestants; and the Church of England, in spite of the sound

and safe evangelicalism of its early missionaries, was spending a
good deal of its energies in internal controversies. The Presbyterian
and Methodist churches commanded a larger allegiance among the
English-speaking settlers, but had no great success elsewhere. The
Ukrainian community was sharply split between the Orthodox
and Greek Catholic churches and, perhaps more than any other
ethnic group, found religion as much a divisive as a cohesive force.
The substantial German element was also divided; Lutheran con-
gregations tended to be organized on traditional lines, and cooperation between them developed slowly. The Roman Catholic church
was of more universal appeal; it was the church of the French-speaking, but it numbered among its members representatives of a great
variety of ethnic groups and social backgrounds.

On the surface the prairie west appeared to be Protestant, and
it was in Protestant circles that assimilationist programs had their
greatest popularity. Such programs were intended to produce a
uniformly English-speaking and Protestant society, British in its
political allegiance but soundly American in its social attitudes.
"American" is used here in the sense the word was understood in
Protestant Ontario: suspicious of hierarchy in social as in ecclesiastical organization, but recognizing that Providence rewards the
virtuous and the diligent. No more vigorous representative of this
view existed than George Exton Lloyd, an Anglican bishop who
had no doubt at all that he was a Protestant and who led a vigorous
campaign for the exclusion of non-Anglo-Saxon immigrants and
the speedy assimilation to his exacting standards of those who had
unfortunately already found Canadian homes. Extremism of this
stamp aroused no widespread enthusiasm and met the chilling indifference of governments schooled in the conviction that religious
controversy was as dangerous to the national fabric as strife over
language or race. The fate in 1934 of the short-lived Saskatchewan
government of the ultra-Protestant J. T. M. Anderson suggests that
the majority of voters in that province shared this view.

There are more subtle ways of promoting assimiliation than
by compelling people to speak a particular language or to attend
a particular church. The desire to belong to the group — to share its

life and to win its approval — seems to be a common human aspira-
tion; and to wish to share with others the cultural heritage which
one enjoys is scarcely an ignoble impulse. Assimilation in this sense
is a kind of growing together that may be seen as the foundation of
any healthy society. The road to this kind of assimilation does not
lead through conformity, though conformity may appear to be an
easy means to it. If conformity were always to the highest, it might
be defensible — but the society produced would also lack variety.
Even if the majority invariably chooses the best, and this seems
on the whole unlikely, the determination of what is best has defeated
philosophers more subtle than most members of the electorate.
Conformity is more probably the road to mediocrity, to a comfortable but unexciting sameness that would give human existence a
rather less than vegetable quality. No doubt for many, perhaps
even for the majority who live in the present state of even a relatively
affluent society such as that of the Canadian prairies, this would be
an improvement. It is not, however, an inspiring ideal.

My argument has been that the Canadian West has been able
to escape the extremes of pressure for conformity because it is
a part of a country that, by the happy accident of a bi-cultural presence in its dominant region, has been obliged, in order to maintain
its viability, to avoid policies productive of cultural conflict. Under
the shelter of the bi-cultural umbrella, the mosaic of prairie settlement has retained much of its color and richness. Its pattern is
abstract, still very much in the eye of its beholder; and, like most
abstracts, its interpretation is not a matter of certainty but depends
on the values of the interpreter. The prairie Canadian, I suggest, is
in an excellent position to cultivate values that will enable him to
appreciate the excellencies of his possession. Not only must he
cherish and preserve his own inheritance, as Lord Dufferin so wisely
counselled the Icelanders to do, but he must be alert to appreciate
the inheritance of others. This goes far beyond tolerance. It is not
enough that he simply accept difference in others; he must learn
actively to enjoy it. He may thus experience the richness and variety
of his cultural as well as his physical environment. The extremes of
levelling out have luckily been avoided, and enough remains to

provide ample opportunity to take a positive leap in the opposite direction.

The Canadian prairie west has been a melting-pot, but the necessities of Canadian politics have damped down the fires beneath it. No gale of nationalism has fanned those flames. The region has been spared the consequences of official intolerance of cultural difference. The values that in these circumstances can be developed have more than a regional significance. Canada's national situation suggests that if there is to be a norm of Canadianism it must involve an acceptance of difference within the Canadian culture and indeed a cultivation of a consciousness of the positive value of difference. A Canadian nationalism so oriented could have a usefulness beyond Canada's national boundaries. To preserve and develop this kind of Canadianism is not visionary and impractical. It is indeed highly practical, for it is a condition of the continuance of human development not in Canada only but in the planet at large.

The Recent West

THE SIGNIFICANCE OF THE SMALL

TOWN IN AMERICAN HISTORY

by

JOHN D. HICKS

Morrison Professor of History, Emeritus, in the University of California (Berkeley), the author is one of America's most distinguished historians. Among his publications are a classic monograph, *The Populist Revolt* (1931), and a famous textbook in United States history. His teaching career was mainly at three state universities — Nebraska, Wisconsin, and California. His autobiography, from which much of this paper is drawn, is under publication by the University of Nebraska Press.

You MAY BLAME this essay, if you like, on Page Smith, for it was his book, *As A City Upon a Hill,* that suggested the theme. In reviewing this book for the April, 1967, number of the *Pacific Northwest Quarterly,* I had this to say: If Frederick Jackson Turner in his prime had written this book, or, more likely, had compressed the idea which it elaborates into a short paper, he would no doubt have called it "The Significance of the Town in American History." For a generation or so it would have won wide acceptance, after which numerous revisionists would have subjected the "town hypothesis" to searching criticism. Before long the "town myth" would have been triumphantly exploded. Towns, really, the more dogmatic would say, never played any important part in American history at all. In fact, towns could hardly be said even to have existed.

"Turner was wrong." After that, the neo-Turnerians and the re-revisionists would have taken over.

There is some evidence to indicate that writers of American history are beginning, if only beginning, to take a somewhat more sophisticated view of their subject. There is no one key to American history; many forces have worked together to make it what it is. The English heritage cannot be discounted, but neither can the fact that the New World was long separated from the Old. The importance of immigration, the operation of the industrial revolution, the effect of westward expansion, all these factors and many more played significant roles. Pioneers did go west, they did conquer a continent, and it did make a difference. Furthermore, they also clustered together in towns, from the earliest beginnings on down, both in the older colonial sections and along the frontier. This, too, made a difference. Finally, when some of the towns grew into cities, what a difference that made!

Page Smith, in his delightful book, makes no pretense of saying "with final authority what the town has meant in American life," nor can I hope to do so. But perhaps I can build a little on the foundation he has laid. I should like to note first that the town — or the small town, as I have preferred to call it — cannot be separated from the country around it. The town was only the nucleus of a cell; its function was to serve as a trading center for the larger agricultural community that surrounded it. Town and country melded together; they had been one in Europe and they became one in America. Early America, indeed, continued for a long time the Old World practice of the farmers themselves living in the towns and going out each day to work the fields. This pattern, however, did not survive the abundance of land in America and the defeat of the Indians. Instead, a division of functions developed. The farmers built their houses on the farms and lived adjacent to the fields they tilled. The townspeople, on the other hand, existed primarily to serve the needs of the farmers. But the two were essentially one unit; the town could no more have lived without the surrrounding countryside than the countryside could have lived without the town.

My second observation, closely akin to the first, is that the small town, with negligible exceptions, was primarily dependent on agriculture. If Smith has any other definition than size to indicate where the town leaves off and the city begins, I have failed to note it. But, as I see it, the town becomes a little city whenever outside industry begins to invade its borders. After that change, it is never a town again. It still remains a town as long as it merely processes the produce of the farm. It can digest a flour mill to grind some of its grain, an elevator to help ship away the excess, a creamery to turn its milk into dairy products, and a poultry house to market its chickens and eggs. It can harbor a slaughter-house to provide meat for local consumption and whatever facilities are necessary for the loading and marketing of livestock. It can still be a town after it has undertaken to erect a water tower and to operate a water system, or to set up a municipal power plant and introduce electric lights — a target not long overlooked by the power trust. But the town's days as a town are numbered the minute a factory moves in, even a box factory. Middletown, made·famous by the book the Lynds wrote about it, was not a town at all; it was a little city.

I think I should emphasize, also, one other point: the dependence of both town and country on manpower and horsepower. Until well after the end of the nineteenth century, horses drew the plows that tilled the soil, and men usually held the plow handles. Horses pulled the riding-plows, the cultivators, the mowing-machines, and men drove the horses. Men, women, and children milked the cows, slopped the hogs, gathered the eggs, churned the butter, and all that. Horse-drawn wagons brought farm products to market and farm families to and from town. In the towns the same situation prevailed. Every family that could afford it had a horse or two and some kind of buggy or road-wagon. Every store depended on horse-drawn dray-wagons to bring goods from the railroad station, and maintained a horse-drawn delivery wagon to carry goods to its customers. What work the horses couldn't do, the people had to do. Town-and-country life meant hard work, work in which every able bodied citizen was expected to share.

As Page Smith puts it, "the basic form of social organization experienced by the vast majority of Americans up to the early decades of the twentieth century" was the country town. When George Washington was President, at least nine-tenths, or more likely nineteen-twentieths, of the American people lived in the town-and-country complexes, while the "cities in the wilderness" which housed the other tenth or twentieth were neither very large nor very sophisticated. Perhaps during some of the earlier decades we should include, along with horse-power, ox-power and slave-power, and in some important aspects the pre-Civil War South was atypical. But census statistics are convincing. Throughout the entire nineteenth century more Americans lived in town-and-country than in the cities; only in the twentieth century did the proportions change. For the nation as a whole, 54.3 per cent of the people were still town-and-country dwellers in 1900; only 45.7 per cent lived in the cities. Also, it seems reasonable to suppose that, even into the nineteenth century, a majority of the city-dwellers had come from the country. As Richard Hofstadter once observed, the United States was born in the country and moved to the city.

It is my theory, and I think Page Smith would agree with me, that the old agricultural America developed in its town-and-country units a viable civilization, a civilization fairly well equipped to meet the needs of the people it served. Our present urban society will have to go a long way to do as well. Most influential in defining and maintaining the town's ideals were the church, the school, and the home. On the debit side, one might list the saloon, the pool hall, and the livery stable. The rest of Main Street in a sense was neutral, not too pious to turn a decent profit and not too grasping to provide good service.

And now may I claim an old man's privilege to wax auto-biographical. Ten years before the turn of the century I was born in the microscopic town of Pickering, Missouri, far up in the north-western corner of the state. My ancestors on both sides were farmers for many generations back; none of them, as far as I know, came to the New World later than the eighteenth century. My father was a Methodist preacher who had been a farmer before he became a preacher; my mother's father was a farmer for all of his life. In my youth I lived in eight different small towns of the kind I have described, five of them in Missouri and three of them in Wyoming. Not much of what I have to say about small towns and their country surrroundings comes out of books; most of it I can document only from memory, but the impressions I recall are still very vivid. For example, I know from experience and observation that young men who grew up in the town often found jobs on the nearby farms, that old men retired from the farms to live in the towns (where they made keeping taxes down a life work), that town boys married country girls, that country boys married town girls, that town and country came together on Saturdays in the stores, on Sundays in the churches, and for a favored few the other five days in the schools. The solidarity of the town-and-country unit was merely a fact of life.

The part played by churches in the old agricultural town-and-country America can hardly be exaggerated. There were from three to five Protestant denominations represented in each community. Catholic churches were rare, for most country people were Protestants and most Catholics lived in cities, although in two of the Wyoming towns we lived in there were small Catholic parishes. The variety of denominations gave the incentive of competition to church activities, which among the dominant Protestants began with something for the faithful to do all day Sunday. During the weekdays there were supplementary activities — prayer meetings on Wednesday night, choir practice on Thursday night, church dinners and socials to raise money for some worthy project at irregular but frequent intervals, and in the fall those long-drawn-out revival meetings, the purpose of which was to save the souls of the sinful and to gather into the fold the current crop of lambs. Whatever doctrinal differences might divide the churches, they agreed completely on a strict moral code, based on the Ten Commandments and the Sermon on the Mount. And they proclaimed these views, in season and out. The boys and girls who grew up on this kind of moral diet rarely had to think twice to know the difference between what was right and what was wrong.

The schools, although publicly supported and strictly secular, lost few opportunities to reinforce the moral teachings of the church. There was little Bible reading or prayer in regular sessions, but school books never failed to plug for the same kind of right living and decent behavior that the churches emphasized. McGuffey's Readers were no longer in general use, but their successors followed similar rules in choosing uplifting and character-building selections. The copybooks from which children learned to write provided as samples of good penmanship the wise admonitions of the ages, often drawn from *Poor Richard's Almanac*. Even the problems posed by the arithmetics made it clear that the harder you worked the more you made — the "Protestant ethic," I suppose.

In the country the one-room, one-teacher district school was still dominant. In such school my parents got all the formal education they ever had, while my mother for eleven years taught in one after another of them before she married my father. Right after the turn of the century one of my older sisters taught country school for seven years, and shortly afterward I, too, followed the family precedent. By this time we had moved to eastern Wyoming, where I learned something about the significance of the frontier long before I had ever heard of Frederick Jackson Turner.

My first schoolhouse was built of logs, with a dirt roof feebly covered by grass — the kind of house that elicited from Mark Twain the comment, on his first trip to the West, that never before had he seen a house with its front yard up on top. None too sure of myself, and never having had a course in education (not that it would have made much difference), I was greeted the first day by a five-year-old with the disconcerting inquiry: "Say, Mister, is you a man or a kid?" I really didn't know. We carried our drinking water from the nearby Powder River, and let the "powder" sink to the bottom of the pail before we took a drink. Our school was a hundred miles from the nearest railroad "point" and all supplies had to be hauled in by wagons, or more expensively by stage, all horse-drawn, I hasten to add. We had two small squares of dilapidated blackboard and homemade desks, conscientiously hand-carved to meet the taste of each new user.

But in those days I saw progress as a result of my teaching, progress such as I have seldom seen since. I taught children to read who had never known how to read before, and I knew I had taught them something. I taught them long division and fractions, and I knew by the light in their eyes when they had caught on. I taught them about the stars and the movements of the heavenly bodies, and I got from one undersized lad of nine, who had listened with rapt attention: "Gee, I just thought the blamed things was pasted up there!"

Town schools were quite a cut above country schools. By the time I went to school they were graded, usually with one teacher for each of the first eight grades and two or three more for high school. Consolidated schools had not yet appeared to bring city-type education to practically the entire nation. Our teachers were often drawn from the town itself and, even when they were not, we came to know them well outside as well as inside the schoolroom. I can remember the names and a good deal about the personalities of every teacher I had from the first grade on through high school. In the high school from which I graduated we had only two teachers for a total of thirty or forty pupils, but our teachers were mature men who tolerated no nonsense. I remember with particular fondness the singing lessons in which the whole high school joined, with the teacher getting the pitch from a tuning fork, and do-re-mi-ing us through lesson after lesson in an old-fashioned singing book. I remember, too, the "rhetoricals" that we were required to put on at stated intervals, with each person, in his turn, speaking a piece or participating in some group performance. Occasionally I got myself involved in a debate; one question I recall arguing was "Resolved, that the men of ancient times were greater than the men of modern times." I stood firmly by the moderns, but a smart senior girl — I was then only a sophomore — made both me and the whole modern world sound foolish.

The third great influence in rural America, and perhaps the greatest of all, was the home. Town-and-country fathers were ever-present factors in the upbringing of their children — there was none of this long-distance commuting. Fathers came home to lunch, only the midday meal was not lunch at all, but dinner, and was so called; the evening meal, much less pretentious, was called supper. Country children had to take their lunch to school, but in the towns the children all trooped home at twelve o'clock, then back to school at one o'clock — school was rarely more than five blocks away. Perhaps I was somewhat more favored than most small-town boys, for my father had his study at home and was as ever-present a figure as my mother. But to a degree this was true of all town-and-country children. The children were no less the father's than the mother's responsibility. Divorces were rare, and widows with small children tended to remarry. Married women rarely left the home to work elsewhere, and most children, whether they lived in the towns or on the farm, enjoyed the security of a home — usually, for good measure, a very religious home.

Work because it needed to be done, and work for its therapeutic value, were also specialties of the town and the farm. Girls helped their mothers with the housework; boys had endless chores to do. Horses, for example, took a lot of caring for. Think of the endless man-hours, or boy-hours, it took to fuel up and service those old hay-burners: storing hay in the hayloft, pushing it down into the mangers, currying the horses, cleaning the stable, harnessing the horses and "hooking them up" to wagon, buggy, or implement, and so on infinitum. In those days a good healthy boy — and I was one such — was expected to saw and split the wood used for fuel, bring it into the house each evening, get up early to start the fire in the kitchen stove, milk the family cow, then drive her across town to the pasture before going to school, then after school drive her back from the pasture and milk her again. My mother, a frugal soul, sold milk at five cents a quart to cowless neighbors, and it was my job also to deliver the milk. Then there was a garden to be tended, a lawn to be mowed, and a buggy to be washed. When I read today of gangs of city boys breaking into houses, cluttering up the roads with hot rods, and robbing pedestrians, I am more reconciled than I used to be to the tasks that destroyed so much of my time when I was a boy.

Frequent visits from close relatives, most of whom lived nearby, characterized the town-and-country homes I knew. I am quite sure that family relationships meant more to the rural Americans of my youth than they mean to the city people of today. No doubt the greater mobility of the present age has served to scatter kinfolk over much wider areas now than formerly; partly on this account, town-and-country Americans probably knew their relatives for better than urban Americans know theirs. There is much talk nowadays of young people trying to establish their identity. For residents of the towns and farms of yesteryear this was certainly no problem. Each person was identified with a home, with a family, with a church, with a school, with a community. Everybody knew who he was and he knew that everybody knew who he was. "Remember," my father said as he sent me off to college, "remember who you are and what you are." How, I wondered, could I forget.

Perhaps I have painted a too utopian picture of rural America. There was, of course, another side quite as demonstrable. We had our full quota of stinkers; the Devil was on the job in the country no less than in the city. The water of the "ol' swimmin' hole" was no dirtier than the speech and conduct that went with it. You could learn a lot of filth, too, if you hung around the pool hall or the livery stable. The facts of life were an open secret; not the bees and the flowers but the birds and the beasts gave you demonstrations. Or if you didn't get the message clearly enough by observation, one of your associates would remove all doubts. Early marriages, followed by healthy seven-month babies, were commonplace. If the language used by a farmhand in encouraging a mule to do his duty omitted any obscene epithet, the oversight was purely intentional. Herbert Quick tells of five close boyhood friends who turned out to be drunkards and thieves. I can't quite equal that, but I had a cousin who robbed a bank — from the inside.

As everyone knew, the Devil made his headquarters down in the licensed saloon. Against this bastion, the church made constant warfare. Signing a saloon petition was a sure means of getting one's name taken off the church roll; there was no trial about it, the name was just scratched off. Party membership hardly counted in local politics; indeed, one might almost say that to all intents and purposes the words "Wet" and "Dry" had supplanted in local elections the words "Democratic" and "Republican." In only one of the

Missouri towns in which we lived was there a licensed saloon, but in Wyoming it was different. There were several saloons in each of the three Wyoming towns we lived in, and brothels in two of them. Well-attested rumors had it that sheepherders or ranch hands in town for a spree were mercifully relieved of their excess cash, as soon as they passed out, to insure them against a too-prolonged debauch. As my preacher father viewed the scene, the Devil had the town in his clutches, and working against His Satanic Majesty was uphill business. When a Methodist bishop rebuked the preachers of the Wyoming Annual Conference for saving so few souls, Father's retort was that it was easier to make a dozen converts in Missouri than to get a single Wyoming sinner to repent.

What I am trying to say is not that the town-and-country environment of rural America was either all good or all bad, but merely that it provided a viable society, a way of life that over a long period of time was able to survive and to meet the basic needs of its members. Hardly anyone would say as much for our cities today. The number of small-town boys who have made good — Smith has a chapter on the subject — seems to indicate that the small-town environment that shaped their characters had something of value to contribute. The firm conventions of the town may have kept the love of freedom it bred from turning into license; its easy acceptance of the crossing of class barriers may have helped to maintain the spirit of equalitarianism; its insistence on the Christian virtues, including hard work and thrift, may have paid good dividends. At least one can say with confidence that the small town was a good place to be *from*.

For the fact remains that the young people who lived on the farms and in the towns were usually frantic to get away. Farm work was just too intolerably hard and the rewards too meager. The much-exploded "agrarian myth," which exalts the farmer to the highest pinnacle in the national pantheon, was not the invention of the farmers, who knew pretty well what a raw deal they had drawn, but of the editors, the politicians, and the city slickers who, in one fashion or another, farmed the farmers. Life in the towns, while less boring than life on the farms, was still too deadly dull; there just wasn't enough excitement to go around.

Why, then, did not rural America explode in discontent? To some extent, in such movements as the Populist revolt, it did; but fortunately it had a safety-valve, not just the old safety-valve of a move to the West, which in its time did indeed serve such a purpose for country people, if not for the city workers, but the new and more important safety-valve of a move to the city. It was toward the city that the ambitious and discontented town-and-country youth looked with longing. There were jobs in the city, jobs that paid well, even for high-school dropouts with only a strong back and a willing spirit. For those who finished high school there were still better jobs, and of those who went away to college very few returned. Most of them, according to Page Smith, became professional men — doctors, lawyers, preachers, teachers, and the like — not business leaders, for it took a city environment to breed these entrepreneurs. Among the country boys who made good, I can count my cousin Edmund Knobel, for example, who went to the University of Missouri and became a soils expert. As such, he traveled the length and breadth of the land analyzing soils and publishing his findings in government bulletins. Then there was my best friend and fifth-grade seatmate, Phil Sheridan Gibson, of whom I lost track for forty years, then discovered him again as Chief Justice of the California Supreme Court. There was another small-town boy from Missouri, Harry S. (for nothing) Truman, who went into politics, played it straight even in Kansas City, and rose to the Presidency of the United States. And what about Dwight D. Eisenhower, a small-town boy from Kansas, who went to West Point, led the American forces in World War II, and also became President? And, while we are on the subject, what about LBJ and HHH? Just think of all the hell they would have raised had their energies been bottled up in their own home towns! It's a hazard even when they go back home for vacations. Ask any citizen of Johnson City, Texas.

But we must not forget that the town-and-country economy

from which these worthies came has to all intents and purposes disappeared — the victim of power machinery, the automobile, good roads, and urban standards. What passes for rural life today is so different that its very existence tends to betray us. The old town-and-country environment is as much a thing of the past as the frontier Turner wrote about, and its influence, like that of the frontier, has steadily diminished. The city has taken over; city standards, city morals, city ways dominate everywhere. Those of us who grew up in the old town-and-country environment are fast dying off.

Perhaps, however, you who have grown up in the cities — asphalt flowers, Charles A. Beard once called you — even if you are now disciples of the new history, the new economics, the new political science, or the new left, you will allow us this crumb of comfort. We've all heard a thousand times over the old saw: "You can take the boy out of the country, but you can't take the country out of the boy." I wonder if even the triumph of urbanism today can take all the country out of America. Is there not something left in our American way of life, wherever we find it and however urban it may have become, that reflects in some degree our rural heritage, a heritage that in every region once had its roots in a primitive agricultural frontier? Perhaps in this sense the old America I knew in my youth still lives.

GEORGE W. LITTLEFIELD:

FROM CATTLE TO COLONIZATION

1871–1920

by

DAVID B. GRACY II

Archivist of the Southwest Collection at Texas Technological College, the author earned the bachelor's and master's degrees at the University of Texas, then continued working toward the doctorate at Texas Tech. He assisted in editing the third volume of *Texas Indian Papers* (1959), edited *Maxey's Texas* (1965), and has written *Littlefield Lands: Colonization on the Texas Plains, 1912–1920* (1968) as well as several articles for learned journals and the supplement to the *Handbook of Texas*.

AT THE DAWN of the twentieth century, the Panhandle-Plains of Texas remained one of the last strongholds of large cattle ranching enterprise in the West — a virgin territory unspoiled by the farmer's plow. But the westward-surging farmer was ready to challenge the cattleman for use of these semi-arid yet fertile plains. Many ranchers, seeing potential profit rather than ruin in the prospect, established land companies, carved portions of their sprawling ranges into farm-sized plots, and, with eyes and pocketbooks wide open, encouraged the settlers' advance.

A clear example of this transition can be seen in the activities which Major George Washington Littlefield began in 1912 on his Yellow House Ranch forty miles northwest of Lubbock. The transformation of the Yellow House Ranch represents the climax both of a remarkable career and of a significant frontier movement: the career of the proprietor and the movement of land-hungry farmers into the ranching realm of the Texas Panhandle-Plains.[1]

George W. Littlefield, born in Mississippi in 1842, moved with his family in 1850 to a plantation in Gonzales County in south-central Texas. After service with the 8th Texas Cavalry during the Civil War, young George returned home on crutches to take up the sedentary life of a cotton farmer. Tilling the soil proved lucrative for four years, but three consecutive seasons of drouth, flood, and worms left him heavily in debt.[2] To salvage his tottering financial situation, Littlefield in 1871 gathered some 1,100 head of cattle and plodded them northward to Kansas. With the money from the sale of the animals, he paid his trail crew, settled his debts, and still had $3,600 left, as he later reminisced, "to begin business."[3]

Under LIT and LFD brands Littlefield subsequently established several ranches in Texas and in New Mexico.[4] During the last three decades of the nineteenth century, despite drouths and blizzards on the plains and panics in the financial world, he continued to increase the number, the size, and the quality of his ranges and of his herds. He reached the pinnacle of his career as a cattleman in 1901 when he purchased the 312,000-acre Yellow House Division of the famous XIT Ranch.[5]

---

[1] This paper derives from researches resulting in the author's recent book, *Littlefield Lands: Colonization on the Texas Plains, 1912–1920* (Austin, 1968). An earlier work by J. Evetts Haley, *George W. Littlefield, Texan* (Norman, 1943), is essentially a contribution to the history of ranching in the Southwest.

[2] David B. Gracy II, "With Danger and Honor: George W. Littlefield, 1861–1864," *Texana*, I (Winter-Spring 1963), 1–19, 120–152; and David B. Gracy II, "George Washington Littlefield: Portrait of a Cattleman," *Southwestern Historical Quarterly*, LXVIII (October 1964), 238–239. See also Haley, *George W. Littlefield*, 47–49. Littlefield was able to lay aside his crutches in 1867.

[3] George W. Littlefield, Autobiography (MS., George W. Littlefield Collection, University of Texas Archives).

[4] Both the LIT and LFD brands were taken from letters of Littlefield's last name. *Early Recollections of J. Phelps White* (n.p., n.d.), 10.

[5] George W. Littlefield, Autobiography (MS. in possession of Miss Ruth Key, Austin, Texas); Arthur P. Duggan to Littlefield, April 16, 1913 (Littlefield Lands Company Records, in possession of the author); and *Early Recollections of J. Phelps White*. See also Haley, *George W. Littlefield*, 80–187 *passim* and Gracy, *Littlefield Lands*, 4, 7.

Despite his amazing success in the livestock trade, Littlefield did not entrust his entire fortune to this single enterprise. Though he wrote in 1906 that the "Cattle business is the best and safest business in Tex — In fact nothing else compares with it,"[6] he maintained an interest in farms in central Texas, in property in Austin, and in the American National Bank of Austin, which he organized in 1890 and served as president and chairman of the board thereafter until his death in 1920.[7] Thus he was first of all an entrepreneur and second a cattleman. It was Littlefield's business sense which led him to climax his career by turning the advancing farmer's frontier to his profit.

The opening of the Yellow House Ranch to settlers was likewise to climax the movement of farmers into the Panhandle-Plains of Texas — a fifty-county area bounded roughly by New Mexico on the west, Oklahoma on the north, Oklahoma and the prairie plains on the east, and the line of the Texas and Pacific Railroad on the south. Though a few sodbusters had found their way into this semi-arid region by the late 1870's, the first land boom there did not begin until 1887.[8] It was over within seven years, stifled by a scorching drouth and by a plague of devouring grasshoppers. Most of the pioneers of this early boom, rather than wait out the drouth, raced pell mell for home and water, leaving behind little permanent settlement.

By the middle of the first decade of the twentieth century, the land rush was on once more. Settlers again began infiltrating this region in 1902 when the state government refused to renew land leases to ranchers. By 1906 the drouth had been forgotten, and some Easterners were optimistically observing that the weather of

---

[6] Littlefield to Mrs. Shelton C. Dowell, June 21, 1906 (Dowell Papers, Texas State Archives).

[7] Gracy, "George Washington Littlefield: Portrait of a Cattleman," *Southwestern Historical Quarterly*, LXVIII, 240–248.

[8] It is interesting, perhaps even significant, to note that the first notable influx of settlers is coincident with the beginning of the end of the range cattle industry resulting from the calamitous winter of 1886–87. See Edward Everett Dale, *The Range Cattle Industry* (Norman, 1930), 108–111, 130, 146.

the sunny plains was becoming "more seasonal." Experimental farms and early settlers had shown that the rich soil could produce wonderful crops by a perfected system of dry-land farming. Acreage in the virgin region was considerably less expensive than that in the settled areas, and money had become more readily available. The land agents were now better organized and understood more fully the country they were promoting. Meanwhile the psychological effect of the announcement of the closing of America's frontier had stimulated a mania for ownership of land, and agricultural areas in the counties to the east of the region had been occupied. Furthermore, cattlemen in numbers were ready and willing to market blocks of land. Thus the Panhandle-Plains of Texas was ripe for a record-breaking land boom.

The Panhandle-Plains was soon the fastest growing section of the state, the population increasing from 34,000 in 1900 to 134,000 by the census of 1910. In 1909 it was reported that as many as 400,000 land-hungry Americans were flooding every year into the West, a healthy percentage of them into the Panhandle-Plains, in a mad scramble for what enthusiastic agents were calling "The Last of the Cheap Land." The end of the boom finally came in 1914 with the outbreak of World War I, but by this time the climax had been reached and farming was well on the way to becoming the dominant industry of this West Texas region.

From 1903 through 1913, towns were platted in the Panhandle-Plains at a rate of at least five per year.[9] The townsite was an integral part of every colonization scheme, and the ranchers of the region gained financially as a result of the success of about half of the towns platted in these ventures.[10] As Walter Prescott

---

[9] To date, the only general study of land colonization in the Panhandle-Plains is David B. Gracy II, A Preliminary Survey of Land Colonization in the Panhandle-Plains of Texas, 1878–1934 (MS., Southwest Collection, Texas Technological College). Only one colonization effort of the 138 investigated showed no attempt whatsoever to develop a town.

[10] Gracy, A Preliminary Survey of Land Colonization in the Panhandle-Plains; *Texas Almanac and State Industrial Guide* (Dallas, 1941), 104–107. See also Ira G. Clark, *Then Came the Railroads: The Century from Steam to Diesel in the Southwest* (Norman, 1958), 259.

Webb suggested in his famous book, this evolution of rancher to townsite promoter followed a natural progression: from free range with longhorns to barbed wire with blooded stock, and then the sale of these ranch lands to sodbusters.[11] The activities of Major Littlefield generally fit the pattern described by Professor Webb.

The genesis of Littlefield's interest in land colonization, according to his reminiscences, is to be found well before he came into ownership of the Yellow House Ranch — as far back, in fact, as the Civil War when he observed in the Western theater the vast destruction and crowded living conditions. Thereafter, on his trips to sell cattle, he watched people pushing westward into the plains states. His belief that some day such people would surge onto the Texas plains was one reason for his purchase of the Yellow House Ranch in 1901.[12]

Seven years later a well-known land agent, William P. Soash, riding the crest of the wave of sodbusters entering the Panhandle-Plains, approached Littlefield with a plan to sell the entire ranch in small plots for $3,000,000. Littlefield turned him down because he feared the possibility of ending up with a few farms scattered over his pasture. He knew the value of an operating railroad to the success of such an enterprise; despite schemes to lace the area with rails, the nearest track was sixty miles distant and was not coming his way. Soash complained that Littlefield did not understand the methods of colonization, but by 1911 the situation had changed. Littlefield had learned the operations of a professional colonizer by watching Soash, in two years, promote and develop the town of Olton, without benefit of a railroad, into a community of 150 inhabitants and the seat of the county in which Littlefield would subsequently undertake his own colonization venture. Furthermore, the Santa Fe Railroad was ready to lay steel from Lubbock northwest to Texico, New Mexico, as the final link in what would then be the shortest route between the Gulf coast of Texas and the

---

[11] Walter Prescott Webb, *The Great Plains* (Boston and New York, 1936), 227–244.

[12] Interview with T. B. Duggan as cited in Gracy, "With Danger and Honor: George W. Littlefield, 1861–1864," *Texana,* I, 143, n.23.

California coast. In June, 1911, Littlefield offered the railroad
a bonus of $100,000 to cross his land. If he had been hesitant to
open his ranch earlier, Littlefield doubtless was committed to the
idea when he extended this offer to the Santa Fe.

The principal reason stimulating Littlefield to market a fourth
of his LFD range to farmers was, without question, profit. But
other considerations apparently weighed on his mind: the desire
to found a town to perpetuate his name, the desire to establish a
college,[13] and the desire to convert as much as possible of his estate
of more than $4,000,000 into cash easily divisible among his
numerous heirs.

Whatever his motives or whenever he finally determined that
the time had come to allow settlers to begin invading his ranch,
Littlefield committed himself to colonization by hiring as sales
manager a relative by marriage, Arthur Pope Duggan, in the summer of 1912.[14] To complete the initial organization of the Littlefield Lands Company, he got his partner and manager of the Yellow
House Ranch, J. Phelps White, to serve as general manager, even
though White did not savor seeing the grass, "our best crop" he
called it,[15] plowed under. Duggan's job essentially was to conduct
the day-to-day affairs of the company, White's to advise and counsel
with him on important matters in Littlefield's absence.

Duggan arrived at the ranch in August, 1912, to begin, under
Littlefield's close supervision, the work of converting a grassy pasture into a farming community. That task, no small one, required
first a decision as to how much land would be initially placed on

---

[13] In this he was unsuccessful. Though he had little formal schooling himself, Littlefield long manifested a deep interest in education. He financed the education of at
least twenty-nine of his nieces and nephews. From 1911 until shortly before his death
in 1920, he served on the Board of Regents of the University of Texas, to which institution he and his wife donated about $2,000,000. Gracy, "George Washington Littlefield:
Portrait of a Cattleman," *Southwestern Historical Quarterly*, LXVIII, 238, 242,
251–252.

[14] To manage his various enterprises, Littlefield preferred to employ members of his
extended family of nieces and nephews since he had no children of his own. Duggan,
who resigned the position of manager of the farm land department of a large Dallas
real estate firm in order to become sales manager of the Littlefield Lands Company, had
married one of Littlefield's nieces in 1902. Gracy, *Littlefield Lands*, 10–11.

[15] *Lamb County Leader* (Littlefield, Texas), June 27, 1963.

sale. The line of the railroad cut diagonally across the northeast corner of the pasture, and to the 32,000 acres thus segregated Little-field added enough land south of the rails to market a total of 79,040 acres. That area then had to be reduced to farm-sized plots. Following the Spanish system of measurement, the land was surveyed into 436 labors (supposed to be 177.1 acres each[16]), which were offered at fifteen dollars per acre as the basic farm unit.[17] Next a determination had to be made as to where on the subdivision the town — of course, named "Littlefield" — would be placed; then the townsite had to be platted. Simultaneously, there was advertising matter to be written and distributed through newspapers, periodicals, pamphlets, broadsides, and mailings. A force of land agents was then assembled to carry word of the new acreage for sale to prospective buyers — commonly called "prospectors." Immediate in the order of need were such substantial improvements as a hotel to house the prospectors who had come miles out onto the bare plains to survey Littlefield lands. Not the least of the improvements, though in the end they proved less than substantial, were 1,000 shade trees, each approximately three feet tall, planted about the townsite. Most prospectors were, of course, farmers; and since proof of the fertility of the soil was their first concern, much initial expense was lavished on a demonstration farm which offered for their close inspection not just a multitude of crops, but a multitude of healthy crops. Coincident, in that semi-arid environment, with the necessity of a demonstration farm was the need for an irrigation well. Indeed, this one item was of such importance to the average prospector, although he could not afford it, that the company at one time considered halting the sales campaign until a flowing well had gushed in.[18] Soon thereafter the first of five wells was successfully sunk.

---

[16] Because of errors made in early surveys of the XIT Ranch, leagues (twenty-five labors each) in the subdivision for sale contained more than the normal 4,427.5 acres. Thus certain labors measured in excess of 177.1 acres.

[17] By 1918 the price of the land had been raised to net Littlefield $26.50 per acre.

[18] The Texas Land and Development Company at Plainview, which offered only irrigated tracts for sale, did not show a profit during this period. Billy R. Brunson, The Texas Land and Development Company (Ph.D. dissertation, Texas Technological College, 1960), 94–96.

The town of Littlefield held its official opening on July 4, 1913. Well over 1,400 persons attended to participate in the pomp and circumstance of the occasion. There was an auction of town lots, a noon meal of barbeque served from the ranch chuck wagons, and a roundup of whitefaced LFD cattle especially staged for this "extraordinary occasion."[19] With such fanfare on the anniversary of American independence, the cattleman and the farmer joined hands on the Panhandle-Plains of Texas.

The sales operation of the Littlefield Lands Company was conducted primarily through agents, acting as middlemen between the prospective buyer and the land owner. Rather than hire such men on salary, the frugal Littlefield made contracts whereby he was only obligated to compensate them with commissions for actual sales. The story of relations between the company and its agents is in large measure a tale of controversy — over contracts, over commissions, over the veracity of agent propaganda. By October, 1913, Littlefield was convinced that "Immigration men are fakers."[20] For their part, the agents found Major Littlefield strictly conservative in his business methods and unwilling to countenance any scheme except "straight buying and selling."[21] Furthermore, they did not approve the moderate pace at which his company made improvements. This conflict serves to point up the two facts that the aging, self-made cattleman scrutinized the operations of his land company as carefully as he did those of all his other various and extensive enterprises, and that, shrewd in deals, he was conservative in methods.

From 1912 to 1917 prospectors flocked to the Panhandle-Plains to survey Littlefield lands; sales progressed at a fairly steady clip despite the collapse of the second land boom in 1914. Purchasers continued to move onto their tracts and to improve them. The Littlefield Lands Company survived the collapse of the boom largely because two divisions of the Mennonite Church were

---

[19] *Hale County Herald* (Plainview), May 8, 1913.

[20] Duggan to R. C. Rawlings, October 16, 1913 (Littlefield Lands Company Records).

[21] Duggan to Rawlings, June 19, 1913, *ibid.*

actively engaged in establishing a colony at the town of Littlefield.
By March, 1917, the Littlefield community boasted an estimated
1,000 inhabitants, a figure twice that of two years previous.

The population had reached its peak. Powerful factors over
which the company had no control, the weather and the World
War, were working to cripple, at least for a time, the growth and
development of Littlefield's enterprise. Through 1917 a drouth,
which had started the year before, grew worse. That fall the company even stopped planting on the demonstration farm so as not
to waste seed. Settlers began to trickle, then flood away. The Holder-
men Mennonites, for example, abandoned their scorched acreage
in a group and returned to Canada. Their resolve to leave was
reinforced by their determination to avoid conscription following
the declaration of war by the United States in April, 1917. Severe
through 1919, the drouth lingered into 1920. Meanwhile the heavy
income and excess-profits taxes, necessitated by American entry into
the War, cut sharply into Littlefield's receipts from land sales.
These taxes, coupled with a marked decline in the number of
purchasers beginning in the spring of 1917, caused Littlefield to
withdraw his land from the market in July, 1918. By 1920 the
population of the Littlefield community had dropped to about one-
half; not more than 400 persons remained.[22]

Before a sales campaign could again get underway following
the War and the drouth, Major Littlefield died on November 10,
1920. During the eight and one-third years that he controlled the
Littlefield Lands Company, the old cattleman cleared about a
quarter of a million dollars from more than 47,000 acres of farming
and grazing land and 148 town lots sold and paid for in whole or
in part. Realizing that a man who did not stay did not pay, Littlefield was liberal in allowing extensions on payments of notes due,
in making loans for improvements, and in seeing that the school

---

[22] After the "cotton culture" took hold, the population of Littlefield again began to
climb. In 1946 the town was made the seat of Lamb County. Presently more than
7,000 persons reside in Littlefield. H. Bailey Carroll and Walter Prescott Webb (eds.),
The Handbook of Texas (2 vols.; Austin, 1952), II, 66; *Texas Almanac, 1966–1967*
(Dallas, 1965), 136.

did not have to close for lack of funds or facilities in these first struggling years.

No violence and little conflict occurred at Littlefield as the farmer and the townsman surged into the rancher's realm to subdue the grassland. There was no call for contention; the cattleman legally owned the land which the farmer sought. Major Littlefield need harbor no fear of a handful of nesters sprinkled over his range, and he could regulate the speed at which the sodbuster moved into his verdant empire. The farmer was more or less at his mercy. But at Littlefield, as was doubtless the case elsewhere, the old-time cattle baron realized that the future followed the plow, and therefore actually assisted the farmer to gain a foothold on the plains. In the large view, the Littlefield Lands Company is representative of the colonization ventures which, during the initial decades of the twentieth century, encouraged the opening of the Panhandle-Plains to settlement.

Through the course of westward expansion in the history of the United States, the cattleman's frontier preceded the farmer's frontier. When the cattleman reached the Great Plains, he found a veritable paradise, and he speedily appropriated the vast grasslands to graze his herds. Countless George W. Littlefields established numberless LFD ranches. While the farmer at first saw in the Great Plains only a forbidding, barren, empty expanse, a kaleidoscope of circumstances — including improved machinery, improved communications, the lack of good government land for sale, and his insatiable desire to sink his plow into virgin sod — led him eventually to attack the region. And once the settler had proved to himself the wonderful productivity of that land, his conquest of it could not be stayed. The cattleman, seeing profit to be made from the invasion, threw open blocks of his ranch land. Colonization companies such as Littlefield's sprang up throughout the cattle kingdom. On the Panhandle Plains of West Texas, the story of settlement is in large measure the story of such land and townsite companies. In the perspective of the western world, as interpreted by Walter Prescott Webb, this last grand transition from ranching to farming was the final act in the closing of the Great Frontier.

THE COMPANY-OWNED MINING TOWN

IN THE WEST:

EXPLOITATION OR BENEVOLENT

PATERNALISM?

by

JAMES B. ALLEN

A native of Ogden, Utah, and an associate professor of history at Brigham Young University, the author served as a Mormon missionary before entering Utah State University as an undergraduate. He earned the doctorate at the University of Southern California with a dissertation which was published as *The Company Town in the American West* by the University of Oklahoma Press in 1966.

DOZENS of small, unsightly settlements of discontented coal miners scattered over the hills of southern Colorado; the copper smelter town of Hayden, Arizona, which was founded in 1911 as a model industrial community, but which also contained a Mexican section of poor roads and disheveled, sad-looking shanties as unsightly as any mining camp in the West; the huge, contented coal-mining town of Dawson, New Mexico; Jesse Knight's strictly controlled, Mormon-dominated community of Spring Canyon, Utah; and the modern mining town of Weed Heights, built in the middle of the Nevada desert by the Anaconda Company: these and literally scores of other Western towns of various sizes and descriptions all shared at least one important element which set them apart from other communities. Each was fully owned and controlled by a mining company, and the social, economic, and sometimes even the political well-being of the town's inhabitants depended on the policies and goodwill of that company. In each there was almost complete lack of self-government. All property was owned outright by the company, and only employees and certain service personnel, such as doctors and teachers, were allowed to live in the town. All business activity was tightly controlled by the company; a company store dominated the economic life of the community. The town existed solely for the support of a mine, mill or smelter, and when that closed the settlement simply folded up and disappeared.

Company-owned towns were not peculiar, of course, either to the American West or to mining, and they did not constitute a majority of the Western mining camps.[1] Still there were enough of them to make a study of their development a significant and instructive aspect of Western mining history. The history of the Union Pacific and its coal towns, while that company may not have been wholly typical, embodies many of the factors involved in this kind of study. A look at the Union Pacific operation provides an appropriate place to begin.

As the Union Pacific Railroad gradually pushed westward in the 1860's, the company found that much of the land granted to it by the federal government contained rich deposits of coal. This was indeed fortunate, for the company needed an assured source of fuel to keep its engines moving across the continent. At first an agreement was made with two private contractors, Thomas Wardell and Cyrus O. Godfrey, to operate mines on company property. In 1869 this contract was assigned to the Wyoming Coal and Mining Company, a corporation peculiarly similar to the Crédit Mobiler. Wardell was retained as general manager, but nine-tenths of the stock was owned by Oliver Ames, brother of Congressman Oakes Ames and president of the railroad, and five Union Pacific directors.

---

[1] For a list of some of the various companies that provided employee housing about 1920, and some of the towns involved, see Leifur Magnusson, *Housing by Employers in the United States,* Bureau of Labor Statistics, Bulletin No. 263 (Washington, 1920), 273–83.

In the true enterprising fashion of the times, exorbitant rates were charged for coal — and the profits went into the pockets of company directors. Accusations to this effect were made by the federal government's representatives on the Union Pacific Board of Directors, who urged the railroad to operate its own mines. Under pressure, therefore, and after new interests had assumed control of the railroad, the Union Pacific created a Coal Department and began to handle its own properties in 1874.[2]

Coal produced by the Union Pacific was not only used for the railroad, but was also sold to the public.[3] The railroad became the most important coal producer in Wyoming, and soon was dominating the life of many communities. For example, Rock Springs, founded in 1868, became a coal town, a railroad center and, to some degree, a cow town. Although it was never company-owned, the Union Pacific controlled it in almost every way. Other communities were strictly coal-mining camps, and their existence depended entirely upon the life of the adjacent mines.

The first Union Pacific coal town was the rough-and-tumble settlement of Carbon, which began with the opening of Wardell's first mine in 1868. Apparently neither Wardell nor the railroad took much interest in such things as town planning or control. Incoming miners found housing practically impossible to obtain, and living conditions rather primitive. Many of the first homes were simply caves with wooden, earth-covered lean-tos over the front. More suitable housing came later, and the town eventually reached a population of about 3,000. After the abrogation of the Wyoming Coal contract, the railroad provided a doctor for Carbon and established a company store. The store became the center of the town's business activity; it was especially crowded on monthly

---

[2] Nelson Trottman, *History of the Union Pacific: A Financial and Economic Survey* (New York, 1923), 42–44; and *History of the Union Pacific Coal Mines* (Omaha, 1940), 43. Wardell naturally contested the abrogation of the contract, but in 1880 the action of the railroad was upheld by the United States Supreme Court.

[3] It has been charged that the company was able, for a time, to maintain a virtual monopoly on the coal business along its lines by charging other producers higher rates for shipping than the actual selling price of U.P. coal. Trottman, *History of the Union Pacific,* 110.

paydays when the miners received their wages from piles of gold and silver coin stacked on a table in the canned-goods section. Carbon also boasted two general stores, a shoe shop, barber shop, blacksmith, dance hall, school, and several saloons. These facilities served not only the miners but also a few Wyoming cowboys, whose activities frequently included "shootin' up the town" in traditional frontier fashion. After thirty-five years the mines were closed, and Carbon was abandoned.[4]

Meanwhile the Union Pacific had opened other coal mines and founded other settlements. Camps with which the company was involved before 1890 included Almy and Dana, Wyoming; the Colorado towns of Northrop, Erie, Louisville, Baldwin, and Como; and Pleasant Valley and Grass Creek, Utah. None of these became fully developed company towns, but in each case the railroad aided its employees by providing some housing and usually a company store and medical services.[5]

By 1890 the company was apparently becoming somewhat concerned over its lack of control over the coal camps. For one thing, these camps did not always attract the most stable or desirable type of employee because of their lack of adequate housing and their isolation. Furthermore, labor disturbances were plaguing the country and agitators had full access to such wide-open towns as Carbon, even though they were on company property. Strikes had already affected the Wyoming coal fields. In 1870, for example, labor disturbances led to the introduction of Chinese workers into Almy, and in 1875 the company brought the first Chinese into Rock Springs to take the place of striking white miners. The result was continued friction and bitterness which ultimately led to a tragic massacre of several Orientals in Rock Springs in 1885. The

---

[4] *History of the Union Pacific Coal Mines*, 28–35.

[5] *Ibid., passim.* At Pleasant Valley, Utah, the company took over the coal mine from another concern in 1890 and soon tried to claim title to the townsite. In the ensuing court case the company argued that it had taken over the mines with the understanding that all property in the town was included in the transfer, but the court ruled against the company.

company eventually adopted the policy of deporting the Chinese, ostensibly returning them to their homes in China.[6] While it cannot be demonstrated that labor problems were major factors leading to the development of more tightly controlled camps, the subsequent use made of company-owned towns by various firms in Wyoming, Utah, and Colorado would suggest this as at least one motive.

The first Union Pacific camp to reach the status of a fully paternalistic, long-lived company town was Hanna, Wyoming.[7] The first mines were opened there in 1889, and within a few years the company had established a community of some 1,500 people. The Union Pacific Coal Company, created in 1890 as a fully owned subsidiary of the railroad, had the town laid out in orderly fashion and erected relatively comfortable, modern homes. What was reputed to be the best water in Wyoming was piped into town from Rattlesnake Creek, some sixteen miles away. The town soon boasted a company store, hospital, and community hall, all of which were typical of company towns. In the early years there was an effort to require employees to do most of their trading at the company store, and the company even tried to prohibit them from sending to mail-order houses. In 1894, however, an independent clothing store operator was allowed to establish himself in town, and in later years a Laramie grocer was allowed to solicit business and to ship to Hanna residents by train. But even after this policy change the operation of the scrip system, together with the fact that there was still only one general store in town, had the practical effect of requiring more residents to do business at the company store.

The Union Pacific contributed in many ways to the improvement of community life in Hanna. It built a lodge hall which housed various fraternal organizations as well as a movie theatre, a pool hall, and eventually a bar. The company built the first school and contributed to the support of the town band, recreational activi-

---

[6] *Ibid., passim.*

[7] Information on Hanna in *Ibid.,* 113-19; interview with Henry Jones, Laramie, Wyoming, July 8, 1961; interview with O. C. Buehler, Hanna, Wyoming, July 6, 1961.

ties, and churches. On the other hand, the company was not reluctant to use its position as landlord to keep union organizers out of
town.

In 1936 an unusual political development took place — Hanna
became an incorporated community. Such tendencies toward self-
government were almost unknown in company towns. The reasons
for Hanna's incorporation are obscure, but one long-time resident,
who served as company clerk for many years, has suggested that
one objective was to bring a saloon into Hanna. Miners were losing
a great deal of work-time by going to the nearby town of Dana where
they frequently over-imbibed simply because the saloon was so far
from home. The Union Pacific did not want to get involved in the
business of selling liquor, but the town government could license
a saloon. In this circuitous way a saloon was brought to town, and
it is reported that lost-time actually diminished.

Whatever the motive for incorporation, the town government
was controlled by the company and, as might be suspected, the
superintendent was usually elected mayor. Hanna continued to
function as a company-owned community until the early 1950's,
when the last coal mine closed. Most such towns would then simply
have been abandoned, but in this case many long-time employees
were ready for retirement and wanted to stay. Others were able to
find employment nearby. When the Union Pacific offered to sell
its houses, many residents took advantage of the opportunity and
purchased the homes they had been living in for years. Hanna has
not yet become a ghost town; it still exists as a quiet, though obviously dying, community.

After the settlement of Hanna, the Union Pacific became
involved with at least six more coal towns.[8] In 1899 a promising
vein was opened at Spring Valley, Wyoming, and the following
year a town was established. The neat little settlement was lighted
with electricity and even was furnished with sidewalks, something

---

[8] Information on these towns from *History of the Union Pacific Coal Mines,* 126–57;
I. S. Bartlett (ed.), *History of Wyoming* (Chicago, 1918), I, 608; *The Deseret News,*
March 22, 1962; and Questionnaire returned by William R. Gibbs, Reliance, Wyoming,
May 20, 1962.

unusual for company towns. Spring Valley appeared to have every opportunity for success, both as a community and as a mining venture, but in 1905 it was abandoned. Oil seeping into the tunnels and the presense of great quantities of explosive gas made the mines simply too difficult and dangerous to work. Cumberland, Wyoming, was also founded about 1900, and its mine was one of Union Pacific's greatest producers until abandoned in 1930. At Superior, Wyoming, mines were opened and homes constructed about 1906 by the Superior Coal Company, which was taken over in 1916 by the Union Pacific. The town was incorporated in 1910, and mining continued until 1962. In 1907 the Union Pacific began development of a mine at Tono, Washington. This town was located in green, rolling hills; its beautiful surroundings, plus efforts of the company to plan the town well, made it a most attractive community. In 1937 it was taken over by the Bucoda Coal Mining Company. Reliance, Wyoming, was founded in 1910 and the company ultimately built a comfortable town of about 145 homes. When the mines were closed in 1954, most of the houses were sold to tenants. Winton, Wyoming, a well-planned community established in 1917 by Megeath Coal Company, was purchased by the Union Pacific in 1920. It was the company's last town in that state.

This brief review of the Union Pacific's company towns suggests a certain progression which probably typifies the development of coal-mining camps in the West. In the early years there seemed to be little concern about town planning or community facilities, and most coal camps were rather haphazard settlements. Gradually a policy evolved which provided both the necessary services for resident-employees and a firm control of community affairs by the company managers. Finally, as seen in the Union Pacific's development of Hanna, towns began to be generally well-planned and well-run, demonstrating that the company had at least some concern for both the well-being and satisfaction of the resident-employees. This, however, is not the complete story. The question of the real purpose or motive behind the establishment of company-owned mining towns needs to be explored. Were these towns used merely as a means of further exploitation by self-seeking industrialists, or were they evidence of sincere efforts toward a positive and benevolent paternalism? Probably this question will never be answered definitively, but a few considerations may be useful.

Motives are difficult to assess. In a recent book I generally accepted the answers given by management as to why company towns came into existence. It was said that the company town was an economic necessity in isolated areas where some workers would not go unless housing was provided for them. The doubtful permanence of mining operations, as illustrated by the fate of some of the Union Pacific's mines, made an employee reluctant to build or purchase his own home. Some mine operators felt that company housing would attract a better class of working men. Many companies needed to maintain control of townsites, particularly in connection with open-pit copper mining, in case the land might someday be required for mine expansion. Poor roads and transportation facilities made it impractical for miners to commute even from nearby communities, and the same factors made necessary the operation of company stores.[9]

These considerations are all valid, and there is no reason to suggest that the motives given by company managers are not accurate — as far as they go. More recent second thoughts, however, compel me at least to raise some speculative questions regarding further motives, which may slightly modify the view presented earlier. I wonder, for example, whether one motive for the creation of tightly controlled camps was not connected with the rise of labor unions, and the desires of some companies to control their workers more effectively during times of industrial strife. It is curious to note that the rise of coal mining in the West almost paralleled the rise of the Knights of Labor. This ill-fated union had organizers in Western coal camps, and its activities, as well as those of other agitators, were a constant source of irritation. Was it absolutely necessary, for example, for the Union Pacific Coal Company so completely to dominate even the building of homes at Hanna, when

---

[9] James B. Allen, *The Company Town in the American West* (University of Oklahoma Press, 1966), 7, 33–34, 50–51.

Carbon had existed in an equally isolated location for some twenty years, and where many private homes had been erected? Sincere benevolence surely played a part, but is it not also possible that a desire to shield workers from the corruptive influence of labor agitators was at least a passing consideration?

The situation in southern Colorado was more to the point. The Colorado Fuel and Iron Company was organized in 1892 as a combination of several mining companies, and it soon dominated the area. Company towns had long been established, and it is to the credit of the company that by the end of the century it was beginning to pay serious attention to community improvement. It nevertheless held tenaciously to its towns, and a federal investigation of the 1913–1914 strikes led to conflicting testimony as to why such ownership was necessary. The company frequently referred to the need to provide housing for immigrant workers, who could scarcely afford to provide it for themselves. These same workers, it was said, were also unprepared to assume the burdens of self-government, making it doubly necessary for the company to operate the towns. George P. West, an apparent union sympathizer who wrote a summary of the federal commission's report, bitterly attacked company motives:

> The Colorado strike was a revolt by whole communities against arbitrary economic, political and social domination by the Colorado Fuel and Iron Company and the smaller coal companies that followed its lead.... This economic domination was maintained by the companies in order that they might be free to obey or disregard state laws governing coal mining as they pleased; arbitrarily determine wages and working conditions; and retain arbitrary power to discharge without stated cause. The power to discharge was in turn used as a club to force employees and their families to submit to company control of every activity in the mining communities.[10]

In reply to the company's allegation that coal miners were not capable of self-government, it was said that this was the same philosophy that justified slavery. The testimony of union officials, as well as

[10] George P. West, *U.S. Commission on Industrial Relations Report on the Colorado Strike* (Chicago, 1915), 15.

that of company officials connected with certain eastern coal mines where self-government had been tried, gave ample evidence that there was the capacity for civic responsibility in camps similar to those of southern Colorado.[11] Edward P. Costigan, leader of the Colorado Progressives, also gave his views to the federal commission:

> There is, of course, in Colorado as elsewhere the general human unrest which is at the base of all progress.... In Colorado in addition to that underlying cause there has been a feudalistic system with absentee control, long prevalent, especially in the southern field, on the part of employers toward their employees; and this system has been perpetuated largely through the political dominance of great industries in that field. Last Spring a State senator, who resides at Colorado Springs, visited Ludlow, and following an investigation which he conducted there after the tragedy at Ludlow, he made a statement to me which I think concisely illustrates the matter I have in mind. He said he had found, after a searching inquiry into conditions in southern Colorado, that the motto of large industrial concerns, especially in Las Animas and Huerfano counties, might be expressed in two words, "We rule." He said the practice of the coal companies, as he knew from his investigation, had been to assert ownership throughout southern Colorado, the ownership of courts, executive and legislative officials, of coroner's and other juries, of churches, of the saloons, of the schools, of the lands, of the houses upon the lands, and eventually a certain ownership over the men who toil upon the lands.[12]

All these charges, of course, were made at a time of great political and emotional stress, and could easily have been exaggerated. Nevertheless there seems to be reasonable ground for the suspicion that some companies obtained and kept control of their coal towns partly as an effort to maintain their independence from union activists as well as other reformers bent on improving the lot of the miner. The suspicion is strengthened by an extensive report on company housing throughout the nation published in 1920 by the Bureau of Labor. When asked about their reasons for providing employee housing, most employers gave the standard answers con-

---

[11]*Ibid.*, 9–12.

[12] Edward P. Costigan, *Papers of Edward P. Costigan Relating to the Progressive Movement in Colorado, 1902–1917,* edited by Colin B. Goodykoontz (Boulder: University of Colorado, 1941), 306–307.

cerning economic necessity and the need to obtain a better class of
men. A few, however, went further, and the report summarized
their views:

> The desire to secure the loyalty of the men is also put forward as a
> reason for housing work, and two mine operators declared that their
> purpose is to control the labor situation better, one emphasizing the
> desire "to have men concentrated so as to have proper supervision over
> them, to better control them in times of labor agitation and threatened
> strikes." It was declared by another operator that the company houses
> had undoubtedly been a factor in winning a strike which had recently
> occurred.[13]

While the report did not state where the housing in question was
located, the point could apply as well in the West as anywhere.

The question of paternalism and its benefits for employees is
complicated, partly because company towns have varied so widely
in almost every respect. In the early years of this century many
companies began to build model communities with well-planned
streets, unusually good homes, and highly adequate water, sewage,
and other community facilities.[14] This was obviously an enlightened
form of paternalism. A few firms have found it necessary even in
recent years to build modern communities in isolated spots, and in
these employee satisfaction is generally high.[15] We are concerned
here, however, with towns which existed forty or more years ago.
It is naturally difficult to evaluate with complete fairness the benefits
or evils of this bygone paternalism, but the six points which follow
should be taken into account.

---

[13] Magnusson, *Housing by Employers,* 21.

[14] This list would include such towns as Clarkdale, Arizona, a smelter town serving the
mines at Jerome and laid out in 1914; Cartago, California, a mineral pumping and
processing town built in 1916; Climax, Colorado, founded in 1920 at the site of the
largest producing molybdenum deposits in the world; Mt. Harris, Colorado, an attractive coal camp laid out in 1914; Conda, Idaho, a phosphate-mining town built in the
1920's; Tyrone, New Mexico, a copper mining town built in 1916–1917 by the Phelps
Dodge Corporation but abandoned in 1921; and Keetly, Utah, built shortly after World
War I by the New Park Mining Company at the site of its lead-zinc-silver operations.
There has been little criticism of these and many other towns like them.

[15] An example is Eagle Mountain, California, where the Kaiser Steel Corporation
established an iron mine in 1947.

1. It should be remembered that the ownership of a town was actually only incidental to the total operations of a large company or corporation. Town planning, and individual and community welfare, were not normal corporate concerns, and only gradually did top management become aware of the increased work efficiency and better public relations that could come from taking these things into consideration. Not until around 1910 did the model communities mentioned earlier begin to characterize the mining fields. It should also be observed that mine owners, often living in the East, probably had little first-hand information about actual conditions in many camps, and this lack of awareness by absentee landlords probably contributed to some of the abuses.

2. Economically, the operation of employee housing did not bring substantial profits to mining companies, although it was not always as great a liability as might be expected. While it is impossible to obtain exact accounting figures, a few calculations on the basis of some published figures are possible. The Bureau of Labor's 1920 report included a study of sixteen coal camps in Colorado and Wyoming, twelve of which were operated by one large company.[16] Of 995 dwellings for which building costs were reported, 404 cost between $250 and $500, 453 between $500 and $750, and 110 between $750 and $1,000. Costs varied according to size, construction material, and whether the homes were detached or built as row houses. Rent varied from less than three dollars to eighteen dollars per month, but slightly over half of the units fell into the group which rented for between eight and nine dollars. In the twelve camps belonging to the large company, town maintenance costs amounted to thirty-nine per cent of the total rent receipts for the period 1911–1915. A Wyoming company reported that maintenance took forty-one per cent of its rent receipts in the period 1913–1916.[17] For purposes of rough calculation, if it is assumed that the average was a $700 unit which rented for eight dollars per month,

---

[16] While the report does not state the name, it probably was the Colorado Fuel and Iron Company. This company was the largest in the region.

[17] Magnusson, *Housing by Employers*, 96–100.

and that fifty per cent of this amount went into community maintenance of all sorts, the company would clear approximately forty-
eight dollars per year from the units — and it would take a little
over fourteen years to make up the original cost. Obviously, the
company would have received no interest on its investment over
those years; but after that, unless the houses were replaced or the
mines closed, the continuing profit per year would provide a 6.8
per cent annual return on the original cost of construction. While
this is not a particularly attractive investment opportunity, especially in view of the fact that these figures do not include depreciation or taxes, it nevertheless indicates that housing did not present
a net long-range loss to the companies involved.

Figures given in 1927 by Colorado Fuel and Iron present a
slightly less desirable investment situation. In that year the company asked for an increase in rental fees, which had been set in
1915 at two dollars per room per month. The company noted that
it had lost several hundred thousand dollars on houses over the past
ten years, and felt that it was entitled to a return on its investment
in houses occupied of five per cent per annum and should be able
to charge three per cent annual depreciation. Adding these figures
to maintenance expense and taxes, it was calculated that the company should charge at least three dollars per room. A series of conferences with employee representatives resulted in a compromise
of $2.50.[18]

Finally, it is obvious that companies sometimes took high risks
in providing extensive housing, for some mines were abandoned
very quickly. At Tyrone, New Mexico, for instance, the Phelps
Dodge Corporation began development of a copper mine in 1914
and spent over $250,000 on housing alone. Total cost for develop-
ment of the entire townsite came close to a million dollars, but the
town was abandoned in 1921.[19] Company housing, then, would

---

[18] *Colorado Fuel and Iron Industrial Bulletin*, XI, No. 5 (June 1927), 13–14; and
ibid., XI, No. 8 (October 1927), 14.

[19] Leifur Magnusson, "A Modern Copper Mining Town," *Monthly Labor Review*, VII,
No. 3 (September 1918); Works Progress Administration, Writer's Program, *New
Mexico: A Guide to the Colorful State* (New York, 1953), 418.

seem not to have been a lucrative investment for mining companies, but neither does it appear that many of them sustained excessively heavy losses over the long run.

3. The operation of company stores cannot categorically be classified as evidence of either benevolence or coercive exploitation. It is clear that stores were there not only to serve employee needs but also as business ventures. Frequently stores were operatd by subsidiary companies whose major purpose was merchandising. It was probably rare that such companies lost money. Even during the Great Depression losses on employee credit were surprisingly low, ranging, on a national average, from 0.9 per cent in 1931 to 1.6 per cent in 1932.[20] Prices in company stores were generally higher than those of independent stores,[21] and any expenses involved in transportation to isolated areas were easily absorbed.

It was possible to use the company store as a tool of economic exploitation in at least three ways: employees might be coerced into trading at the store as a condition of employment; prices could be set excessively high; and liberal credit, especially through the issuing of scrip prior to the regular payday, could keep an employee perpetually in debt, making it necessary for him to continue to work for the company. The scrip system was abused further through the discounting of scrip for cash, either by the company store or by private concerns who could get a face value refund at the store.

The evidence seems clear that even down to the 1920's there was pressure, even coercion, to trade at the company store.[22] An extreme example was reported in Colorado, where a store manager who was on the school board forced removal of a teacher because she refused to trade with him. The daughter of another store manager, who was under age and lacked a teaching certificate, replaced

---

[20] "Company Stores and the Scrip System," *Monthly Labor Review*, XLI, No. 1 (July 1935), 49.

[21] A federal survey of company stores in the East, published in 1935, showed higher prices ranging from 2.1 per cent to 10.4 per cent. *Ibid.*, 51.

[22] Allen, *The Company Town*, 132. See also West, *U.S. Industrial Commission*, 68–71.

her, even though the county superintendent and the people of the camp protested.[23]

A serious accusation made by employees and unions was that wage deductions and credit were intentionally calculated to keep cash away from the employee. Scrip was a form of credit, for it could be issued to employees prior to payday. Even after Colorado Fuel and Iron eliminated the scrip system in 1913, it was charged that the continuing credit system was still operated in such a way as to give few miners cash anywhere near the amount of their actual earnings. The allegation was that this was deliberate industrial bondage, designed to force miners to continue to work for cheap wages. It is difficult, however, to find substantial evidence for such charges. It seems, rather, that only a small number of company town residents in the West actually owed their souls to the company store. At Hanna, Wyoming, the number was less than five per cent, and the company tried to encourage employees to stay out of debt. The whole system, in fact, was considered nothing but a headache by a long-time company clerk who reported that "belly-aches and gripes" by employees who had extended themselves too far was one of his chief sources of trouble.[24] It is apparent, furthermore, that whenever credit is available a certain class of improvident worker will involve himself too deeply in debt, no matter what the circumstances.

Financial records of most companies are practically impossible to obtain, but the available books of a few old-time companies throw some light on the nature and extent of wage deductions around the turn of the century. The Detroit Copper Mining Company was the predecessor of Phelps Dodge at Morenci, Arizona. Records for 1897 and 1898 indicate that most employees had the largest share of their wages eaten up by various deductions. For the month ending June 30, 1897, for example, the total payroll amounted to $36,371.35.

---

[23] West, *U.S. Industrial Commission*, 71.

[24] Jones interview.

Deductions at the company store amounted to $16,752.15; other deductions included board, rent, hospital, insurance, library fees, drafts, and cash advances (the later amounting to $1,645.85), and made a total of $23,595.05. This left only $12,776.30, a little over one-third of the payroll, due on payday. The record of individual employees is equally interesting. John Daugherty, a foreman who worked thirty days for four dollars per day, earned total wages of $120; his deductions included thirty dollars for room and board, $11.35 at the store, and $2.50 hospital and insurance fees, for a total of $43.85; and he received a draft for $76.15 on payday. Bruno Cardona, on the other hand, had worked for twenty-seven and one-half days, earning $61.85; his store bill amounted to $27.75; and his hospital and insurance fee of $2.50, plus a previous advance of $33.60, left nothing to be had on payday. Well over half the men on the payroll received nothing, although some of them had apparently worked only part of the month and had received cash or draft advances upon termination.[25] The fact that the company was so liberal with advances does not indicate a particularly repressive or coercive economic policy. A year later the situation was slightly better in terms of money received at the end of the month, for approximately forty per cent of the payroll was distributed on payday rather than taken out in deductions.[26]

Scattered records of another Arizona operation, the old Twin Buttes Mining and Smelter Company, are also available. Twin Buttes was not a full company town, for the company did not provide housing, but its records reflect some interesting things about the company store and its patrons. In January, 1906, Juan Cano worked twenty-eight days and earned a total of fifty-six dollars, but he charged fifty dollars at the store and received six dollars at the end of the month. The meticulous record of his charge account reveals his family's diet and other household needs. The family existed largely on eggs, meat, potatoes, chili, bread and coffee, with

---

[25] Detroit Copper Mining Company, Time Book & Pay Roll, June 30, 1897, University of Arizona Library, Tucson, Arizona.

[26] *Ibid., June* 30, 1898.

a little fruit once in a while. Eighty-five pounds of beef were purchased during the month, at a rate of ten cents per pound! Other purchases included candy, gum, beans, sugar, lard, flour and soap. Juan's wife was apparently a seamstress, for they purchased thread, ribbon, calico and gingham. Juan also liked to dress up now and then, for he purchased a tie; and he rolled his own cigarettes rather than smoke a pipe or cigars, for he bought plenty of tobacco and cigarette papers. In short, all his needs were provided at the company store and there was little need to go elsewhere even if he could. The six dollars he had left probably went a long way, especially if he had built his own shack to live in. In case he needed it, the store carried almost every other essential item, including fish, stationery supplies, milk, guns and ammunition, canned goods, stamps, stove polish, shoe nails, lily cream, harmonicas, and "cathartic pills." Most of the store's business was credit, but very few employees charged their total paycheck.[27]

In 1914 the president of Colorado Fuel and Iron denied charges that employees were receiving only a minimal amount of cash. He insisted that in the previous fiscal year they had received 80.9 per cent of their earnings in cash, and that only 11.73 per cent had been deducted for store purchases.[28] These figures seem low, and the report did not indicate the basis for his claims. The following year the Reverend Eugene Gaddis, superintendent of the company's sociological department, declared before a federal commission that miners spent an average of thirty to thirty-five per cent of their wages at the company store, although it is not clear whether this was all through credit.[29] In 1933 the per cent of total payrolls expended in company stores was about the same. The national average, based on a survey of 812 stores, was then 29.6 per cent. In the western coal fields, five New Mexico stores showed

[27] Twin Buttes Mining and Smelting Company Papers, University of Arizona Library, Tucson, Arizona.

[28] *The Struggle in Colorado for Industrial Freedom* (Bulletin issued by coal operators during the 1914 labor difficulties), Bulletin No. 15, Sept. 4, 1914, 2.

[29] West, *U.S. Industrial Commission,* 70.

28.8 per cent, six Utah stores showed 32.0 per cent, eight Wyoming
stores reported 29.1 per cent, and Colorado reported the largest
figure of 37.4 per cent in five stores. Four establishments at copper
camps reported 30.8 per cent.[30] A reasonable interpretation of the
available evidence would certainly indicate that even though company managers sometimes demanded trade at the company store,
especially in the early days of company towns, the policy was not
widespread for a long period of time in the West, and only a
minority of employees were held in economic bondage through
perpetual debt.

4. There is ample evidence that town ownership was used
by some companies as an economic tool against union organizers.
It was not uncommon for coal companies to lock striking miners
out of town, since they were not working for the company and
therefore had no legal right to enter company property. In such
cases it fell to the unions to construct tent towns for evicted miners
and their families. It was at such a camp that the tragic Ludlow
Massacre of 1914 took place.[31] In a strike against the Utah Fuel
Company in the winter of 1903–1904 strikers were evicted and,
in addition, were offered one-way railroad tickets out of the state
for only one-quarter fare.[32] Miners who had been allowed to build
their own homes on company property were kept away from them,
and if not sold in six months the houses were to be turned over to
the company.[33] At Morenci, Arizona, the Phelps Dodge Corporation reversed things during a bitter strike in the winter of 1915–
1916. Since the strikers were in control of Morenci, the company
proceeded to build a tent village at Duncan for the benefit of

---

[30] "Company Stores and the Scrip System," 48.

[31] Allen, *The Company Town,* 65.

[32] The Denver and Rio Grande Western Railroad owned the fuel company.

[33] James B. Allen, "The Company Town: A Passing Phase of Utah's Industrial Development," *Utah Historical Quarterly,* XXXIV, No. 2 (Spring 1966), 158–159. An
interesting sidelight on this strike is the fact that young local Mormons were brought
into the Sunnyside mines as strikebreakers on the assumption that their religion almost
automatically kept them from being influenced by unions.

refugee miners who wanted to work.[34] The use of company housing
at a tool against unionism obviously was not permanently successful, but for a while it served some company interests well.

5. Company-owned mining camps, especially before the turn
of the century, were often poorly planned, unsightly and unsani-
tary, although the appearance of particular houses and lots often
depended as much on the personality of the employee as upon company policy. It was not uncommon for towns to go for years without grass, shrubs or trees. Open drainage ditches, which often
harbored garbage and other filth, sometimes ran through the center
of town, and garbage collection came infrequently if at all. On the
other hand, by the turn of the century many companies were
beginning to provide good fences, regular garbage collection, sani-
tary drainage systems, and trees and shrubs for those who would
plant them. In spite of these efforts some residents seemingly lacked
any desire to plant greenery, paint their homes, or help keep things
neat and clean. On the other hand, many went far beyond company-
induced incentive in making their homes more attractive. The federal coal commission concluded in its report, published in 1923,
that "even the best of company communities . . . often have bad
spots; and even the worst camps may have little oases of cleanliness
and attractiveness."[35]

6. Finally, it is clear that many companies provided abundant
services for employees which were not available in other rural communities, but this very paternalism was not always appreciated
and was frequently abused. Colorado Fuel and Iron provided such

---

[34] James R. Kluger, "The Clifton-Morenci Strike of 1915–1916" (unpublished Master's
thesis, Department of History, University of Arizona, 1965), 59–63; and Roberta Watt,
"History of Morenci, Arizona" (unpublished Master's thesis, Department of History,
University of Arizona, 1956), 66–72.

[35] United States Coal Commission (John Hays Hammond, Chairman), *Report of the
United States Coal Commission, Dec. 19, 1923* (Washington, 1925), 1429. An interesting illustration of this point is in Lucille Richins, "A Social History of Sunnyside"
(unpublished paper filed at the Utah State Historical Society), 10–11. The author tells
of the poor care taken of company houses by certain immigrants from southern Europe
who were not used to American standards. She was disgusted by such things as the
keeping of hogs and chickens in the house, as well as the use of bathtubs to scald hogs
at butchering time. Such practices caused one company to remove bathtubs from houses
rented to these immigrants.

services as local kindergartens, language classes for immigrants, the sponsoring of women's clubs and other social organizations, extensive recreational facilities, and inexpensive medical, dental and eye care. Many isolated company towns had electricity long before the REA made it common in other communities throughout the country. It was probably inevitable, however, that such paternalism should cause its own problems, as certain employees were bound to take advantage of the company in every possible way. A humorous but probably typical story is told of a Mrs. Miller who lived in Hanna, Wyoming, before the days of electric light meters. Tenants were charged for electricity according to the number and size of light globes hanging in the house at the time of the check. There were no telephones in town, but apparently the local underground worked well to inform residents when the auditor and company clerk were on their tour of inspection. One morning they knocked at Mrs. Miller's door, announcing that they were going to check the lights. "Great Heavens," said Mrs. Miller in feigned dismay, "I was cleaning my house this morning and I broke every bloody light!" Every drop cord in the house was swinging back and forth. From then on, reported a company clerk in later years, "you didn't catch many lights, but you saw a lot of cords going back and forth." [36] This local tale may be exaggerated, but it illustrates the not unusual efforts of many residents to take advantage of company paternalism.

Looking back, the image of the company-owned mining town in the West is still, in a sense, an enigma. Some towns were well designed and well kept, while others were simply rows of shacks along haphazard dirt roads. Some companies provided abundant services and opportunities for employees, while others only grudgingly provided a few. Some employees found themselves perpetually in debt to the company store, while others in the same town were completely free.

Was, then, the institution of the company town an evidence

---

[36] Jones interview.

of benevolence, or was it simply a way to exploit the worker for the benefit of the company? The answer seems to lie in the motives of the companies themselves. Managers erected towns not out of any primary altruism, but because they considered it an economic necessity. Company housing did not provide profit, but neither was it a great economic loss if mining continued for a number of years at the same location. The company store was usually a profit-making venture, and it is clear that in some cases employees were coerced into trading with the company. Some companies used their ownership of homes and towns as a powerful weapon against union organization, thus further exploiting employee dependence upon their good graces. In the long run, however, avarice seems to have been more the exception than the rule, and in many company towns good living conditions and adequate public services were provided from the beginning. Older towns saw substantial improvements early in the twentieth century. The services of company stores, hospitals, and other community organizations and activities frequently made life not only tolerable but even pleasant. Nevertheless, all these services were in part exploitative, for they were designed to produce more satisfied employees and hence more productive employees. Perhaps we should look back on the company town of forty or fifty years ago as neither outright benevolence nor negative industrial exploitation, but rather as a curious experiment in what might be called "benevolent exploitation."

KENNEDY AND JOHNSON:

A POLITICAL LOOK AT

THE RECENT WEST

by

JOE B. FRANTZ

A native of Weatherford, Texas, and long a professor of history in the University of Texas, the author also has been director of the Texas State Historical Association and editor of the *Southwestern Historical Quarterly*. He has published numerous books and articles on regional and national topics. In 1968 he was granted leave to report to the White House to assemble materials for the Lyndon B. Johnson library at the University of Texas.

THE House of Representatives is a gigantic personnel pool — almost half-a-thousand Congressmen tied to their districts, plus all the administrative assistants, committee clerks, and secretaries, all scurrying about with more confusion than Boston's North Station on a ski weekend when the fall is fresh and full on New Hampshire's slopes. On the other hand, as every pretentious analyst has written, the United States Senate is the world's most exclusive club. Nearly two hundred years old, it is limited to one hundred members — two only from each state in the Union. (Even the *Institut Français,* noble and *distingué* though it may be, permits four hundred members from a nation whose population is one-fourth the size of the United States.) Here men get to know each other. Under the spell of partnership or principle they may disagree heatedly;

but when the moment of ardor has passed, they join ranks as surely
as though they had taken a blood oath in the Mafia or some teen-age
sorority. Witness, for instance, the notorious Bobby Baker case.
Almost every Senator demanded a thorough probe — of the executive branch, of the outside influence peddlers. But when the investigation threatened to turn inward, the Senators barricaded their
doors against the probe faster than an Irish clan against an English
policeman. Senators are brothers; they fight like brothers, but they
also know each other and protect each other like brothers.

Thus it was that John F. Kennedy and Lyndon B. Johnson,
who had served briefly together in the House of Representatives,
came to *know* each other in the Senate of the United States after
the election of Kennedy to that reverend body in 1952. Senator
Johnson had preceded the late President by four years. In the Senate
the two men, sharing membership as members of a minority party,
first really came together, or collided, whichever way you choose
to interpret their overlapping careers. By this time Senator Johnson
had already emerged as the leading legislative light of the Democratic Party in the Senate, ably advised by his politically astute and
powerful fellow-Texan, Sam Rayburn. The two made a team that
knew how to put over programs.

On the other hand, Kennedy was looked upon as a cross
between intriguing and promising. His name had been known
since New Deal days because of his father's service and his father's
insistence on always taking a whole big brood of Kennedys along
with him. Young John had already had a break-in experience as a
Congressman from Massachusetts, and in attaining his Senate seat
he had defeated another proud and even more historic name, the
very personable and able Henry Cabot Lodge. The Kennedy campaign tea parties and the Kennedy approach to pragmatic wooing
of the women's vote had become a topic of some national interest,
largely because it brought a fresh quality onto a scene whose
politicking is too often repetitious.

But at this juncture, and until January 1961, John F. Kennedy
was officially a junior Senator who looked to his more powerful
senior, the Senator from Texas, for general guidance and assistance.

The fact that Johnson was the youngest Democratic leader of the Senate in history and would shortly become its youngest Majority Leader did not take away from the fact that the junior Senator from Massachusetts was a youth indeed. The fact, too, that Kennedy was handsome, unmarried, and much in demand socially did not detract from his interest as good copy for the press and television. It was Johnson as Majority Leader who gave the junior Senator's career a major advance by naming him to the valued Foreign Relations Committee.

The contrasts that shaped the two men are well-known. Senator Johnson was a marginal Westerner, living a little more than an hour's drive west of the Balcones Fault line which geographically, geologically, and culturally divides Texas into the South and the West. He definitely lived in western country, deficient in rainfall, spacious and sparse, good for grazing and deer hunting and not much else. The LBJ Ranch might not be a true ranch in the western concept of size — unless you're a Californian who calls everything larger than a parking lot a ranch — but it was a true ranch in its approach to agriculture. Except for some peach growers, no one in his area knew any past nor foresaw any future for ordinary farming. You could raise white-faced Herefords if your land had some springs or streams, or you could raise sheep and goats if your land belonged to the less watered, rocky patches. Beyond that, besides egg-sized peaches suitable chiefly for brandy, about your only crops would be pecans and prayer. The fact that Johnson's home district also encompassed land to the east of the Balcones Fault, a region which in reality is a continuation of the broad southern Mississippi Valley, and the fact that Texas itself had once been a member in good standing of the Confederate States of America meant that perforce Johnson must represent some Southern attitudes and that he must also bear the political onus of being tagged a Southerner.

Senator Kennedy, of course, belonged to an entirely different background. Although he came from enormous wealth, his family had risen recently enough to remember the aspirations and frequent inconveniences of being Boston Irish. He represented an area in which ethnic differences were both sublimated and intensified in a contradictory fashion. He represented an area where people worked for wages, and expected their children to work for wages also. He represented urban America with all its stresses, sophistications, and strengths. There was just enough gap in the age of the two Senators that the junior Senator had missed the shock of the Great Depression, and had been a presumably happy prep school and college boy when Lyndon Johnson was sticking his neck out with New Deal fervor. JFK's approach to the problems of hard times were arrived at intellectually and rationally rather than emotionally and subjectively.

So far as can be ascertained, as fellow Senators in the same party the two men worked together with reasonable harmony and friendliness. Probably warmth was missing, but this is not too surprising. As the leader of his party in the Senate, Johnson worked long hours and did little else than work. Kennedy fitted work in with other endeavors, including his well-publicized romance and marriage to the future First Lady. Each man at times represented his sectional interest, though both obviously were struggling to rise above mere sectional representation. Examining their records in general, one finds that they tended to vote together on most issues, but varied on specifics. It is a reasonable assumption that Kennedy followed the lead of his party's chief representative in the Senate and pursued a separate path only when party leadership as represented by Senator Johnson did not take a determined party stand. These were the days of the Eisenhower administration when most of the time Eisenhower's progressive support came from the Democratic leadership in both Houses. The policy of loyal opposition as practiced by Rayburn and Johnson took the form of support where White House suggestions seemed to them in the national interest. They objected only when opposition did not mean purposeful obstructionism.

Two items, one anecdotal and the other political, can be cited for whatever they are worth in assaying the amount of warmth and understanding between the two Senators. On one occasion a Texas professor complained to George Reedy that Senator Johnson lacked a sense of humor. In denial Reedy offered this story: As Majority

Leader, Johnson naturally insisted that all Democratic proposals pass through his hands. One day he was standing at his aisle desk at the front of the Senate chamber when Kennedy, like a respectable junior, came quietly down the aisle to ask permission to introduce a resolution commemorating some anniversary of Arthur Fiedler and the Boston Pops orchestra. Johnson pretended not to·hear the request. Kennedy repeated himself in a louder tone, and again Johnson, inclining his ear closely toward the junior Senator's head, did not get it quite clear. A third time Kennedy made his request, this time loud enough that other Senators within the immediate area could hear. Johnson, now with an audience, grinned at his colleague from Massachusetts and with an affectionate slap, said, "Oh come, John, this is the United States Senate. We can't take its valuable time for resolutions on every fife and drum corps in the United States!" (I might add that I have told this story to dedicated Kennedy adherents who did not find it the least bit humorous or heartwarming.)

The other story, authenticable, is rooted in the exciting contest between Kennedy and Estes Kefauver for the Democratic nomination for Vice President in 1956. As you will recall, that contest very quickly evolved into a two-man fight. The Texas delegation, which had been looking the other way, dramatically switched its allegiance to Senator Kennedy at the personal urging of its principal delegate, Lyndon B. Johnson. At the moment, the decision of Johnson to support Kennedy was considered to be a crucial breakthrough; but other states then began switching one way or the other, with enough of them going for Kefauver to give the Senator from Tennessee the nomination. Most pundits agree that Kennedy was the long-range winner by not running for Vice President in a losing cause.

Before you accuse Senator Johnson of trying to put the junior Senator out of future running for President, you must recall that Johnson's personal hero was Franklin D. Roosevelt, who himself had once been persuaded to accept a Vice Presidential nomination in a losing cause, and yet Roosevelt has come down in history in political circles as "The Champ." Johnson, like Kennedy, was too historically astute not to realize that a national race, albeit a losing one, in which the contender is not the front runner, can give a man a national name without any of the burden of being tagged a loser.

Between them, the two men seemed to divide their strength sectionally — Kennedy to the East and North, Johnson to the South and West. Johnson, for instance, discussed western problems with an easy familiarity that made him immediately acceptable as a fellow-Westerner. He had worked on western road gangs under the broiling sun; he had doctored cattle; and he had alternately raged and prayed as the weeks crawled by with hardly a cloud in the sky, while his land parched and withered away. When he was in the West, Kennedy countered his lack of western exposure by reiterating in almost every speech the undeniable fact that two of the greatest friends — he always insisted, the two greatest — of the West had been New Yorkers, both named Roosevelt. The inference was inescapable: if you want a third great friend, go a little farther east to Massachusetts.

Many people might claim that Johnson had one overwhelming advantage. As Senate Majority Leader after 1954, he was in a position to grab much more publicity and credit for any developments and legislation that might take place. This argument can be disposed of by the fact that he was also much more exposed politically, and that his kind of exposure was the same kind that had ruined the Presidential ambitions of such stalwarts as Henry Clay and Robert Taft.

So much for generalities. Let's look at the record, as another Presidential aspirant often said. Nearly a decade ago Wesley Calef wrote:

> It is difficult to avoid the conclusion that national policy with respect to the public domain for the past 75 years has been a disappointment. As citizens we can take pride in our reservation policy for the national parks, the national forest, wildlife refuges, and reclamation and power projects. But our policies of disposal and management of the public domain present the opposite picture. Federal land policy has satisfied neither the proponents of state ownership nor the advocates of federal management or private ownership; neither Easterners nor Westerners; neither cattlemen nor sheep ranchers; neither the range livestock industry nor the conservationists. Federal management has produced

little revenue, has not benefited the West in any fundamental way, has done relatively little to strengthen and stabilize the western range livestock industry.[1]

Calef could have updated his statement to 1968 and have come up with the same conclusion. Neither Kennedy nor Johnson, as Senators or as Presidents, addressed themselves to this problem with any great aggressiveness. This particular problem continues as it always has. On the other hand, the budgets for such divisions of our public life as the Bureau of Land Management, the Bureau of Reclamation, the National Parks Service, and the Forest Service have consistently doubled, trebled, and risen even more spectacularly, invariably with the support of these two men, so that the West can be said to have profited from their presence.

The counter to this claim is that both men were by nature spenders from the public purse, and that they invariably increased budgets because of their inherent prodigality. And there is the even more conservative retort that both men were dedicated to the extension of federal control at the expense of local and private enterprise. This charge can be refuted, however, by pointing out the, although the Bureau of Land Management has "found it difficult if not impossible to build support for its program which might counterbalance the opposing political power of stockmen," nonetheless the budget of the BLM "roughly tripled" under the serene and passive administration of President Eisenhower.[2]

One of the issues which has always concerned the West, and which can provoke arguments without end, is the construction of dams, particularly for production of power. To some people in arid lands, federally-constructed dams are sacred ones — no more to be condemned in concept than motherhood or Mormons. To others, inundating lands with dammed-up water, especially at federal expense, is so much "big dam foolishness," as the signs along the river Kaw proclaimed a decade ago. Throughout, one fervent and

---

[1] Wesley Calef, *Private Grazing and Public Lands* (Chicago, 1960), 285.
[2] *Ibid.*, 260.

consistent adherent to the construction of dams at federal expense
has been Lyndon Johnson. When in 1958 Senator Johnson published "My Political Philosophy," he wrote the following:

> Our nation, like all nations, is possessed of certain resources — resources
> of nature, resources of position, and resources of the human mind.
> Without conquest or aggrandizement, we cannot add to these basics.
> Thus whatever we are to be we must build from those things at our
> disposal, and to content ourselves with less than the ultimate potential
> is to deny our heritage and our duty.
>
> Obviously, having come from a land like Texas, I feel this strongly.
> Of all endeavors on which I have worked in public life, I am proudest
> of the accomplishments in developing the Lower Colorado River dur-
> ing the 1930's and 1940's. It is not the damming of the stream or the
> harnessing of the floods in which I take pride, but, rather, in the end-
> ing of the waste of the region.
>
> The region — so unproductive and insignificant in capacity in my
> youth — is now a vital part of the national economy and potential.
> More important, the wastage of human resources in the whole region
> has been reduced. New horizons have been opened for the fulfillment
> of young minds, if by nothing more than the advent of electricity into
> rural homes. Men and women have been released from the waste of
> drudgery and toil against the unyielding rock of the Texas hills. This
> is fulfillment of the true responsibility of government.[3]

Shortly after Johnson went to Congress as a youth not quite
thirty, he wangled an appointment with President Franklin Roosevelt to discuss extension of cheap public power to his district through
the use of federal funds. The state of Texas had already undertaken
a series of dams on its Colorado River for reclamation and flood
control, plus a parallel purpose of producing cheap electric power.
However, the bureau chiefs felt that Johnson's Hill Country was
too sparsely populated to be provided with power; it simply was
not economic. The freshman Congressman showed Roosevelt pictures and detailed figures, and, in a manner which has become
familiar to the nation since, told the President that he wanted a
better life for the children of his constituents than he and his father
and his grandfather had known.

---

[3] *The Texas Quarterly,* I, no. 4 (Winter 1958). Reprinted in Lyndon B. Johnson,
A Time for Action (New York, 1964), 10–11.

The result was approval of the necessary federal funds to bring electricity to his district and a farm-by-farm stumping of the district to form co-ops in what he often called the battle of public power against the privately-owned "power trust," which always suggested Wall Street and "the interests" to his constituents. Soon he had the largest co-op in the nation, the Pedernales Electric Co-Operative, with headquarters in Johnson City and rates twenty-five per cent cheaper than they had been in neighboring areas. Shortly afterwards, his work culminated with the purchase by the Lower Colorado River Authority of the plants and equipment of a complex of privately-owned electric companies in sixteen Texas counties, most of them in Johnson's Tenth District. Before his first two years were up, he had obtained more than $70,000,000 for his Hill Country district in federal loans, grants, and projects — a bit of a record for a freshman in those days. As he observed, in typical Johnson fashion, all he wanted was for the farm women to "lay aside their corrugated washboards and let their red-hot cookstoves cool off while they iron on a hot August afternoon" and to enable the farmer who "has been dragging water out of a well with a bucket all his life" to "get himself an electric pump to do the work" as well as all the "power he can afford to buy to run it."[4]

It is in this field of reclamation and power that the Johnson-Kennedy Senatorial association is most notable. To such proposals Johnson brought fifteen years of official involvement. Kennedy's interest was more recent, largely because he was younger but also because he represented an area in which capturing water has historically been less crucial. Usually the two men voted together on projects involving the West, though not always. For instance, when Senator Wayne Morse, then a recently converted Democrat, proposed an amendment to the bill authorizing the Secretary of the Interior to construct the Santa Maria land reclamation project in Southern California so that no single landowner might receive water for more than 160 acres, or 320 if married, Johnson voted against the amendment. Kennedy was absent, though it was announced

4 Clarke Newlon, L. B. J., The Man from Johnson City (New York, 1964), 73–77.

that if he had been present he would have voted for the amendment. Senator Morse contended that his amendment would protect small farmers against excess usage of water by large land-holding corporations, but the Senate turned him down by almost three-to-one.

On relatively routine measures, such as the 1954 pact authorizing the construction, repair, and preservation of certain public works and rivers and harbors for navigation, flood control, and "for other purposes," both JFK and LBJ invariably voted *yea* together. A study of their voting and occasional debating records indicates that the similar voting records were more a matter of party accord than of any ideological warmth. The only divergence here appears in the 1957 River and Harbor and Flood Control Act in which LBJ voted with a two-to-one majority, with JFK again being absent but Senator Mansfield announcing that if Kennedy had been present he would have voted *nay*. On the 1954 River and Harbor and Flood Control Act, Kennedy offered an amendment which would have required United States Steel to pay half the cost of some dredging in the Delaware River rather than having the federal government pay the entire cost. Kennedy and Johnson and nineteen others voted for the amendment, which was soundly trounced.

About the same time a bill was sent up from the House providing for development of the Priest Rapids site on the Columbia River in Washington. In debate an amendment was proposed by Senator Warren Magnuson which in effect stated that even though the proposed dam would not be federally owned and operated, still the federal government should have a voice in the sale of power from the dam. Johnson and Kennedy voted for the Magnuson amendment, which lost by 29 to 45.

Then came Hell's Canyon which, along with Dixon Yates, caused the biggest public power controversy of the Eisenhower administration. Toward the end of his administration President Truman had approved plans under which the federal government would build a high multi-purpose dam costing $500 million on the Snake River where it follows the Idaho-Oregon boundary. The Idaho Power Company said such a high dam was unnecessary, and that private companies could do a more efficient and cheaper job with three smaller dams. Meanwhile, such advocates of public power as the National Hell's Canyon Association and the National Rural Electric Co-Operative Association were pushing for the high dam. With President Eisenhower supporting private exploitation, the Federal Power Commission in 1955 granted a license for private production of power in Hell's Canyon. The advocates of public power tried to push legislation in favor of the federally-built and federally-operated dam through Congress for three years from 1955 through 1957. They lost every time. Some evidence of local feeling may be gleaned from the fact that Eisenhower's Secretary of the Interior, Douglas McKay, resigned to contest Wayne Morse for his Senate seat. McKay's defeat has been charged to his advocacy of private power.

On the 1957 vote, which passed the Senate by a count of 45 to 38, Senator Johnson did not vote because he was paired with the absent Senator William Knowland; but, as he explained, "If I were at liberty to vote, I would vote *yea*." During the debate on the bill, the Majority Leader spoke in its favor. Senator Kennedy was silent. Kennedy's objection to Hell's Canyon was one of economy — he thought that here the government could save money. But, as he ruefully admitted to Theodore C. Sorenson, "We made a lot of enemies for nothing."[5]

On one other occasion on the issue of federal dams, the two Senators diverged. In 1955 Senate Bill 500 authorized the Secretary of the Interior to construct, operate, and maintain a Colorado River Storage Project and participating projects. This project was pushed by many conservatives, including President Eisenhower, because of its interstate quality and the undeniable fact that the lands were being ruined by timber overcutting and overgrazing. In an area without much moisture, any washes in the forest or any disappearance of grasslands were scars that perhaps would never heal. Was this land to become another vast emptiness like the dust bowl from Kansas through Okie country into the Texas Panhandle? To head off such a result, President Eisenhower signed an appro-

---

[5] Theodore C. Sorenson, *Kennedy* (New York, 1966), 50.

priation bill of $760 million for the Upper Colorado River irrigation and reclamation project that would provide reservoirs, dams and power plants, and transmission facilities for the area. Johnson voted for the bill, which passed by better than two-to-one. Once again Kennedy was absent, though Senator Clements announced that if Senator Kennedy had been present, he would have voted *nay*.

The accomplishments of the Upper Colorado River Storage Project are well known. As of this moment there are at least twenty-eight participating projects designed to benefit nearly 1,500,000 acres. Better than half of this total has already been irrigated. When completed, the hydroelectric power plants should have an installed capacity of about 1,300,000 kilowatts. Already Flaming Gorge dam has been completed; and its reservoir, ninety-one miles long, has been designated a National Recreation Area. The three dams of the Curecanti unit along the Gunnison are probably two-thirds completed. Navajo dam, a 402-foot-high earth dam, was dedicated in late summer of 1962, while Glen Canyon dam has backed up Lake Powell for 186 miles to build an incredibly beautiful reticulation of green and blue water, varnished red cliffs, and other worldly shapes that bids fair to become a major tourist area.

Under the compact, Arizona gets a fixed consumptive apportionment, while the remainder is divided as follows: fifty-one and three-fourths per cent for Colorado, twenty-three per cent for Utah, fourteen per cent for Wyoming, and eleven and one-fourth per cent for New Mexico. Thus the Rio Colorado, which drains one-twelfth the area of the United States of the melting snows which winter piles high on the Rockies each year, is being transformed into exciting, available land. If "His Majesty's opposition" had chosen to be obstructionist in the 1950's, the West today would not have had these booming areas and these enticing prospects. With Democratic assistance, however, the projects were authorized under Eisenhower, and have been or are being completed under Presidents Kennedy and Johnson.

Among other issues of special interest to the West has been the chronically plaguing question — as urgent in 1968 as it was in 1954 or in the Truman days of 1951 when the pertinent act was passed — of the importation of agricultural workers from the Republic of Mexico to assist during the period of maximum agricultural labor need on the North American side of the border. In March, 1954, a join resolution amending the 1951 act was passed by a vote of 59 to 22. It authorized the proper United States agency to recruit Mexican farm labor in the event that the governments of the two countries could not agree on certain points. Probably reflecting proximity to the problem, Johnson voted for the resolution while Kennedy supported the losing view. Neither, however, spoke out on the question.

In 1956 a bill came up which aimed at providing an improved farm program. In its essentials it was non-controversial, passing with only two votes against it. It is worth little to note that both Kennedy and Johnson voted for the bill, but one point is noteworthy. Of the eight amendments offered to the bill, six passed. What is important here is that on the eight amendments, Kennedy and Johnson voted differently five times. Significantly, of the three votes on which Kennedy and Johnson agreed, the amendments were offered by Senators Hubert Humphrey, Wayne Morse, and the late Robert Kerr, all more or less Westerners.

Such a loaded question as the offshore oil of the tidelands, which certainly had its western overtones because of the involvement of Texas and California as two of the three most affected states, did not get into the legislative chamber when the Democrats held a majority. Although all the non-tidelands states were arrayed against offshore oil rights — Arkansas, for instance, bringing suit to prevent a submerged lands act as an "attempt to abdicate the sovereignty of the United States to a few of the states" — the Supreme Court settled the issue short of legislative action by declaring in principle for the offshore rights of the several states. I need hardly point out how virulent feeling ran in Texas over the threatened seizure of its tidelands by the federal government. In 1952 Governor Allan Shivers went to Illinois to visit the Democratic nominee for President, Adlai Stevenson, to see where he stood on the tidelands issue. When Stevenson declared for the federal government, Shivers led a successful movement to take Texas out of its traditional

Democratic rank in 1952 and again in 1956. But in both contests Senator Johnson, although regularly accused of being friendly with his state's oil interests, refused to desert his party and campaigned hard for Stevenson. Many Texans and other Westerners thought that Johnson was a traitor, as they would again when he accepted the Vice Presidential nomination under Kennedy.

In the latter days of their Senatorial careers both Kennedy and Johnson voted for admission of Hawaii to statehood. In this vote Johnson left behind such colleagues as Senators Byrd, Russell, Smathers, Sparkman, Talmadge, Thurman, and a man that he was then close to, J. William Fulbright, all of whom turned thumbs down on admitting Hawaii to full participation in the American political system. The two men also agreed on the Wheat Act of 1959, which President Eisenhower vetoed as a "proposed return to the discredited high, rigid price supports [which] would hasten the complete collapse of the entire wheat program." Later, in one of Kennedy's very first campaign speeches, in Spokane, he stated:

> It is time for a fresh and imaginative program to meet the programs of our Nation's wheat farms. It is time for a program which views the farmer as a great national asset — not an unwanted burden on the taxpayer. It is time for a program which views an abundance of wheat as an opportunity to provide hungry people with a decent diet — not as an unwanted stock of useless grain to be stored and forgotten. It is time for a program which sees in America's farms a true source of American strength — not a source of difficulty.[6]

He repeated this statement in such states as Minnesota, South Dakota, Montana, and North Dakota, adding at Fargo that from "the way we would handle the problem facing the wheat growers, . . . I think comparable programs could be worked out for other commodities."[7] He reminded his listeners in Billings, Montana, that Roosevelt had called a historic conference fifty-two years earlier

---

[6] *Freedom of Communications: Final Report of the Committee on Commerce, United States Senate;* Part I: The Speeches, Remarks, Press Conferences, and Statements of Senator John F. Kennedy, August 1 through November 7, 1960 (Washington: U.S. Government Printing Office, 1961), 133.

[7] *Ibid.,* 329.

for the development of the natural resources of the United States, and then once again was heard the oft-repeated phrase:

> It is ... a source of satisfaction, I think, to all Americans that the two Americans of this century that did more to develop the resources of the United States, to conserve them, and protect them for other generations, both came from New York State, Theodore Roosevelt and Franklin Roosevelt.[8]

When as President he named the forthright young Congressman from Arizona, Stewart Udall, as his Secretary of the Interior, the West knew that it had a friendly administration. Later Kennedy and then Johnson both tried to deliver on their campaign promises as far as the restrictions on executive action and the compatibility of Congress permitted. Both have been staunchly pro-West in their administrations. The patterns that were established during their Senatorial days have demonstrated continuity right down to the present. The remarkable fact has been that despite differences in backgrounds and the different focus which each man brought to the problems of the West, their programs have been almost identical in principle and in degree. This may say more for the party than it does for the individual President; but it also tends to give the lie to those people who have confused styles with attitudes, thinking that because one man's style differs from another, then his heart and his mind and his principle must also differ.

Certainly for the past decade and a half the recent West has been favored by policies, engineered first in the Senate and then from the White House, that have given the West some of its better days. It is hardly necessary to go into what the two men have accomplished in such fields as industrial development, military appropriations for the western areas, and other moves which have primed the economic pump of the West. California leads the nation in defense industries development; Texas is second. Oklahoma, a semi-arid state, has the greatest artificial lakes development of any state, and booming water-related industries to match. Every state has gained enormously in some wise.

---

[8]*Ibid.,* 331.

Between now and November the nation will be victimized by an almost intolerable smog of political charges that will have just enough truth to confuse and deliberately mislead. What I have wanted to do here, while still remaining more concise than Castro, is to prepare the reader for those obfuscating days ahead by an unemotional look at the West's recent past. While he may not agree that credit for the spectacular onrush of the West — at a rate far in advance of the national average — is due either to Kennedy or Johnson, it is indisputable that the Western policies of the two men harmonized from the beginning and that their areas of agreement have far exceeded their areas of divergence.

THE MODERN TEXAS RANGERS:

A LAW-ENFORCEMENT DILEMMA

IN THE RIO GRANDE VALLEY

by

BEN H. PROCTER

Phi Beta Kappa graduate and All American end at the University of
Texas, the author played professional football before proceeding to the
doctorate at Harvard University. His dissertation, *Not Without Honor:
The Life of John H. Reagan,* was a prize-winning publication of the University of Texas Press in 1962. He has contributed many articles to
learned journals, encyclopedias, and such collaborative works as *Heroes
of Texas* (1964), *Missions of Texas* (1965), *Forts of Texas* (1966), and
Battles in Texas (1967). He is a professor of history at Texas Christian
University where he has taught since 1957.

THE TEXAS RANGERS, announced State Senator Joe Bernal of
Bexar County, are "the Mexican Americans' Ku Klux Klan. All
they need is a white hood with 'Rinches' written across it."[1] "They
were formed in the old days of the Texas Republic to keep the
Mexicans in line," asserted Robert Analavage, an assistant editor
of *The Southern Patriot.* "They merged with the Confederate
Army . . . to fight to preserve slavery, and in the Twentieth Century they have been used repeatedly as strikebreakers."[2] "Abolish
the Rangers," demanded the delegates at the Tenth Annual Texas

---

[1] *Texas Observer* (Austin), June 9, 1967. *Rinches* is the phonetical pronunciation of
Rangers in Spanish; otherwise, the pronunciation would be Raan-hares.

[2] *The Southern Patriot* (Louisville), August 1967.

AFL-CIO Convention at Fort Worth.[3] "One Riot, No Rangers — One Strike, Many Rangers," read a picket sign protesting a speaking engagement of Governor John Connally at Laredo.[4] Mexican-Americans "today are under siege at Rio Grande City by the Connally pistoleros (gunmen) and the [Homer] Garrison gunslingers who subject them," charged Albert Pena, a San Antonio county commissioner, "to harassment, fear, intimidation, a little head cracking and jailing on nebulous charges."[5] And so the barrage of abusive statements and damaging allegations continued ad infinitum throughout the "long, hot summer" of 1967 as Texas Rangers, world famous as fearless peace officers, were sharply reprimanded by labor leaders, state and national politicos, liberal Democratic organizations, church groups, and even university professors.[6] Not since 1934, just prior to their reorganization as a modern investigating and law enforcement body, had the Rangers received such unfavorable publicity — and to a man they did not like it.

Yet on several previous occasions the Rangers had weathered severe criticism and profited from the ordeal. Each time political involvement had been their Achilles' heel and almost their undoing. In World War I, for example, Governors Oscar B. Colquitt and James E. "Pa" Ferguson had enlarged the force to 1,000 men ostensibly to deal with troubles along the Rio Grande. But actually the Rangers were used at times as currency to pay political debts, as a cheap method of elevating aspiring Texans to state peerage, as a kind of exclusive club for political hacks and cronies of the governor. While the force included some outstanding lawmen like Captains Frank Hamer, Will Wright, and Tom Hickman, sometimes a Ranger commission became a license to rob or kill.

On January 31, 1919, State Representative J. T. Canales of Brownsville initiated a legislative inquiry regarding Ranger activ-

---

[3] *Fort Worth Star-Telegram,* August 5, 1967; also see *ibid.,* August 14, 1967.

[4] *Austin Statesman,* June 10, 1967.

[5] *Houston Chronicle,* June 5, 1967.

[6] In Legislative Branch of the Texas State Library at Austin, see file entitled Texas Rangers, especially those newspaper articles dated April-July, 1967.

ities on the border. To fellow committee members he presented eighteen charges including drunkenness, disorderly conduct, and brutal physical assault, torture, and murder of numerous prisoners. Two months later, as a direct result of these hearings, the legislature reorganized the Rangers by limiting the force to five companies and seventy-five men. Because committee witnesses had charged that from 1914 to 1918 the Rangers had killed possibly 5,000 people (almost exclusively of Mexican descent), the act provided that any citizen could file a complaint against an offending officer and an investigation would ensue.[7]

In 1932 the force again became embroiled in politics, openly backing Governor Ross Sterling for re-election against Miriam A. "Ma" Ferguson. When "Ma" and "Pa" moved to Austin in January, 1933, the Rangers went the way of all political appointees who had crossed their boss and lost. Three days after taking office, Governor Ferguson discharged the entire force of forty-four men — those who had not already resigned — and once again the Texas Rangers were a source of patronage, corruption, and ridicule.[8] The effect upon state law enforcement was, of course, catastrophic. During the next two years crime and violence became widespread, bank holdups and murder commonplace. Few states had a more vicious assortment of gangsters or provided a safer sanctuary for the criminal element. For instance, residents in the Dallas–Fort Worth area alone included George "Machine Gun" Kelly, Raymond Hamilton, and the "mad-dog killers" Clyde Barrow and Bonnie Parker. And who besides "Ma" Ferguson was responsible for this breakdown in the public defense? To most Texans the answer was obvious. As

---

[7] As discussed by Walter Prescott Webb in his 1935 book, *The Texas Rangers: A Century of Frontier Defense* (2nd ed.; Austin, University of Texas Press, 1965), 513–516; and Stephen W. Schuster IV, "The Modernization of the Texas Rangers, 1930–1936" (unpublished Master's thesis, Texas Christian University, Fort Worth, Texas, 1965), 6–9. For the complete testimony of the Ranger activities on the border, see *Proceedings of the Joint Committee of the Senate and the House in the Investigation of the Texas State Ranger Force*, Texas State Archives, Austin.

[8] Schuster, "Modernization of the Texas Rangers," 17–21; Seth Shepard McKay, *Texas Politics, 1906–1944: With Special Reference to the German Counties* (Lubbock: Texas Tech Press, 1952), 237–240; William Warren Sterling, *Trails and Trials of the Texas Rangers* (Houston, 1959), 276.

one newspaper sarcastically remarked, "A Ranger commission and a nickel can get . . . a cup of coffee anywhere in Texas."[9]

In January, 1935, however, Governor James V. Allred soon obviated the causes of such derision. Having campaigned the previous year to "overhaul" the state law enforcement machinery, he pushed through the legislature an act creating the Department of Public Safety (DPS). To supervise administrative policies and procedures he appointed a three-man Public Safety Commission, which in turn selected a director and an assistant director. The DPS had three basic units — the Texas Rangers, the Highway Patrol, and a newly created Headquarters Division at Austin which was to be a modern scientific crime laboratory and detection center.[10]

As for the Rangers, reforms were definitely in order — so much so that Walter Prescott Webb, in his centennial history, sadly predicted their demise as a separate law enforcement entity. They would become, he feared, merely a segment of the much larger Highway Patrol, that group which the Rangers contemptuously referred to as a "bunch of motorcycle jockeys."[11] But Webb was wrong; Governor Allred and his Public Safety Commissioners made sure of that. On October 7, 1935, when they met in Austin to formulate Ranger policies, the modernization of the force began. The state was divided into five, then later into six, districts wherein a Ranger company had specific responsibility and jurisdiction. Each group usually had a captain, a sergeant, and a number of privates who resided at different towns in the area. For several years the number of appointments remained flexible until the commissioners finally decided upon a fixed complement of sixty-two men: six captains, six sergeants, and fifty privates.[12]

[9] Sterling, *Trails and Trials,* 519; Schuster, "Modernization of the Texas Rangers," 25–33; Webb, *Texas Rangers,* 519–544.

[10] William E. Atkinson, "The Texas Gubernatorial Campaign of 1934" (unpublished Master's thesis, Texas Christian University, Fort Worth, Texas, 1965), 52ff; Schuster, "Modernization of the Texas Rangers," 34–45.

[11] Webb, *Texas Rangers,* 567; Schuster, "Modernization of the Texas Rangers," 53.

[12] Schuster, "Modernization of the Texas Rangers," 53, 56; interview with Sergeant Jim Riddles and Private Bill Wilson, Austin, Texas, September 10, 1966; Ranger Rosters, 1935–1939, MSS., Department of Public Safety files, Austin.

Allred's commissioners set higher standards for individual Rangers. For appointment examinations and recommendations, not political pull, were important; for promotion, seniority and performance were the determining factors. To be considered for the force, an applicant had to be thirty to forty-five years of age, at least five feet eight inches tall, and "perfectly sound" in mind and body. Each man received instruction in the latest techniques of fingerprinting, communications, ballistics, and records. And he had to be a crack shot. Lack of higher education or formal schooling did not penalize an applicant, except possibly on the written exam, because the extent of his literary efforts would be the writing of an "intelligent" report. For most Rangers, this task was neither difficult nor time-consuming. Captain Frank Hamer, for instance, explained the laborious tracking and the carefully planned ambush of Clyde Barrow and Bonnie Parker in this manner: "We've done the job." [13]

Today the Texas Rangers are experienced peace officers, trained in the latest methods of crime detection and armed with modern technological equipment. Unlike those Rangers of the Republic and frontier days, or even of the 1920's, they usually ride in high-powered automobiles instead of on horses, are armed with advanced and deadly weapons, and have developed sophisticated techniques of interrogation. The men have retained, however, the traits and qualities of character that in 1935 Webb lamented were being lost; indeed, in many ways they appear to be cut from the same rough mold as their predecessors. Basically they are uncomplicated men — direct, straightforward, and not especially concerned about social amenities. They use the English language simply as a tool for direct communication, not as a device to trick or deceive (hence their difficulty at times with newsmen or reporters who tend toward sensationalism). Grammatically they are an English teacher's nightmare; yet they clearly express themselves, some-

---

[13] Schuster, "Modernization of the Texas Rangers," 54–55; C. L. Douglas, *The Gentlemen in the White Hats: Dramatic Episodes in the History of the Texas Rangers* (Dallas, 1934), 201.

times punctuating their sentences with colorful if not downright earthy expressions. Although outwardly friendly and easygoing, they are suspicious of strangers and hesitant to talk ("You might have been one of those damn New York magazine writers"); but once a person wins their trust, they will go out of their way to be helpful.[14]

But make no mistake about these men. They have been, and are, the scourge of those outside the law, obviously feared, sometimes hated, always respected. They are proud men — proud of their traditions and their fellow officers' accomplishments, proud of holding a job that all other Texas lawmen desire. They have an intangible, almost unexplainable quality of toughness about them. Possibly it is the way they handle themselves. Some are no longer lean and trim, a few are wrinkled and graying, one is even potbellied. Yet all exude a poise, a composure of confidence. Or perhaps it is the realization that these men have confronted the toughest criminals in the state, that their tradition of "One Riot, One Ranger" has steeled them toward danger and death. As one Ranger rather graphically put it (and with obvious pride), "Hell, Ben, whenever there's a mean ass, then they call on us."[15] But whatever the reason, these men do have the reputation of toughness and bravery, of dedication to law enforcement, of being the elite of Texas lawmen. Their esprit de corps is almost unbelievable; they will admit, in fact, that becoming a Texas Ranger has completely transformed their lives. "You feel lucky to get the Ranger badge. So many want it," Ranger Sergeant Jim Riddles candidly stated. "So you take an internal vow that whatever happens you won't break your oath to uphold the law."[16]

In 1967, however, no matter how respected or feared they had become, no matter how outstanding their record of law enforcement, the Texas Rangers found themselves in an impossible situa-

---

[14] The author has arrived at these judgments after having interviewed many of the Rangers in 1966–1967.

[15] Closed manuscript in possession of Ben Procter, Texas Christian University, Fort Worth, Texas.

[16] Interview with Riddles and Wilson; interview with Captain Robert A. Crowder, Company B, Dallas, Texas, September 11, 1967.

tion. It all began on June 1, 1966, in what appeared to be a routine dispute between management and labor. At the 1,600 acre, well-irrigated La Casita Farms near the small Starr County community of Rio Grande City, a strike occurred among the stoop farm laborers. Eugene Nelson, a thirty-six-year-old labor organizer who had participated in the California grape pickers' strike earlier in the year, arrived in the Valley and immediately organized some of the workers into a union which was affiliated with the California-based National Farm Workers Association. Then he demanded that La Casita, and other growers engaged in fruit and vegetable production, raise wages to the Federal minimum standard of $1.25 per hour. For workers to receive only forty to eighty cents an hour was "ridiculous," he asserted, and charged that such wages were responsible for much of the widespread poverty in the Rio Grande Valley.[17]

When the growers ignored union demands, Nelson knew that for the moment the battle had been lost, that the local economic and political power structure was in no way shaken, and that it never would be unless his small union could receive equally powerful outside support. He therefore hit upon a dramatic plan: a 387-mile march from the Rio Grande Valley to Austin which would emphasize the pathetic plight of the Mexican-American migrant workers — indeed of all the underprivileged and underpaid throughout the state. On Labor Day he and "50,000 to 100,000 laborers" would meet on the steps of the state capitol and demand of Governor John Connally that justice be done and that a special session of the legislature be called specifically to enact an adequate minimum wage law.[18]

On July 10, according to plan, forty-three members of "La Marcha," led by Father Antonio "Tomec" Gonzales and Reverend James L. Navarro, a Baptist minister, set out from San Juan, Texas, probably unaware of the far-reaching consequences their actions would have upon the state. Through fairly extensive newspaper coverage of the movement, Texans were able to follow the progress

---

17 *Houston Chronicle,* June 12, July 11, 17, 1966.

18*Ibid.,* July 11, 1966; *Dallas Morning News,* July 10. 1966.

of the footsore marchers, at first rather amused by the novelty of the idea and the people involved.

What a strange sight the caravan was as it passed along the highway! In front were the Reverend Navarro, exhibiting for all to see both an American and a Christian flag, and Father "Tomec" Gonzales, wearing a cowboy heat, a Star of David, and a sign entitled "Migrant Priest"; straggling behind was a strange assortment of tired humanity in all shapes, ages, and sizes; bringing up the rear was an old bus filled with food, personal belongings, and a large canvas tent-shelter. Each night the weary group would camp outside a community, sometimes receive food from the neighboring townspeople, listen to the encouragement and prayers of their leaders, and then rest up for the next blistering day on the road.[19]

Yet by late August, as "La Marcha" was in its final phase, Texans began to realize that this expedition was no longer a laughing matter. These people were deadly serious; they were demanding reforms. Gradually a kind of emotional furor — disruptive, upsetting, perhaps even terrifying to some — seemed to tinge everything concerning the march. It was increasingly apparent in the statements of church leaders, liberal politicians, and state AFL-CIO officials. Appalled by the poverty of the migrant workers, they called upon the "power structure" to "listen and analyze what the Valley marchers" were trying to say.[20] In reply, the growers and the Texas Farm Bureau argued that, even though such conditions were regrettable, the union demands were economically unrealistic and, if accepted, would drive the growers from the Rio Grande Valley. Besides, who were these so-called strikers? "We don't exactly know," exclaimed Gordon Morrow, a San Benito farmer. "They certainly are not representative of the Valley farm workers."[21] Soon reports began to appear, intimating that "La Marcha" was Communist-inspired and that the peaceful demonstrators, who at times

---

[19] *Houston Chronicle,* July 11, 17, 1966.

[20] *Austin Statesman,* August 31, 1966; *Austin American,* July 14, 1966.

[21] *Dallas Morning News,* August 31, 1966; *Austin American,* August 31, 1966.

asserted that a "social revolution" was at hand in the Valley, might become violent.

To calm the public temper and to investigate these rumors Governor Connally, Attorney General Waggoner Carr, and House Speaker Ben Barnes on August 30 drove to New Braunfels, some fifty miles south of Austin, to confer with the marchers. Immediately after Father Gonzales and Connally embraced each other amidst shouts of "Viva Connally," the governor announced: "I will not be at the Capitol Monday, but if I had been there I don't think I would have met with you because my door . . . has been open to you since the march began." Now the cries changed to "Viva la huelga" (long live the strike). Then Attorney General Carr, who at that time was also the Democratic nominee for the United States Senate, warned the marchers against the infiltration of "agitators and extremists" who might try to disrupt their peaceful protest. Again there were cries of "Viva la huelga." [22]

So with both Connally and Carr apparently trying to win a prize for the political faux pas of the year, liberal politicians across the state rushed to Austin to join the Labor Day finale. The situation was ideal. Before statewide press coverage they would be able to embrace the cause of the poor and downtrodden, of the helpless underdog who was merely asking for a living wage, while damning the callousness of the "power structure." In a surprise move Senator Ralph Yarborough, an inveterate enemy of Connally, flew from Washington to march the last four blocks to the capitol and address the huge crowd. Then other liberal dignitaries and honored guests also spoke, including Representative Henry B. Gonzales of San Antonio, state president Hank Brown of the AFL-CIO, five state senators, a dozen representatives, and the leaders of the march. Even Bobby Kennedy got into the act by sending a telegram of "regret." Yarborough — obviously enjoying the derisive shouts of

---

[22] *Austin Statesman,* August 31, 1966; *Dallas Morning News,* September 1, 1966; *Houston Chronicle,* September 1, 1966; *Houston Post,* September 2, 1966; *Austin American-Statesman,* September 4, 1966.

"Where's John?" — climaxed the emotion-filled rally. "I see a storm coming," he dramatically exclaimed. "I know there is a God. If he has a place for me, I am ready . . . [for] I see the real heroes of Texas."[23]

After this rousing finale the Valley farm workers returned home, greatly encouraged by promises of support and confident that they would soon realize their goals. During the next nine months, however, their every effort met with defeat. Their political alliance was not powerful enough. In helpless frustration they watched the legislature, which convened on January 10, 1967, haggle over, delay and bottle up in committee their minimum-wage bill. And there was nothing they could do about it. The posting of two "wage sentinels" constantly outside the Governor's Office, as "a symbol of olden times when a chief ignored payment of debt," had not persuaded Connally to their cause. Nor did their organized efforts of packing the galleries at committee hearings affect conservative legislators from other districts. Now there seemed to be only one recourse left to them — "la huelga."[24]

Early in May, 1967, the growers at Rio Grande City began anticipating a record-breaking melon crop. Since this produce was highly perishable, it was imperative that the harvest season not run more than four to six weeks. But Gilbert Padilla, vice president of the farm workers' union, had other plans. To La Casita Farms he issued this ultimatum: "Negotiate or let them rot." When Ray Rochester, vice president and manager of La Casita, refused and began hiring "green carders" — Mexican nationals who sought work on the Texas side during the day — a desperate test of strength between the growers and the migrant laborers was inevitable. Anticipating the strike, Padilla had already decided what actions the union must take. With success hinging on the fate of the melon harvest, his men would prevent the "green carders" from working.

[23] Houston Post, September 4, 1966; Dallas Morning News, September 5, 6, 1966; Austin American, September 6, 1966.

[24] Houston Chronicle, September 6, 9, 1966; DallasMorning News, September 7, December 4, 1966; March 16, 26, 1967; Houston Chronicle, January 24, February 17, March 16, 17, 1967.

If, however, the "foreign strike breakers" could not be dissuaded and the gathering proceeded, then every "means of transportation," he publicly announced, must be "closed down."[25]

With violence imminnet, Starr County officials called upon the Texas Rangers to help their small police force keep order, especially since several destructive fires and acts of sabotage during the preceding six months had gone unsolved.[26] Ranger Captain A. Y. Allee of Company D, with seven of his men, quickly responded — and then the trouble began. For "la huelga" was no longer just a strike by poor migrant workers seeking a living wage and a chance to escape poverty; now it had become multi-faceted, explosive, in many ways symbolic. For both the liberals and the conservatives of Texas it had become a political football, for Starr County officials a "hot potato" which might affect local political careers, and for Yarborough a club to swing at Connally. Possibly labor believed that it would help strengthen the cause of unionism in Texas; perhaps socially and politically sensitive university students and church leaders thought of it as a fight for civil rights and human dignity; a number of Mexican-Americans may have hoped that it was the beginning of a social revolution which would topple the feudal economic and political systems in the Rio Grande Valley. But for the Rangers "la huelga" was a bewildering, angering, unpleasant assignment. It had become too complicated; old methods of law enforcement were no longer effective. Captain Allee, a crusty veteran of thirty-five years on the border, soon realized this. As he later told State Senator Don Kennard of Fort Worth: "Son, this is the goddamndest thing I've ever been in."[27]

For three weeks (May 11-June 1) the strike grew in intensity, each incident aggravating the public temper, each arrest increasing the animosity between the strikers and the Rangers. Soon charges arose of Ranger brutality, of violation of civil rights, of favoritism

25 *Dallas Morning News*, May 7, 1967.

26*Ibid.*, March 26, 1967.

27 Interview with State Senator Don Kennard, Fort Worth, Texas, September 14, 1967; closed manuscript in the possession of Ben Procter, Texas Christian University, Fort Worth, Texas; *San Antonio Express*, May 11, 12, 1967.

toward the growers, of strikebreaking. And just as quickly these were denied. After each new clash widely divergent accounts of events circulated, all of them, however, containing a small area of agreement. But since the participants quite naturally magnified the importance of certain happenings, they therefore interpreted them in the light of their own experience.

On May 11 the first in a series of confrontations occurred. Early that morning, after Mexican police had dispersed sympathizing Mexican pickets and had allowed "green carders" to cross the international bridge at Roma, the Rangers cleared the way on the Texas side. They roughly shoved the closely-bunched *huelguistas* aside, while explaining, several union pickets angrily recollected, that it was their duty to get the workers to the fields without interruption. In reply, Captain Allee denied that his men were "taking sides"; they were merely upholding Texas law which forbade secondary strikes, picketing, and boycotts.[28] A few hours later Rangers also stopped a carload of strikers just outside of Roma and arrested the driver for having no license. Rev. Ed Krueger, a member of a special "team ministry" of the Texas Council of Churches, accused Ranger Jack Van Cleve of "throwing his weight around" and verbally scaring him, then became especially incensed when the driver was held in jail for five hours. To Krueger and other *huelguistas*, this was just another method of Ranger strikebreaking.[29]

"Quite perturbed" over these episodes, union leader Eugene Nelson went "looking" for Captain Allee the next morning to lodge a strong protest. When he arrived at the courthouse at Rio Grande City and Allee could not be found, he reportedly lost his temper. Constable Manuel Benavides claimed that he said: "You tell that s.o.b. he had better lay off or there will be some dead Rangers." By late afternoon County Attorney Randall Nye, who was also an attorney for the strike-bound Starr Produce Company, had charged

[28] *Vernon's Annotated Civil Statutes of the State of Texas,* Art. 5154f.
[29] *Texas Observer* (Austin), June 9, 1967; *San Antonio Express,* May 13, 1967.

him with threatening the lives of law enforcement officers. Nelson claimed that he had been misunderstood — that he had told the constable "if the Texas Rangers don't stop, there are going to be some red-faced Rangers around here when the Senate investigators arrive." Nevertheless he spent the night in "a relic from the dark ages," the cockroach-infested Starr County jail.[30]

Beginning on May 18, as union activity increased and the strikers became more militant and hostile, the Rangers tried to keep the peace through mass arrests. Within two weeks they had jailed fifty-seven men and women either for secondary boycotting or for mass picketing which under Texas law prohibited more than two strikers to be "within fifty feet of the premises being picketed, or within fifty feet of any other picket."[31] As a result of these actions, the Rangers received bitter, galling criticism as well as statewide demands for an investigation of their law enforcement methods and techniques. By June there were a number of court suits, with accompanying affidavits, charging them with unnecessary brutality and unlawful confiscation or destruction of private property.[32] Such allegations arose, of course, because there were numerous individual confrontations where the Rangers enforced the law by physical persuasion.

The night of May 26, however, was by far the most explosive — and, in the divergent stories, most confusing. At a railroad bridge near Mission, Texas, the Reverend Krueger, his wife, and eighteen *huelguistas* picketed a train carrying melons from the Valley. Rangers soon arrived and arrested them for mass picketing. In the ensuing roundup, so the strikers claimed, the Rangers slapped several of them (including a former state heavyweight boxing champion) "with tremendous force," and kicked Krueger, then slammed a car door on his leg while threatening to "knock . . . his head off."

---

[30] *Texas Observer* (Austin), June 9, 1967; *San Antonio Express*, May 13, 14, 1967.

[31] *Vernon's Texas Statutes*, Art. 5154d; *Texas Observer* (Austin), June 9, 1967.

[32] *San Antonio Express*, May 26, 31, June 13, 1967; *Fort Worth Star-Telegram*, May 30, June 13, 1967.

At that moment Mrs. Krueger tried to take pictures of the fracas whereupon, she asserted, Captain Allee grabbed her arm and twisted it, then took her camera and exposed the film.

To these allegations Allee replied that he was "a strong believer in enforcing the law and enforcing it as it is written." Then he added: "I don't think we've been wrong in what we've done." In fact, he claimed that he had not planned to arrest Krueger until the minister begged him repeatedly to do so. "I told him," Allee later explained to Jimmy Banks of the *Dallas Morning News,* "if that's the way he felt about it, I'd sure as hell accommodate him." Then the tough Ranger captain grabbed him by the belt and the seat of his trousers and unceremoniously escorted him to a nearby car. As for the tussle with Mrs. Krueger, Allee stated that it was "customary, when you arrest somebody and they cause a commotion, to take whatever articles they're carrying away from them. She put the camera behind her back, so I grabbed it." But at no time, he adamantly asserted, did a Ranger "expose any film." [33]

For the next few nights, as mass arrests continued, Captain Allee and his men, increasingly harried and perturbed by newsmen and cameramen flocking about them as they were trying to do their job, added more fuel to the growing furor. On several occasions they unwisely threatened to confiscate or destroy cameras, all of which seemed to substantiate Mrs. Krueger's charges. [34] Yet of all publicity unfavorable to the Rangers the "Dimas Affair" received the widest circulation. On June 1 Jim Rochester, a foreman at La Casita, claimed that on the previous night Magdaleno Dimas, a Mexican-born convicted murderer who had threatened his life several times, and Benito Rodríguez, who also had a criminal record, had driven up a loading ramp at one of the La Casita sheds yelling "Viva la huelga." Since Dimas was brandishing a rifle, Rochester fired at them, trying to puncture a tire as they sped away. Upon complaint, a Starr County deputy sheriff and Captain Allee tried to find the

---

[33] *Texas Observer* (Austin), June 9, 1967; *Dallas Morning News,* July 9, 1967.

[34] *Texas Observer* (Austin), June 9, 1967; *Dallas Times Herald,* May 28, 1967; *Fort Worth Star-Telegram,* May 30, 1967; *San Antonio Express,* June 22, 1967.

two men. After inquiring at the union office at Rio Grande City where Bill Chandler, an administrative assistant, denied any knowledge of their whereabouts, the two peace officers left, then waited nearby in their car. When Chandler and another man hurriedly left a few minutes later, they trailed them to a house from which Dimas emerged with a rifle. Immediately Allee took over, flashing a spotlight on the men and ordering them to surrender. Taken aback, Dimas dropped the rifle and ran back into the house as Chandler yelled: "Don't shoot, don't shoot, he isn't armed."

During the next thirty minutes Allee followed what he considered to be routine procedure in apprehending someone resisting arrest. From a justice of the peace he obtained a warrant to enter the premises, then moved in. Armed with a double-barrelled shotgun, his favorite weapon, he kicked down the door — and there before him were Dimas and Rodríguez "sitting behind a table with their hands under it." In that split second Allee had to decide whether the subjects had guns hidden and, if so, whether to blast them. Instead of shooting, he ordered them to get up. When they would not, he suddenly "tilted the table back against them," rearranged Dimas' head with the barrel of his shotgun, and physically subdued him. As he later explained, "I used only the force that I deemed necessary to effect their arrest."[35]

Dimas, however, gave a much different version of what happened. Badly beaten, possibly suffering a concussion, he stated that when Allee burst into the house he and Rodríguez quickly raised their arms, lest they be killed. Then several Rangers ordered them to lower their hands and, when they would not, Allee hit him with the shotgun. Other Rangers continued the beating when he tried to protect himself against further blows.

After the "Dimas Affair" the tension between the *huelguistas* and the Rangers quickly subsided — melon season was almost over. By June 17 only three Rangers remained in Rio Grande City.[36] But in the aftermath of this conflict, investigating bodies, both

[35] *Texas Observer* (Austin), June 9, 1967; *Dallas Morning News,* July 9, 1967.

[36] *San Antonio Express,* May 31, 1967; *Houston Post,* June 17, 18, 1967.

state and national, moved into the Valley to question the participants, evaluate the evidence, and pronounce judgment. In the main
the investigators were highly critical of the Rangers, especially
reprimanding them for appearing "on the side of the employers,"
for being "completely out of line" in their dealings with the press,
and for violating the civil rights of the strikers. Yet they did not
challenge the contention that the Rangers were justified in being
at Rio Grande City and that their presence probably prevented
bloodshed. In turn, Colonel Homer Garrison, director of the Department of Public Safety, conducting his own investigation, categorically denied *any* wrongdoing on the part of the Rangers.[37]

So throughout the state Texans have questioned the actions of
the Rangers and have demanded an explanation of what really
happened. Possibly the forthcoming court cases will clarify certain
issues. Regardless of the outcome of those legal decisions, however,
there are certain problems emanating from the Valley dispute to
which state officials and the people themselves must find answers.
For make no mistake about it; "la huelga" has been much more than
a controversy between management and labor, between picketers
and Rangers. Unquestionably the economic upgrading of a minority
group and certain political realities have been involved. But possibly not so obvious has been the interjection of civil rights into
a labor dispute.

Surely Captain Allee and his men did not grasp that "la
huelga" was anything more than just another local disturbance, at
least not by their actions. At Rio Grande City they tried to enforce
the law by time-tested and previously reliable methods. Toward
those *huelguistas* who claimed that the state mass-picketing statute
violated their rights and was unconstitutional, they were unsym-
pathetic and unmoved. Toward those who infringed upon others'
rights, they were stern and, if need be, violent. Their solution was
"to go by the book" — and therein lay their difficulty. Never had
they been confronted with problems involving that gray area, that

---

[37] *San Antonio Express,* June 2, 18, 22, 28, 1967; *Dallas Morning News,* June 22, 30,
July 1, 5, 6, 1967; *Texas Observer* (Austin), June 9, July 21, 1967.

"twilight zone" between civil and criminal actions. The cry, "I have a right to carry a picket sign," had no effect on them; only what the law said. And they were angered as well as dismayed by the criticism and abuse directed toward them. After all, they had kept the peace, protected property, upheld the law — and no one had been killed. What more was expected?

In past decades the answer to that question would have been rhetorical, but not in the 1960's. To a generation facing a Detroit or a Newark, the Rangers had proven ineffective; they had tried "to cope with current problems by using yesterday's tools."[38]

So from the Valley experience the Rangers should profit, for their administrators now have a clear responsibility to establish certain guidelines by which the force can serve more effectively. Of utmost importance is that the Rangers maintain, indeed project, a proper public image. If possible, they should not at times be ordered into quasi-civil conflicts in which they might appear to be "taking sides" or in which economic, social, or political considerations might take precedent over an unqualified enforcement of the law. As public servants they should also exert more patience and self-control in dealing with the news media, ignoring whenever possible the irritating activities of certain individuals. But of far greater concern to state administrators should be the training of Rangers. There is no question that the men of the force are experienced law enforcement officers, that they know their job, that they are topflight in investigating crimes and apprehending criminals. Yet the developments in the Valley have indicated certain weaknesses in current methodology. In some manner the Department of Public Safety must keep these men abreast of current problems as well as possible solutions. And thus for the Rangers would be the legacy of "la huelga," from denunciation and scorn to rejuvenation and reform.

---

[38] Closed manuscript in possession of Ben Procter, Texas Christian University, Fort Worth, Texas.

Comment by

Philip D. Jordan

University of Minnesota

Professor Ben Procter, as might be expected by those who know and appreciate his meticulous scholarship and his steady judgment, has presented a more than adequate summary of the role which Texas Rangers played in a contemporary economic and social dispute which agitated not only the Lone Star State but also the nation. The Wall Street Journal, *for example, on September 13, 1967 gave the Rangers extensive coverage under a three-deck caption: "The Texas Rangers: Lawmen Get Their Man, But Their Tactics are Currently Under Fire. Celebrated Force is Accused of Strikebreaking Assault: It Terms Charges False." And the tragically pathetic situation, described but not analyzed by Mr. Procter, produced a hit record, a sort of ballad, in which pro-union Mexican-American farm workers sing a sad song whose verses relate how they were beaten by damned Rangers and picture John Connally as a "bad governor who hates the Mexicans and laughs at suffering."*

The most significant portion of Mr. Procter's paper lies not in his vignette of the Ranger, nor in his sketch of the force's prideful past, nor in his pointing out of the tradition that one Ranger is competent to handle one mob. The Ranger legends and traditions are well known. Neither does Mr. Procter's major contribution lie in his summary of the causes and the progress of unrest among the workers, although he has done this well in the time allotted to him. It seems to me that Mr. Procter's primary contribution — the very core of his paper — lies in his statements which concern the inability of the Rangers to grasp the fact that the difficulties in the Rio Grande Valley were not just another disturbance; that the Rangers were unprepared to comprehend, as Mr. Procter points out, the "twilight zone" between civil and criminal action; and that the Rangers stood upon "the law" and showed ignorance of contemporary legal philosophy and social thought. The Rangers may indeed now patrol in automobiles instead of on horses and may carry the most effective modern weapons, but unfortunately their minds still seem to work in a rigid nineteenth-century mode. The times have passed them by, and they still believe that enforcement by fear and at pistol point is good police practice.

The "tough" police officer is rapidly becoming an anachronism. The psychology inherent in modern police training, and emphasized in every up-to-date police academy, stresses instruction in human relations, in the soft but firm approach, in the withholding of force until the use of that force is absolutely unavoidable. Apparently the Texas Department of Public Safety is unaware of these developments. The department may not know, for example, that force, if used, should be applied by degrees in accordance with a worked-out formula; that the police of New York City are forbidden to use firearms except in cases of self-defense or to counter a dangerous threat to the community; that the Chemical Mace (a spray which fires repeat shots or a continuous stream of liquid gas which renders a victim helpless for ten or fifteen minutes) is standard equipment for every patrol-man in Charleston, West Virginia; and that the federal government has developed a super water pistol which fires either a stream of incapacitating chemical or a small plastic ball filled with a distinctive colored dye which "breaks and marks the target on impact."

Mr. Procter, properly enough, underlines the need for the better training of Rangers, suggests that Rangers not allow themselves to be drawn into quasi-civil conflicts, and recommends that Rangers establish better relations with the news media. Yet, in all fairness to the Rangers, it must be pointed out that their problems and their deficiencies are the vexations and weaknesses of law enforcement agencies throughout the nation. Peace officers, in both urban and rural areas, face a rising crime rate, attempt to cope with situations with which they are unfamiliar, and are confused by what they believe to be restrictions put upon them by the courts. In addition, again as Mr. Procter makes clear, their public image is less than satisfactory. A recent survey, published in the June, 1967 issue of Trans-Action, seems to indicate that the police are more unpopular than they should be. Upper-income groups seem more favorably disposed than lower-income groups, and non-whites are more critical than are whites.

These comments are germane to Mr. Procter's paper, for his discussion of a law enforcement dilemma in the Rio Grande Valley only reflects a national dilemma. His suggestions are applicable not only to the Texas Rangers but also to peace officers generally. His reflections on the proper role of Texas peace officers in mob and strike situations may properly be extended widely, for it is most certainly true that riots and mob action will increase in America before diminishing — and that law enforcement agencies will be compelled to develop new attitudes and new techniques for their control.

Other Historical Observations

THE WEST AND NEW NATIONS

IN OTHER CONTINENTS

by

EARL POMEROY

Apart from his teaching at the University of Oregon, the author in 1968 was a fellow of the National Endowment for the Humanities, studying the history of the West in the twentieth century. His publications include *The Territories and the United States, 1861–1890* (1947), *In Search of the Golden West: The Tourist in Western America* (1957), and *The Pacific Slope: A History* (1965). He also prepared a new edition of Lincoln Steffens' *Upbuilders* for the University of Washington Press.

WHEN Charles Kingsley became Regius Professor of Modern History at Cambridge in 1860, his literary reputation rested chiefly on his historical novels. Taking his inspiration from Hakluyt, he had distilled the spirit of sixteenth-century chronicles into an epic account of the adventures of men of Devon with John Hawkins on the Spanish main in *Westward Ho!*, which he himself called "a sanguinary book." He continued the romantic approach when he moved to Cambridge; it appeared in the title of his inaugural lecture, on "The Limits of Exact Science as Applied to History"; and his enemies soon indicted him for writing both immorally and inaccurately. His successor, Sir John R. Seeley, author of *The Expansion of England,* concerned himself with history not as romance but as "the school of statesmanship"; he turned from the adventures of

Elizabethan seadogs to the administration of the Victorian empire, and in his inaugural lecture, on "The Teaching of Politics," he dismissed what he called past history as consisting of "controversies . . . closed, questions answered . . ., problems together with their solutions."[1] The master of Trinity, W. H. Thompson, the Platonist, sat disdainfully through Seeley's lecture and as he left remarked, "Dear, dear, who would have thought that we should so soon have been regretting poor Kingsley!"[2]

To propose following the measured footsteps of Seeley — whether as problem-solver or as student of tropical colonies — may seem peculiarly unpromising, especially in the field of Western American history. Most of us have supposed that we needed other models, including some closer to Kingsley in imagination and skill with words. The literary possibilities of our subject-matter tend to exceed our literary grasps so patently and so commonly that one cannot easily imagine an announcement in another field such as a distinguished patron of historical studies made several years ago in offering a prize for a history of the American West "written with distinction and in which sound scholarship may be taken for granted." Perhaps no one, either among or beside the competitors for the prize, has fully explored the implications of that cryptic announcement. It may not, in fact, be easy to imagine taking even sound scholarship for granted, as a speaker at the first meeting of this organization suggested in discussing the topic, "The History of the West: The Worst Scholarship in America,"[3] but the literary shortcomings of Western history have long been conspicuous. Theodore Roosevelt, who privately had regarded the American Historical Association as a conspiracy of "painstaking little pedants" dedicated to lowering the standards of historical writing from those

---

[1] J. R. Seeley, *Roman Imperialism, and Other Lectures and Essays* (Boston, 1871), 312–13, 332.

[2] Robert B. Martin, *The Dust of Combat: A Life of Charles Kingsley* (London, 1959), 268.

[3] Alan Swallow at Santa Fe, New Mexico, October 14, 1961.

of Francis Parkman to those of Justin Winsor,[4] exhorted its members in his presidential address on "History as Literature" in 1912 to bring grace and imagination to the opportunity to portray "the backswoodmen, with their long rifles and their light axes," and "the endless march of the white-topped wagon trains across plain and mountain to the coast of the greatest of the five great oceans."[5]

The opportunity remains, and at first glance it does not seem to lie along the austere paths of modern political science — some of whose practitioners are not so much indifferent to literary grace as suspicious of it, prone to subject it to the inquisitions of content analysis or quantitative semantics. Even Seeley, nearly a century ago, warned that history "should not merely gratify the reader's curiosity about the past, but modify his view of the present and his forecast of the future"; history should be interesting not in the sense of romantic or poetical but "interesting in the proper sense which affects our interests. . . ." If history so written did not interest the reader, the problem according to Seeley was to change him, and not to rewrite history.[6]

Seeley's subject-matter, which is the colonial world overseas (or, more precisely, the organization of the colonial world), contrasts sharply with the American West, and some attempts to compare the two have been quite unrewarding. Following the Spanish-American War, imperialists argued that we should never give up Cuba and the Philippines because we had not given up the Louisiana purchase and the Mexican cession.[7] At the same time our associations with territories overseas apparently tended to handicap Western territories not yet admitted — to prompt members of Congress to object to the use of the Spanish language in New

---

[4] To George O. Trevelyan, January 25, 1904, in *The Letters of Theodore Roosevelt*, ed. by Elting E. Morison, III (Cambridge, 1951), 707–708.

[5] *American Historical Review*, XVIII (April 1913), 487–88.

[6] *The Expansion of England . . .* (London, 1883), 1, 308–309.

[7] Albert J. Beveridge, "The Development of a Colonial Policy for the United States," *Annals of the American Academy of Political and Social Science*, XXX (July 1907), 5.

Mexico as they had not objected a few years before.[8] Whereas some argued that the Spanish islands and Hawaii ought to govern themselves because constitutionally they were successors to the Old Northwest and other continental territories — proposed, that is, to raise Puerto Rico to the status of New Mexico — others inclined rather to reduce New Mexico to the status of Puerto Rico, and thus helped to delay its admission as a state until 1912.

As the constitutional lawyers pointed out, Congress's authority over both the old continental and the new insular territories was plenary, municipal, deriving from the "power to dispose of and make all needful rules and regulations respecting the territory or other property belonging to the United States. . . ."[9] Yet in practice the differences between Puerto Rico and the older territories, and therefore between their governments, were so great that authorities at Washington did not even begin to consolidate correspondence with them until 1934, when President Franklin Roosevelt established the Division of Territories and Island Possessions. Some of the differences appeared in the alternatives to statehood proposed for Puerto Rico in 1966: continuance as a commonwealth, association with the United States by compact, and independence. The model was not merely the Territory Northwest of the River Ohio, but also the Philippine Islands.

The territories of the American West differ more strikingly from today's new and emerging nations, formerly colonies, of Africa and Asia, such as Algeria, that have had choices comparable to the choices available to Puerto Rico; they differ still more from Africa south of the Sahara Desert, for which Seeley foresaw no possibilities of self-government when he considered the arrangements developing in his time for Canada and India. Seeley's academic heirs, the students of comparative political development, describe problems for these new states that were almost entirely

---

[8] Whitney T. Perkins in United States-Puerto Rico Commission, *Status of Puerto Rico: Selected Background Studies . . . 1966* (Washington, 1966), 441–42; Howard R. Lamar, *The Far Southwest, 1846–1912: A Territorial History* (New Haven, 1966), 17–18, 486–87.

[9] Article IV, Section 3.

absent in the early American West. The people of a new Western territory or state might complain, for instance, of their boundaries, but in general they had no crises of identity or legitimacy — of deciding who they were and to what their government owed its authority. They or their ancestors had met such crises before they went west. They were about as well equipped for independence by experience as any people when they went; but to become independent was not what they wanted, even so gradually as the people of, say, Canada became independent, but rather permanent association in a federal union. An American political scientist has recently pointed out that the United States at independence was "historically a new society but an old state."[10] He might have said the same of the American West, whose newest constitutions resemble the oldest of them much more than the Constitution of the United States resembled the Articles of Confederation or any other older systems. By contrast, the emerging nation of "Tropicalia" is an old society and a new state.

Some of the traditions of early English government appeared more in the West than in the East, perhaps as Elizabethan speech long persisted in the back country: the idea of fundamental law (denying power to the legislature), the vitality of local government, for many years the ancient vitality of the militia. For such reasons, then, the beginning of a new Western state was not a time of excessive demands or loads on government. Political parties had relatively few pressing problems to solve; the parties themselves were reasonably well prepared to attack them, both in that their members had long experience to draw on and in that their experience was more in working with government than in rebelling against it.

The Westerners' preparation for self-government, moreover, extended beyond formal political experience. Their social institutions, and those of so-called backward peoples, will not fit into the kind of comparative framework that Marc Bloch used to explain

---

[10] Samuel P. Huntington, "Political Modernization: America vs. Europe," *World Politics,* XVIII (April 1966), 409.

economic events in Venice by examining the limited number of relevant variables among Venice, Florence, and Genoa.[11] Whereas most of the people of Tropicalia are peasants committed to traditional or parochial ways, the American frontier had a large, strong, and modern middle class. The typical Tropicalian cannot easily raise himself from the tradition-bound peasantry, because he is both illiterate and desperately poor; the typical Westerner, at least by the middle of the last century, was not only literate and prosperous by nineteenth-century standards but more so than the average American, and in the Far West less likely to be a farmer. The Tropicalians have crowded into their cities because they are too many for the land, but they have not learned urban ways; Westerners even today still have abundances of land, long after the so-called closing of the frontier. Thus California of 1967, the only Western state except Hawaii more densely populated than the country as a whole, has only about two-fifths the density of Vietnam, about a fourth the density of India. To make a more familiar comparison, California has less than two fifths of the population of Italy, which resembles California in climate and resources but is less than three fourths its size. And unlike Tropicalians, pioneer Westerners moved easily from country to city and back again, bringing the mores of the commodity exchanges into the agrarian rites of homesteading, which a sentimental government had ordained on the assumption that Western pioneers wanted farms in order to live permanently on them.[12]

---

[11] William H. Sewell, Jr., "Marc Bloch and the Logic of Comparative History," *History and Theory*, VI (1967), 214–17.

[12] As Simon Kuznets has pointed out, many settlers on the frontiers of the United States and the British dominions suffered material deprivation comparable to that of inhabitants of underdeveloped countries. "But these troubles were the penalty of pioneering, not of economic backwardness; and the comparison is irrelevant. At no time after these early pioneering days had passed and the settled groups had begun to be significantly large did these countries lag much behind the economic leaders." See his comments in "Underdeveloped Countries and the Pre-Industrial Phase in the Advanced Countries: An Attempt at Comparison," *Proceedings of United Nations World Population Conference, Rome, 1954* (New York, 1955), V, 951. Kuznets has also noted that migration to cities in underdeveloped countries is unnecessarily large, relative to opportunities, whereas migration lags in developed countries, including the United States. Kuznets and Dorothy S. Thomas, "Internal Migration and Economic Growth," Milbank Memorial Fund, *Selected Studies of Migration Since World War II* . . . (New York, 1958), 202–203.

Tropicalia has one political party, experienced less in the responsibilities of government than in the arts of denouncing its former European rulers. Its skills and interests are more oppositional than aggregative or adaptive; its general weakness, like that of the Tropicalian middle class, invites the bureaucracy to dominate the country politically and economically. The West had essentially the parties of the East, and Western parties continually recruited from and competed for the support of other associational groups, such as miners' and stockmen's associations and labor unions, which have no real equivalents in Tropicalia. The Tropicalians seem pre-occupied with politics, although most of them know little about it, and they ask their government to solve all at once problems of the kind that the ancestors of the Westerners had solved over centuries. The Westerners were so busy with other matters that they some-times neglected territorial or state government, although they were well prepared for it; they expected so little of it that at the begin-ning they seldom bothered to adopt essentially new constitutions or laws. Sometimes they neglected territorial government precisely because they were so well prepared for government, because their political and social standards were so high that they could not easily commit themselves to an area that was still backward relative to what they had known in the East. They had made political com-mitments, but to the nation rather than to the territory, or to the Eastern state they had left rather than to the Western state where they worked. Meanwhile they might put much political energy into local government and into voluntary associations, some of which provided services, such as education, that the Tropicalians leave to their national government. On the other hand, Tropicalia has traditional local loyalties so strong, cultural diversities so extreme, that it must suppress federalism rather than import it, but yet has no tradition of self-government at the grassroots.

The farther one gets from national or state into local politics, and from formal political structure into the social basis of politics, the greater the differences appear. Religion is essentially a traditional force in Tropicalia, opposing political integration and development, whereas in the West the churches were both a training ground for politics and the source of new political issues — in education, in social control, in the treatment of Indians. Feeling against racial minorities means something quite different in California or Wyoming, where the Chinese were primarily low-priced unskilled labor, and in Java or Malaya, where the Chinese have been merchants and bankers, corresponding not to the Irish of the nineteenth-century Middle West but to the Jews of early modern Europe.[13]

One may hesitate especially to make bold comparisons at a time when some Americans propose to export the model of American society to parts of the world with much less political experience than North America or Europe, and when even many of those who criticize American policy seem to assume that progress or development consists in becoming like the United States. A political scientist recently has protested that "the effort to see connections and . . . parallels between what happened in America in the eighteenth century and what is happening in Asia, Africa, and elsewhere in the twentieth century can only contribute to monstrous misunderstandings of both historical experiences."[14] Winston Churchill said as much — actually, being Churchill, a little more — when Franklin D. Roosevelt tried to persuade him that the solution to India's problems in 1942 lay in the example of the Articles of Confederation.[15] And a sociologist has charged that students of comparative social development derive their standards so narrowly from particular cultures that they fail to see that in more essential respects many so-called underdeveloped peoples outrank their betters in Europe and North America. "Lacking markedly any clear idea of what [development] means," he says, social scientists "use it as a prestigeful rubric to cover an array of unrelated studies and to conceal a state of obscure thought."[16] In writing about African and Asian countries — and in developing our policies toward them — we have

[13] Bert F. Hoselitz and Wilbert E. Moore (eds.), *Industrialization and Society* (Paris, 1963), 189–90.

[14] Huntington in *World Politics,* XVIII, 409.

[15] Roosevelt to Churchill, March 11, 1942, in Churchill, *The Hinge of Fate* (Boston, 1950), 212–14.

[16] Herbert Blumer, "The Idea of Social Development," *Studies in Comparative International Development,* II, no. 1 (1966), 6, 11.

imposed the standards of European and American development on them, whether Marxist or capitalist, somewhat in the style of that survey of advancing civilization by Donald Ogden Stewart, *Aunt Polly's History of Mankind* (1923), the story of progress from the jellyfish to Uncle Frederick.[17]

If such approaches have not been profitable, we may not come to understand part of our own country (and a part that is not the most backward part of it) by reversing the process, imposing on its history the categories and criteria of social development that social scientists have abstracted from the developmental crises of distant lands. Attractive though the idea of extra intellectual motive power may be, perhaps comparative development is not an ideal star to hitch our covered wagon to. Yet comparisons of different cultures and events can be useful, and not merely to the Tropicalians and their benefactors from overseas. Some recent attempts to draw lessons for the mid-twentieth-century world from events of the 1780's have been quite suggestive, particularly in calling attention to the obstacles to development, European style, in new nations, to fundamental differences as well as similarities among countries — although it is a little startling to find a social scientist referring to the American Constitution as "a system of stabilization feed-backs"[18] or coupling the United States and Nigeria as "reconciliation systems."[19]

A comparative approach may be more rewarding in studies of the American West than in studies of the Federalists not because the West as a whole, or any region of it, is much like many entire

---

[17] As C. E. Black notes, much comparative history operates in a conceptual framework directed to a predetermined end. *The Dynamics of Modernization: A Study in Comparative History* (New York, 1966), 177. The idea of progression was not new when Marx spoke of how a more developed country might present to a less developed country the image of its own future (*Capital*, I [London, 1886], xvii); it recalls Tocqueville, and it also anticipates twentieth-century programs of foreign aid. *Cf.* Reinhard Bendix, "Tradition and Modernity Reconsidered," *Comparative Studies in Society and History*, IX (April 1967), 292–346.

[18] John R. Platt, *The Step to Man* (New York, 1966), 109.

[19] David F. Apter in Bert F. Hoselitz and W. E. Moore, *Industrialization and Society* (Paris, 1963), 139.

foreign countries, new or old (which it probably is not), but because we still do not know enough about some social processes that are analogous — that is, about some of the things that people have done in the West and still do elsewhere — and because the field of Western American history has unusual need for organizing principles. Frederick Jackson Turner offered such principles to it more than anyone else has done, setting an example of analytical vitality both for the amateur historians who had confined local history to genealogy and tales of explorers and Indian fighters,[20] and for the professional historians who tried to force it into a system of institutional molds imported from England and Germany — when they noticed it at all. He took his cues not only from the dramatic historical spectacle of men mastering the wilderness, making the public domain into a private monopoly, but also from the new People's Party of the 1890's and its revolt against the monopolists. Thus he brought to his Western studies the perspective of other kinds of history that Samuel Eliot Morison has recommended — of national and contemporary topics as well as of grassroots (or, as Morison said of his own work, coral reefs and mudflats).[21]

It was commonplace for a while to criticize Turner and his followers for intellectual isolationism, for unawareness of other parts of the world, from the point of view of the non-American historian, and for weakness in method, from the point of view of the social scientist. Yet Turner drew on his knowledge of European history as well as on his pride in America's unique destiny; perhaps he made his greatest contributions in drawing on other disciplines, in a larger-than-American perspective. It is true that he did not see trans-Atlantic analogies as Alexis de Tocqueville did

---

[20] Cf. Turner to Constance L. Skinner, March 15, 1922, in which he distinguished himself from "those who approached the West as fighting ground, or ground for exploration history," and described his paper on "The Significance of the Frontier" as "in some degree a protest against eastern neglect ... of institutional study of the West, and against western antiquarian spirit...." "Turner's Autobiographic Letter," *Wisconsin Magazine of History,* XIX (September 1935), 96, 101.

[21] "Faith of a Historian," *American Historical Review,* LVI (January 1951), 271.

and that, since he was an American rather than a Frenchman, the American social ferment of his time turned his mind not to the future of France but to the difficulties of tracing democracy and protest on the frontier to American roots in Britain. Whereas revolution in France had an international setting, directing Tocqueville toward democratic America among other foreign countries, the atmosphere of Populism was fundamentally isolationist or nationalist. The Western followers of Henry George and Ignatius Donnelly may not have overthrown the "gold bugs," but they helped to overthrow the germ theory of the exclusively European origins of American institutions. Yet Turner drew not only on George and Donnelly but also on the new European historical economists of his day, who had found that the mathematical models of the English classical school did not explain continental developments. As Lee Benson has shown, he derived his argument in part from the Italian economist, Achille Loria, who in turn borrowed from Henry George in tracing the consequences of monopoly in land on European society.[22] His seminar developed within the School of Economics, Political Science and History that he had persuaded the University of Wisconsin to establish under the direction of Richard T. Ely, whom he joined in relating history and the new German economics to each other and to contemporary problems.[23]

The principal new trends in the social sciences of the 1930's and 1940's were so ahistorical or even anti-historical, and most Western historians were so unfamiliar with them, that cross-fertilization was less common than in Turner's time. Essentially regional projects in the social sciences have been relatively few, apart from

---

22 Lee Benson, *Turner and Beard: American Historical Writing Reconsidered* (Glencoe, Illinois, 1960), 1–40; Loria, *Analisi della proprietà capitalista* (Torino, 1889), II, 8–15 ("La revelazione storica delle colonie"). On the emergence of the historical school, see J. J. Spengler in Daniel Lerner (ed.), *Quantity and Quality: The Hayden Colloquium on Scientific Method and Concept* (New York, 1961), 164–65.

23 Richard T. Ely, *Ground Under Our Feet: An Autobiography* (New York, 1938), 179; Merle E. Curti and Vernon Carstensen, *The University of Wisconsin: a History, 1848–1925* (Madison, 1949), I, 630–32, 638–39.

geography and economic history, since Howard Odum's studies of the Southeastern states in the 1930's;[24] interest in rural sociology has declined along with rural population and along with government's interest in restoring the rural community. Sociological studies of new communities organized by the Farm Security Administration, the War Relocation Authority, and other governmental agencies during the depression and during and after the Second World War had large potential meaning for studies of the frontier;[25] but most historians were slow to notice them, perhaps in part because there was so little history in them, so little concern with the pasts of the people who had moved into resettlement projects, concentration camps, or new tract housing. Nevertheless, once the more personal arguments about the specific hypothesis of the safety-valve had declined, it became obvious in the work of such historians of the West as James C. Malin, Paul Gates, Allan Bogue, and Henry Nash Smith that ideas were still crossing academic boundaries, as from ecology, agricultural economics, and literary criticism.

Over the last decade and a half or so, the possibilities of deriving perspectives from other disciplines have greatly increased. Perhaps the most striking developments of potential concern to historians have been in fields that for a generation had been least historical, and especially in political science.

By the middle of this century, in the course of trying to make their discipline scientific, American political scientists had practically stripped their studies of historical content and context. Authors of community studies rigorously suppressed names of persons and places, not merely to respect rights of privacy and to keep faith with their informants, but to emphasize their concern with the atomic

---

[24] See his *Southern Regions of the United States* (Chapel Hill, 1936); and Odum and Harry E. Moore, *American Regionalism: A Cultural-Historical Approach to National Integration* (New York, 1938).

[25] Cf. Allan G. Bogue, "Social Theory and the Pioneer," *Agricultural History*, XXXIV (January 1960), 21–34; Stanley Elkins and Eric McKitrick, "A Meaning for Turner's Frontier," *Political Science Quarterly*, LXIX (September, December 1954), 321–53, 565–602.

uniformity of universal types.[26] Seeking to standardize elementary
political relationships, they tended to abandon the structure and
development of institutions for the behavior of individuals in decision-making, and to prefer those methods and those data that seemed
to fit most neatly into computers. Although the "political man" of
the behaviorists took shape from measurement and induction rather
than, as the "economic man" of the classical economists, from specu-
lation and deduction, nevertheless the two tended to be equally
uncontaminated with social heritage. It was hard to regard either
of them as a human being moving in the disorderly world of history.
As late as 1954, when David M. Potter looked to cultural anthropologists and social psychologists for the most telling recent contributions to the literature of national character rather than to
historians,[27] he mentioned only two political scientists, Denis W.
Brogan and Tocqueville, neither a behaviorist. "I am not quite
clear about political scientists," the anthropologist Alfred L. Kroeber
had remarked in a forum on the study of human behavior in 1951.
"They seem to me a sort of recent deviation from history — people

---

[26] Reviewing three volumes of W. Lloyd Warner's *Yankee City Series,* Oscar Handlin
complained of the authors' "pretence of anonymity and generality," their construction
of "fictive persons," and their "calm disregard of the historical background." *Journal
of Economic History,* VII (November 1947), 275–76. Robert A. Dahl has recently
observed that "the actual content of almost all the studies that reflect the behavioral
mood is a-historical in character" ("The Behavioral Approach in Political Science . . .,"
American Political Science Review, LV [December 1961], 771). David B. Truman
has conceded that historical knowledge was likely to be an essential supplement to
contemporary observation of political behavior, but his emphasis on measurable
behavior tends to thrust history into the background, to be called up only occasionally. Thus institutions "must always be conceived as persons behaving," and the
student of behavior "is obliged to perform his task in quantitative terms if he can
and in qualitative terms if he must" ("The Implications of Political Behavior Research,"
Items, V [December 1951], 38–39). Yet both behavioral political scientists and historians have proposed to rescue actual human beings, whether from sociological (as
opposed to psychological) bias and historical generalization or from presentism and
impressionism. David Easton protested that in situational analysis the individual had
become "a wooden automaton who does not seem to vary in his predispositions or
feelings under any political situation" (*The Political System: an Inquiry into the State
of Political Science* [New York, 1953], 203). The expressed concerns of historians
and behaviorists — and their fears — sometimes seem more alike than their work.

[27] *People of Plenty: Economic Abundance and the American Character* (Chicago,
1954), vii, 22–23.

who want to deal with historical or political material without doing any history."[28]

In the 1950's and 1960's political scientists and historians converged again at several points, some of which would have seemed unlikely a few years before. Robert A. Dahl several years ago identified two particularly promising points of convergence or contact, which he described as nodes about which unity between behavioral political studies and history might grow, targets of opportunity on which the weapons of modern social science might concentrate. One concerned problems that lend themselves to simple statistical analysis, such as studies of elections and movements of population. Another was the field of political change, as in developing nations,[29] which suddenly pressed for attention when recently dependent territories came to constitute nearly half the membership of the United Nations. Neither discipline was well prepared for these new states, although political scientists began to study them earlier than historians. The political scientists were apparently impressed by the large number of case studies available to teams of visiting investigators, and at first were unembarrassed by the problem of working in new foreign languages. In measuring the growing populations of tropical countries, one now had to deduct not merely visiting anthropologists but also political scientists.

Dahl did not say this, but both types of studies that he mentioned offer large opportunities for historians of the West. When the Inter-University Consortium for Political Research at Ann Arbor has put on magnetic tape all Congressional roll calls, the results of all elections, and all the records of national, state, and territorial censuses, the regional historian will easily master data that are more voluminous and more elusive than those of national politics. Perhaps such tabulated regional data will also have more

---

[28] Crane Brinton and others, "The Application of Scientific Method to the Study of Human Behavior," *American Scholar,* XXI (Spring 1952), 218.

[29] "The Behavioral Approach to Political Science...," *American Political Science Review,* LV (December 1961), 771–72.

to tell us in a field where one cannot easily depend so much on published governmental reports, on unpublished correspondence, and on evidence of intellectual or conceptual change as in national history. Some impressions of the possibilities are already available in the work of Allan Bogue, Lee Benson, Samuel Hays, and others who are working with the Consortium and its compilations; in the correspondence of Turner and his student, Joseph Schafer, which shows their enthusiasm for a great systematic inventory of demographic data for the state of Wisconsin; and in the publications that followed, including Merle Curti's book on Trempealeau County.[30]

The possibilities of drawing on studies of political change in developing countries are no less interesting. The historian who becomes familiar — to use Dahl's words — with "the most relevant issues, problems, and methods of the modern social sciences" in comparative politics should find fruitful insights by analogies between national or colonial and regional history. He may find insights to some extent as a historian in any field would, simply because comparative politics is in one of the liveliest areas of the social sciences today, comparable to molecular biology in the life sciences, and because, like the German economics of the 1880's, it has at least possibilities of historical dimension. It requires, Lucian W. Pye says in his study of *Burma's Search for Identity*, "more impressionistic and intuitive treatment than the strict canons of scientific method would permit," blending "the historian's art and the social scientist's discipline."[31] The concept of political culture — in Sydney Verba's words, "the system of empirical beliefs, expressive

---

[30] *The Making of an American Community: A Case Study of Democracy in a Frontier County* (Stanford, 1959). "What kind of people tend to be Whigs, what Democrats, Abolitionists, etc.? This can be ascertained from such studies," Turner wrote to Schafer, "and it would be the first time such correlations have been worked out on any considerable scale." Schafer, "The Wisconsin Domesday Book," *Wisconsin Magazine of History*, IV (September 1920), 63–64. A political scientist, Michael P. Rogin, in *The Intellectuals and McCarthy: The Radical Specter* (Cambridge, 1967), recently has set an example of what historians should have done before, analyzing voting in Wisconsin and the Dakotas over half a century.

[31] *Politics, Personality, and Nation Building: Burma's Search for Identity* (New Haven, 1962), vii.

symbols, and values which defines the situation in which political action takes place"[32] — seems potentially as broad as the anthropological-sociological concept of culture from which it comes and, given historians' traditional bias toward political events, more accessible to them. After painstakingly refining the techniques of functional-system theory, accepting its static bias as the price of precision, social scientists have, in effect, begun doing history again, studying whole political systems in time instead of merely abstracted processes of decision-making.[33]

The Western historian may find ideas in studies of foreign countries, moreover, because he has not looked there for a long time. At symposia on frontiers or regions of different parts of the world, Western Americanists usually seem to know less of other frontiers than foreigners know of the United States. For many years historians of Germany, Russia, Australia, Brazil, Argentina, Rome, China, and other countries have looked to analogies in American expansion, writing of the *Drang nach Osten,* of individualism, and other frontier traits. Perhaps it is time to reverse the process, to redress the balance.

We might simply compare the American West with frontiers of other countries, rather than this one part of one country with the whole of another. Such comparisons of regions or processes of expansion are rewarding, especially in studies of various groups of English-speaking farmers. Their experiences were so similar that a family or a settlement moved from some parts of, perhaps, Nebraska or Dakota would not seem much out of place in parts of Canada, Australia, New Zealand, or South Africa; of course, many

---

[32] Verba in Lucian W. Pye and Sydney Verba, *Political Culture and Political Development* (Princeton, 1965), 513.

[33] Daniel Bell, *The Reforming of General Education* . . . (New York, 1966), 161–62; Lucian W. Pye in Pye and Verba, *Political Culture,* 9–10. Gabriel Almond's model of the functional approach to comparative politics, following on Talcott Parsons' model of systems of social action, seems at first as abstract, as aloof from cultural holism as functional anthropology; but, like the work of many of Parsons' students, it soon confronts historical reality. *Cf.* Almond, "A Developmental Approach to Political Systems," *World Politics,* XVII (January 1965), 183–214.

families made such moves. One could not easily say this of any of the so-called backward nations, unless one looked to limited parts of the West that we seldom regard as typical, such as the delta lands of Mississippi. My argument for going further afield, to less obvious comparisons, is pragmatic. In studying an area as varied as the American West, various approaches are useful, and different phases invite different methods of inquiry. Studies of the advancing Canadian and Australian frontiers, for instance, help especially to illuminate the beginnings of our early miners, cattlemen, and wheat farmers. They tell us less about our commercial and urban Western frontiers, about conflicts of races, and about the complex and populous West that followed the first agricultural settlement; they tell us more of economic and psychological experiences that we have already studied at length than of those that we have studied less. Further, in seeking new perspective we can most profitably go where the intellectual action is, and at this time that is in national rather than regional studies.

As Westerners we especially need new perspective because of the great volume of evidence that we have inherited, an embarrassment of riches that calls for principles of selection. Turner cut manageable cross sections through it, starting the directions of his cuts from such experiences of his time as the exhaustion of free land and the Populist revolt. Such starting points — or, as a social scientist might say, extrapolations — can be fruitful, for Westerners live among survivals of their past, which include tastes and ambitions that became clearer when fulfilled than when merely felt.

Nevertheless the Western present sometimes fails us, or leads us astray. Survivals tell us more of success than of failure, which was also a part of the West. As Josiah Royce noted, the surviving California pioneer tended to remember either the marvelous probity or the phenomenal wickedness of his fellows in early days and to say little of general social irresponsibility;[34] he did not testify much

---

[34] *California, From the Conquest in 1846 to the Second Vigilance Committee in San Francisco: A Study of American Character* (New York, 1948), 214–15.

on more credible traits and experiences, on the kinds of behavior that we find most interesting in new societies today. In retrospect the pioneer passes over the psychological stresses of his youth and still more those of his parents, and celebrates more his mastery over physical hardship. Thus he says much of conflicts with Indians, which George Stewart omitted from his history of the California trail because they did not appear in letters and diaries, and little of loneliness, homesickness, confusion, and disappointment in a strange land. Seeing around him in his old age those who succeeded, if only by surviving, he forgets those who fell by and left; he forgets his own doubts; or like Hamlin Garland — who, even as he resolved to shock Easterners with the truth, could not bring himself to describe the experiences of the pioneer mother [35] — the pioneer passes on to less painful memories. Having changed the land himself, he can look back on beginnings in a new spirit, impressed by the changes and by those who anticipated them, even nostalgic for aspects of the wilderness that once had seemed threatening rather than beautiful or picturesque.

We may pick up alternative or supplementary principles of selection, and alert ourselves to other kinds of evidence and events, by looking more to other countries and other disciplines. There are types of social processes and relationships that tend to appear in widely differing kinds of developing societies, and that the functional approach to comparative politics may help us to notice, to identify. Although no one has established a single scale of development on which we as Americans or Westerners have advanced further in all respects than the Tropicalians have advanced, nevertheless different societies and their members seem to share types of experiences. Thus, after the First World War, Frederick Jackson Turner suggested that the relationship of the nations of Europe with each other in the League of Nations and with their dependencies might help Americans to understand their own development. "If, for example," he said in 1922, "we describe the way in which the sections of the Atlantic seaboard have dealt with those of the

---

[35] *A Son of the Middle Border* (New York, 1917), 416.

interior of the United States in such terms as 'colonization,' 'spheres of influence,' 'hinterlands,' American history takes on a new meaning."[36]

In the twenty-third year of the United Nations, the terms we use to describe the development of new nations are more complex than those that we used to describe the exploitation or control of colonies and mandates in the fourth year of the League of Nations, when Turner made that suggestion; not all of them have much meaning for the history of the West (the "interior," as Turner called it, showing his Midwestern bias). As Douglas Dowd has pointed out, the Western economy was so much an extension of economic activity in metropolitan areas that one cannot describe it regionally as one describes the economy of the South;[37] nor can one describe it pathologically as one describes tropical economies. Perhaps comparison with other areas is useful chiefly to emphasize the generally progressive and advanced state of Western society. While for the most part we can put aside the problem of populations unprepared for industrialization and for citizenship — including perhaps comparisons of charisma as a substitute for experience south of the Sahara and south of the Tehachapi — large comparable processes of economic and political development remain.

As India contributed to England's industrial take-off, so the American West contributed to the take-off of the United States, both by furnishing raw materials and markets and by promoting social fluidity.[38] A turn at mining, ranching, or farming corresponded to a commission in Her Majesty's armed forces or in the Indian civil service, as opportunity for a younger son. Further, the injuries that the expansion of European trade did to manufactures in underdeveloped colonial areas[39] corresponded to the decline of household and local industries in the West after the Erie Canal

---

[36] "Sections and Nations," *Yale Review*, XII (October 1922), 4–5.

[37] "A Comparative Analysis of Economic Development in the American West and South," *Journal of Economic History*, XVI (December 1956), 560–61.

[38] Black, *Dynamics of Modernization*, 112.

[39] Gunnar Myrdal, quoted by Benjamin Higgins in Eastin Nelson (ed.), *Economic Growth: Rationale, Problems, Cases* (Austin, 1960), 50–52.

and the transcontinental railroads.[40] Although Westerners had
much capital of their own, they also sought and received much help
from government. W. W. Rostow points out three American experiences with governmental intervention that suggest analogies for
developing areas overseas: the role of the Army Corps of Engineers,
assistance to agricultural, mining, and industrial technology through
the Morrill Act, and the roles of county agents and mail-order
houses.[41]

One must guard also against overfacile comparisons of politics,
and by comparison take care to expose significant differences. Some
large institutions — constitutions and bureaucratic systems — are
deceptively similar in form from one country or region to another,
while in mode of operation and working relationship to people they
vary widely. Other institutions vary in form or operation while
those who operate them are much alike. In colonial relationships,
as in relationships between new and old anywhere, admiration and
rejection, imitation and deviation, mingle and reinforce each other;
those who deviate are not necessarily unable to imitate. The West
lagged politically at times essentially because its people were
advanced, not retarded. Westerners needed the frenzy of the frontier
press to draw them into politics not because they were unused to
politics but often because they had made their political commitments elsewhere — to the nation or to an Eastern state — and because
they were so busy working and speculating that they had little time
for anything else.

Despite the common practice of transplanting institutions, the
most significant resemblances among members of different societies
may be at the level of individual behavior and traits rather than at
the level of form or cultural norm. As Walter R. Goldschmidt has
noted in some suggestive essays on what he calls comparative func-

---

[40] In the Far West, the decline was both uneven and temporary. The percentage of the
labor force in manufacturing in the Far West in 1880 was considerably greater than
in the entire United States. Harvey S. Perloff and others, *Regions, Resources, and
Economic Growth* (Baltimore, 1960), 120–21.

[41] Rostow in William R. Polk (ed.), *Developmental Revolution: North Africa, Middle
East, South Asia* (Washington, 1963), 55.

tionalism, cultures differ more than people; actual behavior tends towards the center of ranges for all humans.[42] Americans have experienced this simple fact in assimilating millions of immigrants who reveal their essential similarities even before they learn a new language. Everett S. Lee and Thomas C. Cochran have given a worldwide setting to a Western trait by putting the frontiersman on a scale on which he resembles the migrant from abroad and also the migrant who moves from India or China to Africa and from rural to urban Africa: he is young, male, either single or not long married; by migrating he weakens the ties of kinship and loses some of his ascribed status.[43]

We need to know more of migration and of some factors in the socialization of migrants — that is, the process of their making commitments and putting down roots in new homes — such as the family, the school, clubs, churches, and the mass media. We have been learning to ask questions about such factors chiefly in the lives of people in so-called backward or undeveloped societies; but they are factors that appear also in societies like our own and those of our immediate ancestors, especially in the West. In comparative studies of societies in flux, some of the most fruitful opportunities may lie in such processes and factors, those closest to individual psyches and experiences and farthest from law — particularly from our western European and North American kinds of law.

The role of traditional institutions in socialization encompasses a particularly fertile field for inquiry, even though the United States generally, and the West more than the older states, may seem relatively free of traditional and ascriptive bonds. The effect of freedom itself needs exploring. As David Riesman has pointed out, freedom in a mobile society may make Americans depend on mass media

---

[42] "Culture and Human Behavior," in International Congress of Anthropological and Ethnological Sciences, Philadelphia, 1956, *Men and Cultures: Selected Papers,* ed. by Anthony F. C. Wallace and others (Philadelphia, 1960), 98–104; and Goldschmidt's *Comparative Functionalism: An Essay in Anthropological Theory* (Berkeley, 1966), 134.

[43] Everett S. Lee, "The Turner Thesis Re-examined," *American Quarterly,* XIII (Spring 1961), 80–82; Thomas C. Cochran, *The Inner Revolution: Essays on the Social Sciences in History* (New York, 1964), 183–85.

to replace the guidance and support of family and clan.[44] But we
are less free from tradition than we sometimes suppose, looking
through the spectacles of science on countries whose failure to
imitate us we attribute to the dead hand of the past. In the words
of Gabriel Almond, "all political systems — the developed Western
ones as well as the less-developed non-Western ones — are transi-
tional systems, or systems in which cultural change is taking
place."[45] Moreover, traditional institutions may be not merely barriers to progress but media for socialization. This is even more
evident on the frontier, as in the activities of churches, than in large
cities where the political boss fills a social need.[46] As Royce said,
the West had more than its share of the breakdown of social responsibility that Tocqueville saw as a general phenomenon in the
nineteenth century; and many Westerners, then as now, sometimes
clung to tradition in the face of the threats to their values that such
breakdowns entailed, as traditionalists in developing countries rally
against threats to their values.[47] Perhaps both the politicians who
promise to stop disorders in the streets today and the vigilance
committees of the 1850's and 1860's have something in common
with peoples of far-off lands, as well as with the disorderly elements
that they have proposed to suppress.

   As we seek perspective on the experiences of Westerners who
came from Europe, Asia, Africa, and the East, we should re-examine
also those Westerners who came from the West itself and whose

---

[44] "Some Questions about the Study of American National Character in the Twentieth
Century," *Annals of the American Academy of Political and Social Science,* no. 370
(March 1967), 42–43.

[45] Gabriel A. Almond and James S. Coleman (eds.), *The Politics of the Developing
Areas* (Princeton, 1960), 24.

[46] Although Charles E. Merriam pointed out many years ago the social values of urban
political machines, political scientists still try to apply the test of reason to traditional
and ascriptive elements in developing nations. Yet traditional institutions may be
constructive forces, not only in maintaining stability, integration and order, but also
in promoting drastic change, as where the Indian government enlists village physicians
in promoting birth control.

[47] Reinhard Bendix, *Nation-building and Citizenship: Studies of our Changing Social
Order* (New York, 1964), 70; James Q. Wilson, "A Guide to Reagan Country: The
Political Culture of Southern California," *Commentary,* XLIII (May 1967), 45.

experience was not so much socialization as de-socialization: the American Indians. First pretending that they were not there as we took their land, we then — with better intent but perhaps to worse effect — forced them to use the land we left to them in our ways rather than theirs, and thus deprived them of independence and manhood only somewhat less effectively than white colonists had deprived black tribesmen in Africa.[48] While the Indians were neither numerous enough nor adaptable enough to our uses to inspire systematic slavery or apartheid, their experiences and the attitudes of the dominant majorities toward them are parts of Western history that need further telling — and that, in a revolutionary world, we may understand more clearly than our ancestors did.

At the end of the last century, when Western American history became an academic field, what it especially needed was a system of organization to relate it significantly to national history. It had been too much a story of individual adventure. Turner sketched out such a system, deriving it in part from the models of the currently emerging historical school of economics. He emphasized the effects of pioneering experiences in building political parties and other institutions. It was natural for him to emphasize integrative processes at a time when new states had been organizing themselves, the Populist party forming its demands, and the Western economy maturing, from the point of view of agriculture.

Today, in a West that promises to urbanize and industrialize itself beyond the East, agricultural settlement seems less climactic than it did then. In an age whose means for material progress are greater than our ancestors foresaw, but whose hope is less than theirs, we do not so much fear the effects of the end of Western development as regret its continuing advance and the stresses that

---

[48] In prizing the honorable traditions of the British yeomanry, reinforced by the experiences of settlers in the Old Northwest, we may forget the low social status of crop agriculture in much of the rest of the world, including aboriginal America, whether because of the cultural legacy of slavery or because of the prestige of warfare, the chase, and stockraising. Commenting on the migration of American Negroes to cities, Theodore W. Schultz notes that for them agriculture was and is an inferior occupation. "Urban Developments and Policy Implications for Agriculture," *Economic Development and Cultural Change*, XIV (October 1966), 4.

it brings. We see Western development continuing, from a past in which we rejoiced in physical circumstances that shielded and set us apart from the troubles of the rest of the world, into a present in which we cannot so easily distinguish the actions of our own government abroad from those of other governments as we once thought we could — and in which caste, alienation, hopeless poverty, and intercultural conflict appear not only in other continents but also in our own. In a troubled world, some of the processes of development that interest us most are those that pertain more to disintegration than to integration: the breakdown of loyalties, the strains of social tension and social irresponsibility, the pains of anxiety and rising expectations. The opportunity of relating regional history to national history remains, but it has changed. The resemblances today between the San Joaquín Valley and the Ohio Valley are less striking than those between San Mateo County and Westchester, or Watts and Harlem.

It is a long road from pioneer San Francisco to present-day Accra or Lagos. The willow-marked path that the Franciscan fathers walked, and that now leads into the great concrete ducts or traffic sewers that empty into the Golden Gate, seems long enough, and is today such a confusion of plunging metal and oily smoke that we may lose our bearings rather than find them there. A visit to the crossroads or interchanges of the West that is today is enough to make one wish for the West that was, and for refuge from what Mary McCarthy has called the indestructible fecal matter of civilization filling up the once-lovely bay that Portolá and his men discovered nearly two centuries ago. But the frontier was seldom a refuge from change. The young men who came to California for an interval of adventure and romance knew that they were going to spend their lives in the factories and counting houses that were taking over the land; they came hoping, in fact, to gather stakes for their part in the new way of life, or to profit by bringing it here. The forces of a new world were converging in California. As the Dutch economist de Vries recently observed, the gold rush along with the opening of Japan and Africa epitomized a time that brought all of humanity under the general forces of the market, of the school, of war and peace.[49] Within a few years, by the time Henry George and Karl Marx were tracing the power of centralized capital on this bay, California had not even the appearance of refuge.[50] Long before the wanderings of later emigrants took them to Watts, or to Accra or Saigon, the Argonauts found loneliness, insecurity, and frustration far from home.

To put people on a quantitative series or on a worldwide setting can lead to a bloodless kind of history, in which abstractions replace men. It can also turn our attention to some of the most human dimensions of the past — to experiences that we have slighted in favor of those that made for livelier stories of adventure and achievement by those who reported them at the time, or for less revealing and less painful recollections by those who survived them. It may remind us that the appeal and significance of Western history lie not only in the outer uniqueness of events but in the inner universality of experience, of behavior, of feeling. As Walter Prescott Webb, looking back from the depression of the 1930's, advised us to enclose in one frontier of economic history those who gathered and exhausted windfalls on the foothills of the Sierra Nevada, in the Andes, and on the Macquarie plains, so perhaps we can fruitfully explore a great frontier of the social experiences of men and women who have left home and family for developing lands here and in other continents, then and now.

---

[49] Egbert de Vries, *Essays on Unbalanced Growth: A Century of Disparity and Convergence* (The Hague, 1962), 7.

[50] "I should be very much pleased if you could find me something good (meaty) on economic conditions in California," Marx asked Friedrich Sorge (November 5, 1880). "California is very important for me because nowhere else has the upheaval most shamelessly caused by capitalist centralization taken place with such speed." *Karl Marx and Friedrich Engels: Letters to Americans, 1848–1895; A Selection,* ed. by Alexander Trachtenberg (New York, 1953), 126.

Appendix

THE TRAINING OF
WESTERN HISTORIANS

A Seminar Under the Chairmanship of

WALTER RUNDELL, JR.
University of Oklahoma

The purpose of this panel session, thoughtfully conceived and planned by Professor W. Turrentine Jackson, was to raise and examine certain questions which may be regarded as vitally important to the future of Western historical studies. What goes into the training of the Western historians of today, and what should go into their training? Are graduate students sufficiently aware of the original sources, the primary materials available in the field, and how to get to them? Do professors ensure sufficiently close relations with the repositories of these sources, and do we give adequate support and encouragement to historical societies, museums, and state libraries and archives — the whole range of repositories where Western historians might find their materials? How large is the content of Western history, of frontier history? Do we try to set our field within the broader areas of American history, modern history, or the history of western civilization? As an example, I might just mention the refreshing exchange that we had in THE AMERICAN WEST *between Lynn White, Jr., and Owen Ulph* *over medieval technology in the "Wild West." Is this a legitimate sort of comparison, a legitimate kind of bridge to build? Such questions as these have elicited the attention of four distinguished panelists — Professors Carstensen of Washington, Crampton of Utah, Jacobs of California, and Lamar of Yale — each of whom has had much experience in the training of Western historians.**

We should be concerned with the health of our specialty of Western history. I am sure that most of us read the 1964 report of W. N. Davis, Jr., on the West as a field in American history. The findings were not particularly encouraging. I think that we should consider whether the Western History Association has in any way tended to turn back this tide. There are many hopeful signs that we can consider in our discussion of Western history as a viable specialty. One is the commercial prize offered by Alfred A. Knopf in Western history. John A. Hawgood won the first of these $5,000 prizes. The fact of William H. Goetzmann's EXPLORATION AND EMPIRE, a book obviously just as Western as it can be, winning the Pulitzer Prize in 1967 should certainly give a great deal of encouragement to those of us who labor in this field. Here was important recognition that Western history continues as a vital area in American historiography.

The popular consumption of Western history continues unabated. Perhaps this interest constitutes a wellspring of strength from which Western historians should draw some sustenance. Like Antaeus, whose power as a wrestler was renewed each time he touched his Earth Mother, we can draw continuing inspiration from the fact that our specialty does command wide interest, and is manifestly important to great numbers of our countrymen. Our task is to train historians of the West who can capitalize on this inherent interest in a way that will be intellectually respectable. How we should go about this task is the business at hand.*

---

* Neither C. Gregory Crampton nor Howard R. Lamar could be present at the session. Lamar had earlier supplied a paper which the chairman presented. Crampton, unexpectedly called away from the conference, left an outline of his presentation, which the chairman shared with the seminar. Crampton later incorporated these ideas in the paper which is published here.

The Training of Western Historians and the Place of Western History in Institutions of Higher Learning

b y

VERNON CARSTENSEN

University of Washington

In focusing on our mutual problems as historians of the West, a proper question to ask at the outset is whether we as Western historians have problems distinct from and in addition to those of historians who work in other fields. We probably do, but they are not major ones. In talking about Western history we are plagued by problems of definition, and Western studies have been more frequently attacked than most other fields. I take it that we understand Western history to embrace the history of the advance of the frontier from colonial times to at least the end of the last century — or, in other words, the internal colonization of America. Some would take the story to the present in Alaska, appropriately, I think. "The West" is quite properly used from time to time to describe the Trans-Missouri or the Trans-Mississippi country (some Bostonians still seem to think the term includes everything west of the Connecticut River, and in the editorial offices of the *American Historical Review* the term includes everything west of the Appalachians). Although there are courses and seminars that specifically confine themselves to a region described as the West, I take it that we are not talking about such regional historical study.

Despite the continued flow of books, good and bad, from commercial and university presses dealing with the West, study of the advance of the American frontier is less prominent than it was a few decades ago. In the heyday of Western historical studies, say from the 1890's when Turner launched his course and seminar and provided direction and inspiration with his famous essay, until the early 1930's, study of the westward movement was widely regarded as central or at least essential to an understanding of American history. So widespread was Turner's influence through his essays, his teaching, and his numerous students that it was alleged that meetings of the Mississippi Valley Historical Association were convocations of frontier historians or, as someone has phrased it, Turnervereins. But much has now changed. In the 1930's an attack began on Turner's ideas, and for two decades or so his writings came under sustained, detailed, often hostile examination. In some quarters it seemed to be assumed that the advance of the frontier was something invented by Turner, and accordingly, that if the Turner hypothesis were destroyed, the courses and the seminars dealing with the internal colonization of the American continent would be rendered meaningless and could be dropped.

The hot dispute over the Turner hypothesis, with all its theological and sometimes exegetical comment, has subsided, but the relevance and the quality of frontier studies and courses continue to be questioned both from within and from without the field. In 1955 Earl Pomeroy published an article, probably familiar to us all, called "Toward a Reorientation of Western History," in which he offered some melancholy comment on the low quality of much of the work being done in the field and concluded that some graduate students worked in Western history for unheroic reasons including, as he saw it, the fact that the scholarly demands were less exacting than in other rigorously developed fields. He suggested that some of us as teachers had "abetted such tendencies by regarding the field as a refuge for the flabbier minds among our graduate students, by encouraging factual rather than interpretive studies, by conferring academic dignity on vulgarization, by debasing literature into accumulation.'" Other doubters and critics followed. In 1964 W. N. Davis, Jr., published a report of his survey intended to discover whether the West was likely to survive as a field in American history and, as many of you will recall, his conclusion was not optimistic. The next year Mario DePillis read a paper at the annual meeting of the Organization of American Historians in which he asserted that "the academic specialty familiarly known as the American West or Westward Expansion is in a state of crisis." He said that the crisis was "conceptual," that "historiography of the West has become meaningless." Not only has the field of Western history been undergoing this critical scrutiny, but as we all know, the last thirty or forty years have seen the rise of a host of new fields in American history to command the attention and interest of specialists. At the 1967 meeting of the OAH some fifteen groups, societies, associations, and institutes representing these more or less distinct fields offered joint programs. Perhaps the most ironic aspect of the present situation is that, although we now have a professional association of our own, it sponsors a magazine that seems intent upon providing entertainment rather than serving scholarship. In fact, if the fruits of new research appear there, it is purely coincidental. Nor has the creation of a "Review" appendage improved matters much. The list of new books published — perhaps the most useful part of the "Review" — is flawed by being restricted largely to the Trans-Missouri West.

If what I have sketched were the whole story, the prospects for Western historical studies would be bleak indeed. But of course it is not. In fact, in many respects the prospects are quite bright. The amount of available unexplored and unexploited source material is not only enormous, but it is growing as manuscript and other collections multiply and expand. Each successive number of our several historical journals carries reports of new and often important acquisitions. The large increase in bibliographic and other aids makes these materials more easily available, as, of course, do the various duplicating services which we hope one day will place a large part of the National Archives in each of the dozen Federal Records Centers across the country.

Perhaps our most serious question is how best to use this growing wealth of material. And here I have a feeling that I echo what you may call either the platitudes or the rituals of historians generally. All of us need to know more about all history in order to avoid the parochialism that characterizes too much of our work, and here I include historians working in other fields than Western history. We should be spending more time looking at other places in the world that also have experienced large land-settlement movements so that we might learn more about our own. We need to look, for instance, at the experiences of Canada, Latin America, Australia, New Zealand, Siberia, perhaps even South Africa. It is a hopeful sign that economic historians propose to spend some time on just this matter at their international meeting next summer. Many scholars in such related fields as sociology, geography, literature, and law are bringing their insights to bear on aspects of the westward movement, and our own work can be infinitely enriched if we use what they offer. I am thinking in this connection of such works as Frank Kramer's *Voices in the Valley*, which deals with folk belief in the shaping of the Midwest; T. S. Miyakawa's *Protestants and Pioneers*; the work of Andrew H. Clark and his students in historical geography; and the work in American legal history of Willard Hurst and his students. Hurst's great study, *Law and Economic Growth: The Legal History of the Lumber Industry in Wisconsin, 1826–1915,* is both a momumental study and a model of its kind.

The quantifiers also have much to offer by furnishing us with new means of obtaining more precise information. A student of mine once got interested in the business of doing a very simple problem of machine-checking the age and sex characteristics on four or five successive frontiers from the 1830's forward. It was necessary to negotiate with the high priest that commanded the services of a computer and to arrange for the financing. These were difficult problems, although for physical scientists they would have been nothing. Costs amounted to about six hundred dollars an hour. We historians cannot readily afford that kind of service! Negotiations finally over, the data were collected from the census sheets, put on cards, and run through the machine. To our vast surprise we found the computer to be a somewhat prudish beast. It would report on sex differences under the age of fourteen in the South and the West, but it would not give us this data for New England. I do not know whether it felt it was none of our business, or if one simply does not discuss this sort of thing in New England under the age of fourteen.

I confess that I feel old-fashioned and unprogressive, even troglodytic, in having nothing more or better to offer than the proposal that we try to do better, more perceptively, those things that we have been working on all long, and suggest that we welcome, and where possible employ, promising new methodologies and contributions from other disciplines. As I recall, I myself did not share completely Pomeroy's feeling about the near intellectual bankruptcy of Western historical studies when he wrote in 1955. But some of you will recall that he permitted himself a bit of optimism. This I did go along with. "Good books on western history still do appear," he said, "and few fields present so many subjects for other good books still to be written." That is probably still a pretty good statement of the situation.

Training Western Historians: A Western View

by

C. GREGORY CRAMPTON

University of Utah

The basic academic training of historians in the Western field should follow, in principal, the same patterns established for any recognized field of history. And the end product should be that ideal person — the inspiring teacher and the productive scholar. That these patterns have not always been followed, and that the products of departments turning out Western specialists have not always reached the ideal, have caused numbers of historians — and not all of them resident in the Eastern United States — to question the legitimacy of Western history as a field of study. These skeptics point to such things as antiquarian tendencies, localism and provincialism, and preoccupation with too few subjects and theories as weaknesses of the field. In his 1964 article, "Will the West Survive as a Field of History? A Survey Report," W. N. Davis, Jr., reported the results of a questionnaire, summarizing a number of such criticisms of the field by the professional fraternity.

That the West as a field of historical study still has great vitality is quite evident, however. The formation of the Western History Association in 1961 is a case in point. This learned society, dedicated to the promotion of the study of the American West in all its varied aspects, is supported in its objective by more than fifty universities and colleges, libraries, foundations, museums and other institutions throughout the land. I venture to say that no learned society was ever launched with stronger backing. Moreover, the academic and institutional support of Western history is exceeded by an ever-growing popular enthusiasm which reaches an international level.

Yet Davis could seriously ask if the West would survive as a field in the study of American history. The results of his survey led him to be pessimistic. The story of the frontier grows shorter as the national story grows longer, and the sharper immediacy of world affairs, he found, seems to be crowding the more static course offerings to the wall. Those with crusading zeal who teach in the Western field have seen this happen. Departments once great (there are some very notable absentees in the list of those academic institutions supporting the Western History Association) in the field have reduced Western history to token offerings. And occasionally one finds the erstwhile strong, lusty advocate of the field reduced to defensiveness and apology by arrogant colleagues or other factors.

If the field of Western history as an academic area is indeed under attack, some of the criticism must be justified — and the most satisfactory replies to it are going to be found in a grass-roots approach. It would be difficult to summarize adequately the basic objectives of graduate training programs in the fields. That they are varied is evident; course titles alone ("The American Frontier," "Frontiers of North America," "History of the West," "Trans-Mississippi West") suggest diverse approaches and subject matter.

The published products of the academic and professional practitioners are somewhat easier to assess. Any critic will have to acknowledge that the history of the West has been more than a match for most comers. In the interest of space, let us admit the worth of many titles and concentrate instead on some of the deficiencies which might suggest some new areas of training. The works of some of the few greats in the field have been worried to death. Criticism and counter-criticism of Turner, Bolton, and Webb for some years now has been barren and unrewarding. Each of these men laid important foundations; each from his heavenly position must be appalled that so little has been built upon these foundations and that so few additional foundations have been laid by later comers. New theoretical approaches to Western history, in my opinion, constitute one of the greatest needs and might well be introduced more frequently in graduate seminars.

Indeed, new approaches suggest themselves on every side. The West, of course, did not stop growing in 1893; rather it is the fastest growing section of the United States. But is this evident in a course on the Turnerian frontier? While an examination of the retreat of the American frontier is still legitimate, Western history does not end with the closing of the frontier. There is much need to relate the West to the twentieth century and the contemporary scene, but Western historians have demonstrated something of a haughty disdain for the scholarly production coming from such pertinent disciplines as sociology, anthropology, political science, and geography. (The reverse, to a greater or lesser extent, is also true.) Yet the practitioners in these vineyards more often than not are working in subject areas chronologically close to the present and of national and even international immediacy. Urban problems and minority relations are two areas that come to mind. I want to agree with Donald R. McCoy, in his recent article entitled "Underdeveloped Sources of Understanding in American History" (*Journal of American History*, September 1967), that cross-cultural approaches might force substantial revision and erode parochialism.

In my view the West as a field of historical study is bound to survive. Western history is too vital to perish. But its growth can be stunted by the heavy hand of the dead. Those who train the Western historians of the future should try to be as big as the subject and reach imaginatively for the new idea, the new interpretation, the new approach, the new theory and hypothesis. The field itself is great. It is deserving of a greater historical literature than has yet appeared.

Suggestions for a "New Look" at Frontier History

by

WILBUR R. JACOBS

University of California, Santa Barbara

Some of you may recall Alexis de Tocqueville's brief description of different types of historians in his *Democracy in America*. Those who write biography, de Tocqueville argued, tend to look at the past in terms of an aristocratic interpretation or a great-man theory of history, while those who write about movements tend to be the democratic historians who interpret the changing patterns of society. So it is with the story of our frontier development. It seems to me that Western American history is a broad phase of American society's frontier history. In our colleges and universities it is unfortunately often neglected by departments of history today. Where it is offered, it continues to be popular, primarily because it is one of the few courses that interprets American history from the beginning of settlement to modern times.

When one examines the catalogues of the various University of California campuses or of some of the leading universities in the East and West, one cannot help but be impressed by the way American history is being sliced up for course offerings. With such salami-sausage slices of history, it is hard for the average student to see the American past in perspective. One of the reasons why the history of the American West has been very popular with students is because it does offer a strong thread of interpretation linking the whole of American history.

But the increasing emphasis on the American West as a region, centering in the Rockies and the Great Plains in the nineteenth century, has given us a pattern (especially in this Association) that might well be modified. We have allowed ourselves to be warmed by fireside fancy under the influence of legends of mountain men,

miners, cattle wars, and wagon trains. Our magazine, as well as
the handsome prize offered by Alfred A. Knopf for the best book
on the Trans-Missouri West, have tended to focus our attention
on a geographical area in a golden era. As Ray Billington, John
Caughey, Earl Pomeroy, Oscar Winther, and others have suggested,
this emphasis has tended to freeze investigation and blight research
in wider aspects of frontier and regional history. For example, the
study of California history went through this kind of metamorphosis
because of an emphasis on economic growth in the late nineteenth
century. If one examines the list of doctoral dissertations in the
University of California, one will find a conspicuous number of
them concentrating on the boom of the 1880's. That era surely has
had its share of attention. And so has the entire Trans-Mississippi
West become a timeworn and slightly frayed historical theme.

It would be well for us to return to the broad and flexible concept of "frontier" that Turner espoused.[1] The frontier was, and is,
a vibrant expanding and contracting force which encompasses the
whole nation and extends from the seventeenth century to modern
times. With some justification it can be argued that the study of
the nineteenth-century Great Plains and Rockies is static and out
of style. But if we look at the subject in the new style, in terms of
modern techniques of research, we might do as the manufacturer
of the new hula-hoop did: bring the product back into style with
roller bearings inside the hoop. We need to put zip and life into
the whole field of graduate study in American Western history.

We should, I think, give more consideration to the history of
the American West in terms of today's problems. For example, the
field of conservation history and attitudes toward conservation as
manifested in California today can be studied in terms of the nineteenth century, the eighteenth century, and even colonial times.[2]

---

[1] See, for example, Turner's perceptive essay, "The Development of American Society,"
published with Turner's handwritten revisions in Wilbur R. Jacobs (ed.), *Frederick
Jackson Turner's Legacy: Unpublished Writings in American History* (San Marino,
California, 1965), 168–191; Ray A. Billington, *America's Frontier Heritage* (New
York, 1966), 1–22.

[2] Origins of our attitudes toward conservation are discussed in Roderick W. Nash's
brilliant new volume, *Wilderness and the American Mind* (New Haven, 1967).

Among Western historians, much writing has had the effect of glorifying the exploitation of our natural resources. In the field of the fur and skin trade especially, our writers continue to conjure up heroic images to glamorize the men who had a large role in the cruel extermination of much of our wildlife. Nor have we zeroed in on the rascals who robbed us of timber and mineral resources.

Another area of revisionism concerns the frontiers of urban growth. The problems of congestion in Los Angeles and other modern Western cities can be traced historically to the "cities in the wilderness" which Carl Bridenbaugh described.[3] The story of our urban ugliness (and haphazard attempts at civic planning) is a continuous story that goes back to colonial Philadelphia, Boston, and New York. Bridenbaugh, for instance, has described sanitation problems and pollution in the colonial cities. The urban attitudes of those days have a close resemblance to attitudes prevalent today. In colonial times public apathy concerning waste and sewage was only slightly different from our outlook today on the pollution caused by automobiles and industry.

Still another area that might concern Western historians is the cost of higher education — a vital issue in modern California and other states, east and west. This significant but complex phase of our development is also derived from colonial times through the evolution of tax-supported public education. And California's pioneering in higher education is now having a powerful impact on the East, an illustration of the "backlash" of the frontier that Turner described in his writings.[4]

Nor have all the traditional sources been fully exploited. By turning to the origins of America's westward movement — to the colonial period — the true frontier historian finds much to illuminate the development of American life. A study of the origins of the legislative committee system in colonial South Carolina in con-

---

3 Carl Bridenbaugh, *Cities in the Wilderness* (New York, 1938) and his *Cities in Revolt: Urban Life in America, 1743–1776* (New York, 1955).

4 The most complete discussion of Turner's concept of the "backlash" idea is in Wilbur R. Jacobs (ed.), "Frederick Jackson Turner's Notes on the Westward Movement, California, and the Far West," *Southern California Quarterly*, LXVI (June 1964), 161–68.

nection with frontier defense, for example, affords insight into the development of representative government;[5] and a study of the legal problems of the Indians in colonial Massachusetts casts much light on the evolution of the contemporary relationship with the Indians of the West, whether defined as a point in time or in space.[6]

In other words, the American West is a seminal field if we consider it in terms of a great frontier advance and societal evolution. It can contribute to the understanding of our civilization perhaps as much as any facet of United States history. If we continue to focus on the Trans-Mississippi West in the nineteenth century, however, we cannot but neglect the larger picture of the West and its future as a region. A brilliant article pointing toward this larger view was written many years ago by John Carl Parish, the first editor of the *Pacific Historical Review*. In "The Persistence of the Westward Movement," Parish emphasized the changing aspects of a continuing frontier as cities emerged with modified industrial and educational institutions.[7] Unfortunately, a number of our more recent Western writers have tended to set up artificial barriers which center attention on a romantic West of a heroic nineteenth century which all but ignores the manifold richness of the great frontier that captivated Turner, Bolton, and Webb.[8] In a sense, we stand at a crossroads between romantic antiquarianism and genuine United States history.

New methods of research can well lead to a more perceptive understanding of the work ahead. Merle Curti, for example, turned

---

[5] George E. Frakes, "The Origin and Development of the South Carolina Legislative Committee System, 1719–1775," (Unpublished doctoral dissertation, University of California, Santa Barbara, 1966).

[6] Yasuhide Kawashima, "Indians and the Law in Colonial Massachusetts, 1689–1763," (Unpublished doctoral dissertation, University of California, Santa Barbara, 1967). See also Wilcomb E. Washburn, "The Moral and Legal Justifications for Dispossessing the Indians," in James M. Smith (ed.), *Seventeenth Century America* (Chapel Hill, 1959), 15–32, and John W. Caughey, *Opportunities in American Indian History Study* (Los Angeles, 1967).

[7] J. C. Parish, *The Peristence of the Westward Movement and Other Essays,* edited by Louis K. Koontz (Berkeley, 1943).

[8] See Wilbur R. Jacobs, John W. Caughey, and Joe B. Frantz, *Turner, Bolton, and Webb: Three Historians of the American Frontier* (Seattle, 1965).

to data-processing in his brilliant book on Trempealeau County, Wisconsin. By so doing, he altered established concepts of Wisconsin frontier history. It had been long accepted that persons of German origin had risen to positions of dominance and influence in that state, but the computer showed that Polish and Irish immigrants made similar progress.[9] Individual historians, if provided with special grants and technical assistance, can use such techniques. We *can* revitalize the history of the American West.

As Henry Nash Smith has pointed out in his perceptive volume, *Virgin Land,* much of what we have accepted as history is actually myth and symbol.[10] But we have yet to give full recognition to this historical fact. Once we have made this meaningful step, we can turn our sights on a new history of the frontier. By using the techniques of literary scholars, we can examine the wide spectrum of coloration that links history as fact and history as symbol and myth. Smith has shown us that too much of what we have accepted as history borders on romantic fantasy. Yet even historical romanticism can be significant if we recognize it for what it is.

We have, therefore, a challenging task ahead of us in creating a new synthesis of the America's Western frontiers. Like the clean hard rattle of raked gravel, the hard impact of meaningful research can be heard if we face up to the competitive standards established by researchers in other phases of American history. There is every hope that the course of Western American history will be favorable. Like other fields of American history, it will not entirely escape the

---

[9] Merle Curti, *et al., The Making of An American Community: A Case Study of Democracy in a Frontier County* (Stanford, 1959), 192, 443.

[10] "The master symbol of the garden," Smith writes, "embraced a cluster of metaphors . . ." (*Virgin Land: The American West as Symbol and Myth* [Cambridge, 1950], 123.) According to one of its leading practitioners, the field of "mythography" is "a coalition of several independent disciplines — anthropology, archaeology, classics, folklore, history of religion, philology, philosophy, and psychoanalysis." (Herbert Weisinger, *The Agony and the Triumph: Papers on the Use and Abuse of Myth* [East Lansing, 1964], 199.) Weisinger's illuminating discussion of Freud, psychoanalysis, and history (pp. 143 ff) is well worth consulting. A penetrating critique of images and symbols in history and historical writing was made by Alfred Kazin in his review of Alan Trachtenberg's *Brooklyn Bridge: Fact and Symbol* in the *New York Review of Books,* July 15, 1965, 6–8. Both Weisinger and Kazin stress the point that it is now possible to study history without consulting conventional historical sources.

ravenous maws of literary scholarship or of computer data-processing.[11] But it can be improved by using such techniques. In short, Western American history can become what we want it to be.

---

[11] An eloquent criticism of the social-science approach to history, and the use of data-processing techniques, is made by Allan Nevins in "The Old History and the New," *The Art of History: Two Lectures by Allan Nevins and Catherine Drinker Bowen* (Washington, 1967), 1–19.

Training Western Historians: An East Coast View

b y

Howard R. Lamar
Yale University

I wish to deal with the problems of training students in Western history on the eastern seaboard. From this angle two problems are immediately obvious: the location of the sources and the difficulties involved in travel for research purposes. In varying degrees these problems always face us and all of our students. But Western history is so concerned with the land and environment that no bona fide doctoral candidate has any right to complete a dissertation without both consulting the libraries and archives there and without living in the West for a long enough time to get more than a superficial impression of it and its many regions. It seems to me that while students can get all kinds of fellowships to go abroad — at Yale our students in European history must live six months or a year abroad whether their dissertation topics necessitate this or not — we do not have similar provisions for residence in parts of the West.

That is a roundabout way of getting at a more fundamental matter, which is that nearly all good Western and frontier historical writing presupposes an accurate and detailed knowledge and sense of American geography. Whether one is discussing the Age of Exploration, the fur trade, the Oregon Trail, the cattle drives, the gold rush, the Mormons, or the local economic diversities within territories and states, these subjects call for an intimate acquaintance with the terrain, distance, and physical factors. Turner provided one answer by drilling his students in maps, and Billington's *Westward Expansion* is full of the kind of maps that are essential for any understanding of Western history. It was the author's knowledge of the land that helped to make Webb's *Great Plains* such a powerful book. But courses in historical geography are out of fashion, and the chances are that few Eastern students do more than read about the physical factors in Western history. A student at Yale entering Western history might have no first-hand knowledge of the physical West at all. It seems, therefore, that some formal training in American historical geography, or at least fuller and more professional concern with physical, enviromental and soil factors, must be stressed. Turner, Bolton, Webb, and Merk all emphasized these factors, and today Malin, Bogue, and Fite use them with great effect.

There is no substitute, of course, for the knowledge gained by traveling or sojourning in the American West, but the expense of giving Ph.D. candidates a royal tour of the Chosen Land puts this out of the question. Since I do not think that this problem is unique to the student living in the East, I would like to see us consider some way whereby we might send students to regional summer institutes or conferences which would offer courses in regional history, regional or general geography, Indian ethnology, agricultural economics, and Western research sources. Just as the student of Russian history might take summer courses at Moscow or Leningrad, the doctoral candidate would benefit from dealing with several distinguished men in Western history while gaining some firsthand knowledge of the region. The good Western historian has to have that "sense of place" that C. Vann Woodward talks about in *The Burden of Southern History*. I would like to see us provide the student with the opportunity to develop a similar sense of Western place and space.

As Western history becomes broader and more complex, it is evident that our students need some professional knowledge of such specialized topics as Indian history and customs, tribal locations, and federal Indian policies. Yet courses in American Indian ethnology — even if our students had time to take them — are not generally geared to Western history. Historical studies in this area by such men as Jack D. Forbes, William T. Hagan, Francis Paul Prucha, and Allen Trelease suggest just how much we are missing if we leave out this side of the Western story.

Still another problem of background training is that of language. A large number of graduate students are attracted to Western history because, on the face of it, they do not need to be competent in a foreign language. But the American frontier in its formative stages was a babble of many tongues: French was spoken in areas of the Mississippi Valley and Russian was common in Alaska. Any student of the Southwest obviously needs to know Spanish, and a social historian of the Dakotas had better know German and one of the Scandinavian languages. One could even argue that the ideal California historian should know Spanish, Italian, French, Chinese, Japanese, and Hippie. I am not, of course, suggesting that any of us learn several new languages, but for any one of our students to master the history of certain regions, special language training may be in order if we are to broaden our coverage and deepen our understanding of all sides of Western history.

One last comment on the background training of students. Our colleagues in colonial and national history are attracting bright people just now who want to use computerized methods of statistical analysis and data-processing. In our own field, the agricultural historians have done this with rewarding results. On the whole, however, it appears that we have neither stressed the potentialities of these techniques nor have we consciously collected materials which lend themselves to this type of study. Western history is in part the story of large-scale economic enterprises, booming urban centers, political protests, and ethnic groups as varied and as complicated as those which Lee Benson found in Jacksonian New York. While I would hate to see us turn into "head counters," we would be helping both Western historiography and the modern training of students if we pursued the possibilities of the computer in our field.

I bring up these problems for two reasons. First, although we are accused by our brethren in other fields of history of being concerned largely with narration and of teaching and writing in a simple, non-interdisciplinary manner, I think that we can demonstrate convincingly that our work is fully as demanding and complex as that of the colonial or national historian. Secondly, the prognosis for our benefiting from an interdisciplinary training and approach is very good indeed. While some of the techniques may be new, it was in fact Frederick Jackson Turner who actually first used the interdisciplinary approach really effectively in the study of American history.

The problem which troubles me most as a trainer of students in Western history is that of finding a proper conceptual approach to the field. If we pursue the story of the West chronologically, should we start with the "first West" of Jamestown and Plymouth or with the country west of the Mississippi, thus relegating to our colonial colleagues the coverage of the first New World frontier? Then there is the question of how far forward we should take the story — to 1890, to 1900, or to 1967? Most of us seem to be pushing the coverage of the field to the present time. But here the properly trained student must perforce be able to handle government reports of all kinds on such technical and specialized topics as agricultural policy, irrigation, and Indian affairs. Then, at the state level, do the political histories of Ronald Reagan and Shirley Temple come under our jurisdiction, or do we leave that to the local and national historians? Can we as teachers competently cover the political, economic, and social history of the vast area of the West in one course? Or, if we have regional courses, how many can the regular teacher offer and how can the student take them all? Were we to resolve some of these questions, we might better know where Western or frontier history ends and other kinds of American history begin. I, for one, would like to see us relate the complex period of the modern West to its colorful past — and thereby lay some claim to being contemporary historians as well as to being frontier historians.

That the panelists dealt with vital issues and engaged the interest of at least 150 auditors is testified to by the following comments from the floor. Since the supply of recording tape had been exhausted before the discussion period, the floor discussants kindly supplied the chairman with written copies of their remarks. These are presented here in approximately the same order as they were in San Francisco, but a few have been re-arranged for better continuity of thought. To avoid duplication, the chairman has regretfully found it necessary to omit some comments.

*   *   *

Ray A. Billington, *Huntington Library*

All speakers, and particularly Professor Carstensen, have properly stressed the obvious fact that one basic problem in the teaching of Western history in the conceptual fuzziness of which we all are guilty. In their comments, the speakers have apparently used the term "West" and "frontier" as equatable. This same confusion exists in our college catalogues. When I began teaching at Northwestern University more than twenty years ago, I gave a course on "The History of the West" using an inherited description in the college announcements. At the end of the first quarter a student approached me in obvious dissatisfaction to complain that this was advertised as a history of the West, yet at the end of the first term we had only reached the Appalachians. I suspect that similar complaints can be heard in colleges today. Actually the two subjects are easily defined, and should be separated. Courses on the "history of the frontier" can be readily justified, courses on the "history of the West" less easily so.

A course on the "history of the frontier" should properly begin with the first European intrusions in the New World and trace the course of settlement across the continent to the closing of the frontier in the early twentieth century. This is an important aspect of American history, demonstrated often to be of lasting significance in altering the American character and the nature of institutions. Yet too often the course is over-popularized, in an apparent effort to live up to what many students call it: "Cowboys and Indians." If proper stress is placed on the changing nature of the settlement process, on the transfer of culture and cultural institutions, on the emergence of economic surplusses and their effect on eastern markets and labor supply, on the sectional conflicts that resulted from the occupation of differing physiographic regions, on the political results of expansion, and on the many other aspects of the subject that proved either enduring or national in scope, then courses on the history of the frontier are assured a solid intellectual content and a relationship to the present that justify their inclusion in any curriculum.

Courses on the "history of the West" are less easy to justify in the eyes of many contemporary scholars. These same scholars will readily welcome into their departmental offerings a course on the history of the South, for the regional characteristics which distinguish that section from others are still readily observable. Not so the West. There, traits and institutions seemingly are those of the national norm; hostile critics ask why a course on the history of such a region should be given when the region itself merges rapidly into the larger country of which it is a part.

Those of us who know the West, or who read in Western history, recognize that there is a difference. This is a mystic quality, one that Frederick Jackson Turner recognized but could never exactly define. In the West there is a greater social mobility, an easier communication among peoples, a spirit of progress, an emphasis on social democracy. Those unfamiliar with the West or its literature will deny this, but we know that there is a difference. Our problem is to convince others that this difference is actual, without at the same time overstressing the West's distinguishing features to the degree that they are distorted.

This is no easy task, but it is by no means impossible. Instructors must not merely recite the history of a region; they must be familiar enough with other regions to sharpen in the minds of their students the differences that they observe. They must be prepared to show that there has been a "Western spirit," and that such a spirit still animates life in the Plains and the Rockies, in the Great Basin and along the Pacific slope. Only when instructors succeed in this, and only when they define their own concepts of "West" and "frontier" properly, will courses in these two subjects warrant a place in the modern curriculum — and only then will they deserve the attention of better students attracted by the promise of intellectual stimulus rather than mere amusement.

* * *

JOHN W. CAUGHEY, *University of California, Los Angeles*

The best advice I ever had as a graduate student came not from any of my mentors but from another graduate student. Lawrence Kinnaird persuaded me to desert political science, then not much more than political history in disguise, and join him in developing a minor in anthropology. Different in method and outlook, this field gave me better insights, better understandings. I see it now as worth more than any two or three of the six history fields in which I stood examination. I have not always succeded in transmitting that advice to my students. Many come to me already committed to fields in history and nothing else. I am convinced, however, that interdisciplinary or cross-disciplinary study makes better Western American historians.

The issue of the West as frontier alone, stopping at 1890, or as frontier and region, has already been commented upon by two of the panelists and by Ray Billington. The problem, as I see it, is not whether we can conceptualize the West both as frontier and region but whether in reality both features were present. Unless we encompass the modern West, clearly more region than frontier, what we offer is likely to be nothing but "Cowboys and Indians" and what we have to say is likely to be antiquarian and sterile.

Howard Lamar is right in saying that students in our field need to see the West. With its pilgrimages to Santa Fe, Denver, Salt Lake, Oklahoma City, Helena, El Paso, and San Francisco, the Western History Association sees to it that we older Westernists get around. More could be done for students. I urged all my students to come along with me to this meeting, but not a one took me seriously. The Western History Association is affluent enough to subsidize students. For a starter I suggest student rates for the tours and student plates at the banquet.

Sixty years ago Booker T. Washington was advising his people, "Improve yourselves and you will be accepted." At the same time W. E. B. DuBois was saying, "Demand your rights as Americans." Perhaps the most needed advice to prospective specialists in Western history is not to be apologetic about the field but to develop backbone. I set a bad example by identifying myself as a professor of American history. I could say Western American history. I don't see many medievalists or modern Europeanists or American intellectual historians teaching out of field. Yet most of us have allowed it to happen to us. To cite an example from long ago, my introduction to Walter Prescott Webb occurred when I enrolled in his class in European history at the University of Texas. The history of the West need not continue to be the least prestigious historical field.

*   *   *

Oscar O. Winther, *Indiana University*

Some pessimism has been expressed and comment made concerning the apparently declining status of Western history as revealed, for example, in W. N. Davis' article, "Will the West Survive as a Field in American History?" I tend to view Davis rather optimistically. I think that the West has done well when one takes into account the fact that many other fields of history — economic, social, intellectual, urban, and others — have arisen since Turner's day to demand pieces of the historical pie. In particular I agree with Howard Lamar, who takes it for granted that Western history as a field is a fact of life.

Students wanting to work in the field continue to emerge at graduate schools without any particular identification with the present geographic West. Moreover, Western historians can be and are being trained in all regions of the United States. Considering the ease with which present-day scholars move from one library to another and the ease with which research materials can be imported, institutional location is not as important a factor in the training process as it once was. I do believe, however, that trainees in Western history should travel widely, as Lamar has suggested, and that they should follow in the footsteps of Herbert E. Bolton in examining the areas concerned with their researches.

I do not believe that a student should necessarily do his dissertation within a particular subject on which his mentor is doing research. Inasmuch as the work is supervised by a committee of scholars, it is not likely that the candidate will get by with loose workmanship. As Wilbur Cortez Abbot once remarked in his seminar, "One doesn't need to be able to lay an egg in order to determine whether or not an egg is rotten." In any case, I do not want a student of mine to say to another: "Have you read my seminar paper in Winther's new book?"

The training of Western historians can at times become too narrow. Some of the most enthusiastic of our present-day scholars in Western history have been converts from other fields of specialization, and some very excellent work has also been done by specialists in other fields. I am thinking of such men as David Potter and Thomas D. Clark, both of whom have brought out excellently edited diaries pertaining to the California Gold Rush, and also such non-Western authorities as Carl Becker, Samuel Eliot Morison, Samuel Flagg Bemis, T. P. Abernethy, Roy F. Nichols, Arthur S. Link, Howard Quint, Harris Warren, Frank Vandiver, and Lynn White, Jr. If, therefore, a student wishes to prepare for Western history, let the curriculum be broadly based. It is just as important for prospective Western history majors as it is for majors in other areas to read widely and to take work in European, Latin American, and Far Eastern history.

Finally, I look upon the training of a doctoral candidate as a lifetime partnership with his mentor. Even though we figuratively kick the stool out from under the student upon completion of the Ph.D. degree, we all know this is not really done. We continue to offer our gratuitous criticism and continue to help our students move up the professional ladder. Our letter files testify to this. I am proud, for instance, that five of my former graduate students are participating in this year's WHA conference. One of them, I am especially proud to say, is the incoming president of this Association.

*   *   *

Kenneth N. Owens, *Northern Illinois University*

The observations and comments of other speakers encourage me to offer remarks upon two points. First, Professor Winther has urged that we not begin to specialize in Western history so soon in collegiate training. While endorsing his recommendation, let me add that neither should we wait so long to introduce our students to scholarship in this field. The truth is that many of us share a tendency to teach a popular-style course at the undergraduate level. We are inclined to make the history of the West for under-graduates little more than "Cowboys and Indians." In the process we encourage a stereotype of the field which students unfortunately may often carry with them into graduate training. Then our unpre-pared students may indeed be shocked in their first graduate semi-nar to realize the true demands of scholarship. They find out for the first time that it is assumed, as another speaker has mentioned, they have read dozens and dozens of scholarly works which may seem far removed from epic tales of Dodge City. We should not wonder that many students will react with shock and confusion to such demands; this was not the type of Western history which they had been led to expect.

If we are to improve the quality of professional training, it seems to me that we should think of beginning at the undergraduate level. We should attempt to let even introductory students realize in some degree the intellectual demands and scholarly concerns in our field which we understand as professional historians. Otherwise, it remains our own responsibility that students and colleagues alike may identify our field as one with popular attraction but little relevance to significant historical issues.

These remarks are related also to my second point. Professor

Lamar, Professor Billington, and others have drawn attention to the "conceptual crisis" in the field of Western history or frontier history. Let me suggest that this "crisis" may not be nearly so critical as might be supposed. It may indeed be a sign of renewed strength and intellectual vitality in our often berated field.

To explain, let me recall one or two familiar facts. The Turnerian hypothesis — and through it the first definition of frontier history in the United States — took shape in a particular intellectual climate, the climate of the progressive generation. The spokesmen of that generation shared broadly a certain group of social opinions and preconceptions that may be recognized as a progressive consensus. Turner himself, I scarcely need remind this audience, was but one among the progressive historians who maintained that each generation will try to form its own conception of the past, that "each age writes the history of the past anew with reference to the conditions uppermost in its own time." And it was Turner's brilliant accomplishment to create in the frontier hypothesis an interpretive view of United States history which expressed clearly and forcefully the concerns and conditions of his generations by applying the views of the progressive consensus to an explanation of the national past. Largely because of the vitality of this progressive consensus, Turner's genius was able to develop a particular view of American frontier history which has persisted ever since as a strong tradition in the study of the American West.

Yet in our own time there is no longer such a general intellectual consensus as that common to the progressive generation. Among the generation and a half of historians represented in this room, there is not the same sort of broad philosophical agreement that Turner shared with his contemporaries — even with historians such as Beard and Becker. Between ourselves there is a far wider divergence of social opinions and political views and far greater differences of opinion concerning the relationship between material and cultural factors in shaping historical trends. We will not agree so readily among ourselves as to the basic moving forces of history. This lack of consensus, this divergency of pluralism of views, is perhaps now the essential reason for what we have called the conceptual crisis in our field. For myself, I find this pluralism no critical matter. Rather it is encouraging, for it should be a stimulus to fresh ideas and new perspectives for scholarship in Western American history.

Let me add that in training our students we should be honest in making clear the dimensions of intellectual differences in this field. After all, the most important problem is to make clear to students what it requires to be a historian. Whatever our differences in ideas, we each follow the career of a historian. To borrow a phrase from the hippies, each of us does his own thing. Given the pluralistic and changing nature of our present intellectual climate, we must recognize an ideal of toleration rather than consensus. And we should aim, I am suggesting, not to indoctrinate our students but rather to train them, through admonition and example, so they will each be professionally equipped to do their own thing.

*   *   *

W. TURRENTINE JACKSON, *University of California, Davis*

The observations made up to this point have served, it appears to me, to highlight a basic problem that is inherent in the training of historians of the American West. All of us are aware that an effective historian of the region is going to need interdisciplinary training. A plea has been made for anthropology, another for geography. Eastern students need to attend summer institutes located in the West so they can explore the historical geography of the region; Western students, on the other hand, need to examine the rare documents and manuscripts that are now housed in the National Archives and in at least one New England university library. It might be added that exposure to a first-rate course in American literature emphasizing western, or frontier, themes is likely to provide interpretations and stir up the imagination of the student.

The point that must be made, however, is that we are training *historians* first, and incidentally specialists of the American West. Our professional colleagues in the discipline of history expect our students to be trained in the entire United States field, with a sophisticated understanding of the latest scholarship, along with some knowledge of related fields in Latin American, European, and Asiatic history. We work with graduate students within departments of history, not in institutes for the study of the American West. Rather than focusing on the region and using various allied disciplines to make our training of a new generation more effective, perhaps we need to give more attention to the latest research methodology — in the behaviorial sciences, for example, and in the quantitative research by computers currently being used throughout the entire discipline of history — and to discover ways in which such techniques can be applied to the American West.

If there was ever a generation of professional scholars who have more vigorously re-examined the past in an attempt to explain the present than today's younger United States historians, I am not aware of it. It is past time for Western historians to join the crowd. The drains upon one's time, finances, and energy make it impossible for the graduate student of history, who is interested in Western America, to become sufficiently competent in his chosen discipline and at the same time to achieve even a minimal competence in all the other disciplines that will shed light upon the Western past. We must resolve this dualism in our training of students. As professional historians, most of us are associated with universities or research centers; we have an obligation to decide whether we are training in a discipline or concentrating on a geographic region. The problem is acute.

*   *   *

RONALD H. LIMBAUGH, *University of the Pacific*

Teachers and students of Western American History have an unfortunate tendency to devote almost exclusive attention to environmental and geographic problems: exploration, transportation, settlement, use and abuse of natural resources, and the ups and downs of community growth. These unquestionably are important Western topics, but overworking the environmental approach to Western history can distort historical perspective. It reinforces the erroneous but popular view that Western history is merely a study of how pioneers learned to cope with a hostile world in various forms, including virgin forests, arid deserts, rugged mountains, and "wild" Indians. Worst of all, it underrates the intellectual and emotional impact of the West on the East.

Bernard DeVoto, Henry Nash Smith and many others have shown that fanciful notions about the West, especially in the first half of the nineteenth century, were often more decisive than concrete facts in shaping policies, attitudes, or actions affecting the West. Easterners and Westerners alike constructed an imaginative West to satisfy deep-seated moral, intellectual, or spiritual needs. These myths and half-truths, consciously or unconsciously developed, colored American thinking in such diverse areas as economics, diplomacy, literature, and social relations. Mody Boatwright, for example, has remarked that the literary version of the American West, by perpetuating the myth of rugged pioneer individualism, perhaps undermined the American concern for social justice in the twentieth century.

Greater awareness and understanding of these psychic forces are needed to add depth and dimension to Western studies. Concern for non-environmental issues will also help to erase the stigma of provincialism by providing an interdisciplinary approach to Western history and by focusing attention on the important intellectual relationships between East and West.

*   *   *

Thomas H. Peterson, *Arizona Pioneers' Historical Society*

A number of the excellent comments made in this enlightening seminar have emphasized the broader aspects of the study of Western American history, and this is as it should be. I think, however, that one important point has inadvertently been overlooked. This is the continuing need for sound scholarly work on the smaller subjects, the less conspicuous personalities, and the less momentous events of Western history. Since it is almost impossible for a scholar working on a broad theme to investigate all the primary sources which may be pertinent, he must necessarily rely — and sometimes even heavily — on the limited and particularized research of others. Public libraries and historical societies are often best equipped to supply the research materials for such studies of limited scope and local interest. These institutions are likewise in the best position to encourage and support these studies, but to do so their directors need also to be encouraged and supported by the professorial members in our midst.

Another point, perhaps related, concerns the growing importance of historical archaeology to the Western historian. In recent years the curators of museums have been increasingly aware of the value of artifactual discoveries to the assessment of the historical as well as the pre-historical past. A close study of the actual implements, products, and weapons in use at a particular place is often vital in the interpretation, or re-interpretation, of the history of that place and its environs. As more and more historic sites are excavated, many under the pressures of urban renewal, more data becomes available through the reports of the archaeologists in charge. Historians of the West cannot afford to ignore such data. Some of it may determine just how a local history should be written.*

*   *   *

* Dudley C. Gordon, of the Southwest Museum, also spoke to this point. In describing a trip to England in the summer of 1967, he commented on The American Museum in Britain, two miles outside Bath. This museum depicts early American cultural history through such room exhibits as a country store, Shaker home, herb store, textile room, New Orleans bedroom, and New Mexican *morada*. Visitors are permitted to handle some of the artifacts. Gordon contended that students of the American frontier need first-hand familiarity with the artifacts of the westward movement as well as with its literary sources. He suggested that the Western History Association might sponsor an exhibit at the Bath museum.

JOHN C. EWERS, *Smithsonian Institution*

As an ethnologist and a museum man who is not involved in the classroom teaching of history, I feel a bit like an eavesdropper sitting in on this fascinating discussion of both the theoretical and practical problems of training Western historians. But I should like to express two thoughts. First, I am happy to learn that a number of you think that some courses in ethnology would be useful to students of Western history. Not only do I agree, but I may add that I think a few good courses in Western history would be very helpful to students of the ethnology of any Western tribe. The time has passed when any ethnologist can make a real contribution to his field by describing Indian cultures in a chronological vacuum, or without reference to influences from the white man's world.

I am interested also in the expressions of belief that historians may have devoted too much attention to the contributions of a very few earlier historians to the development of concepts of the West. We have a very similar problem, I think, in anthropology. Too much mythology passes for history in some of our studies of the history of American anthropology. Too many students seem inclined to attribute every important concept to Lewis Henry Morgan, Franz Boas, or Alfred L. Kroeber. It is no sacrilege to the memory of any of these leaders in the field to suggest that other men and women also contributed worthwhile ideas to our fund of anthropological theory. Yes, some of these ideas probably originated at my own Institution — on the Mall in Washington. The time is ripe for separating some of the facts from the myths in the history of American anthropology. And perhaps men and women trained in the discipline of history as well as that of anthropology can be of very real assistance in this task.

*   *   *

MARION J. RIGGS, *National Park Service*

I hope that another comment from an anthropologist — this one an archaeologist — may be permitted here, particularly in view of the comments expressed in favor of interdisciplinary approaches. One way to help your students, of course, is to talk to them often and give them more advice earlier in their careers. Another way (and a way which the anthropologists seem to have made more use of than I have seen at this conference) is to encourage those students to attend conventions such as this. What a marvelous opportunity for them to see, to meet, and to listen to men whose books they had read! They can also see what they are "in for" as professional scholars. I must say that it has been a little lonely at this meeting, not seeing many others who appear to be in the graduate-student category.

*   *   *

TIMOTHY J. CARMODY, *Rockhurst College*

As one who is still an undergraduate student, I agree whole-heartedly with the suggestion that universities set up fellowships of some type to enable graduate students to live for a time in the West and thereby obtain some first-hand knowledge of the area they are studying. How can one pretend to teach the history of the mining frontier if one has never panned for gold, crawled back into an abandoned shaft, or gagged on sourdough and beans? How can one pretend to understand the cattleman's frontier if all one knows of branding and cutting is what one has seen on television? How can one pretend to know the trials of the Mormons in Utah if one does not know the mechanics of irrigation or the barrenness of the Great Salt Lake valley? I vigorously support the idea that means should be provided for graduate students in Western history to come to the West.

There is reason to doubt, however, that large amounts of money are needed to inaugurate such a system of study. I have two friends who are as crazy about travel in the West as I am. Every Easter we take two weeks to drive, hike, and climb over sections of West Texas, New Mexico, or Colorado. For twenty dollars apiece we eat well enough, take quite a few color slides, and still manage to sleep in ghost towns, explore old mines, and talk to the natives of the area. I surely agree that some type of endowed program would be advantageous, but why hamper ourselves by starting out with such grandiose schemes as fellowships and summer workshops? How about a simple and reliable guidebook instead?

I should like to make a second point — one which I can see clearly because I am an undergraduate and not a teacher or research historian. It seems to me that the historians of the American frontier often come across to their students not as professional scholars but as hobbyists. Yours is a work of love — but where is the work? The field of Western history demands disciplined scholarship just as other fields, but does the undergraduate know this? I do not think so. The comment has been made that students of Western history should be trained in ethnology, archaeology, geography, and languages. But this is not brought to the attention of students at the undergraduate level, where such subjects should be learned! The average undergraduate says, "Why study languages? The pioneers all spoke English. Why study ethnology? They were all Anglo-Saxon. Why study geography? It's people that count." These are attitudes which are more common than may be imagined. Such attitudes tend to divert serious students and cause them to think that there is no academic challenge in the field of Western history.

I would plead with Western historians, therefore, not to hide your light under a bushel. You have a legitimate discipline, not a mere hobby. Start blowing your horn about the scholarship implicit in your work, and for heaven's sake quit making like it is all just a lot of fun! Certainly it is fun, but it is also very rewarding work. Get this across to your future students. Further, advise them that such outside subjects as ethnology may be studied at the undergraduate level. What makes me uneasy is the implication that a rounded education has to wait until graduate school. Is the college becoming a mere prep school for graduate work? Is it now the case that one can obtain a broad education only *after* receiving the bachelor of arts?

*   *   *

JOHN FRANCIS BANNON, *Saint Louis University*

The observations of several of the young folk would seem to point up one very significant aspect of this matter of the training of Western historians. We may be waiting too long — without recruits, we will have no graduate students to train. Perhaps we should be a mite more alert to the fact that interest in Western history may be engendered at a pre-graduate level, and give some serious attention to "selling" our field to promising undergraduates. In our present system the undergraduate is often the forgotten man. We lecture at him, and then seem to hope that he will stay out of our way as we go about our own research and devote ourselves to our graduate students. A little time with the undergraduate major who has a Western interest or bent can prepare him for a superior performance in a later seminar.

Repeated mention has been made of the value of anthropology to Western historians. Thoughtful counsel of the undergraduate, when his program of study is still somewhat fluid, could encourage him to obtain at least an elementary acquaintance with that discipline; the same could be said of other useful supporting fields. We will all gain thereby in having better rounded graduate students come into our seminars and thus be able to do more for them at that level.

INDEX